Pra

"Rarely is there a book that captures the moment as well as Dr. Matthew Arau's *Upbeat! Mindset, Mindfulness, and Leadership in Music Education and Beyond*. As we all navigate confronting our challenges and realities in meaningful ways, Dr. Arau balances theory and practice and gives us tangible ways to understand and be, and help our students be, our best selves. Mindfulness is the gateway to help us be present for music education, and this book is a present to us all."

— Scott N. Edgar
Associate Professor of Music, Lake Forest College

Director of Practice and Research,
The Center for Arts Education and Social Emotional Learning

Author of *Music Education and Social Emotional Learning: The Heart of Teaching Music*

"I enthusiastically recommend joining Matthew Arau as he takes the reader on an insightful, inspiring, and quite possibly life-changing journey. *Upbeat!* is a must-read for all who wish to become highly effective 'conductors and composers' of their lives."

— Dr. Paula A. Crider
Professor Emerita, The University of Texas

"Matthew Arau convinces all of us that we possess this amazing gift of positivity. Reverberating with this potential, we are taken step by step through the many challenges and choices music teachers face to create a lifestyle and teaching approach leading to professional fulfillment. This book needs to be read (and reread!) by novice and veteran teachers alike. Very highly recommended!"

— Mark Fonder
Professor Emeritus, Ithaca College

"There is nothing more important than leading through connection with our students. When connection happens, students feel valued, and the art of collaboration leads to a music-making experience that has more depth and meaning. Dr. Arau's book shows us how the positive synergy of the 4 C's of Upbeat Leadership create an extraordinary musical organization built on a strong culture of excellence. A must-read!"

— Scott Rush
Author of *Habits of a Significant Band Director*

"*Upbeat!* is a treasure trove of information that helps music teachers reflect and renew themselves and their music programs. After the upheaval caused when COVID hit, educators and students found themselves with even more stress as they struggled with personal and school-related challenges. Dr. Arau's book addresses many of the obstacles we face and provides practical solutions that, when intentionally practiced on a regular basis, can be the game-changer that helps teachers find more sustainability for their work and gives practical exercises and tools for assessing and addressing the things that can be done to intentionally support students and programs. You'll keep coming back to this book for the great stories, quotes, and advice."

— Lesley Moffat
Jackson High School Band Director
Author of *I Love My Job, But It's Killing Me* and *Love the Job, Lose the Stress*

"*Upbeat!* is unquestionably the one-stop-shop book for the music educator who seeks to inspire not just the musician but the wholeness of each individual. Dr. Matthew Arau masterfully crafts one of the most comprehensive books ever published with an abundance of resources and references that will positively impact those who experience this treasure of a book."

— Jon Gomez
Former Director of Bands, Dobson High School
Gomez Consultation, L.L.C.

"Everyone who reads this book will be forever changed! Matthew unlocks the musical superpowers inside all of us as he inspires students and teachers alike to pursue their passions through music. We G.E.T. to experience his infectious optimism and genuine spirit of gratitude through his stories and lessons of leadership, mindfulness, and inspiration. The transformational truths found within each chapter will empower readers to anticipate the next upbeat in every aspect of their lives. This is a must-read for anyone who cares and dares to make a difference!"

— Scott R. Sheehan
Music Educator, Leader, Advocate
Director of Bands and Music Department Chair,
Hollidaysburg Area Senior High School

"*Upbeat!* is a wonderful collection of hands-on, immediately applicable ideas and strategies for all those involved in the music profession. The leadership strategies found in this book are relevant, not only for the private teacher but also the music educator and the seasoned conductor. This comprehensive book on leadership, motivation, and successful life skills should be required reading for *all* teachers, music educators, and future music educators. The views in this important book admirably express the significant impact we as teachers make on our students and their future. I plan to add this book to my required reading list for my music education students."

— Mary Land
Associate Professor of Music Education
Conductor, University Concert Band, Western Michigan University

"I've had the great fortune of working with Dr. Matthew Arau for many years and have witnessed in person the impact he has on both students and music educators. *Upbeat!* captures the essence of Dr. Arau's uplifting and powerful message and shares actionable strategies to create a positive imprint on our students' lives through music. I would absolutely recommend this book to any music educator looking for more effective ways to shape the success of their program and create deeper engagement with their students!"

— Erin Cole Steele
Director of Educational Programs, Conn-Selmer, Inc.

"G.E.T. ready for a meaningful literary journey with Dr. Matthew Arau, as he provides readers with a roadmap to positively shift one's mindset and develop the thoughtful music educator. *Upbeat! Mindset, Mindfulness, and Leadership in Music Education and Beyond*, is a great addition to your academic library. Each chapter is an inspiration to music students, music educators and leaders of all sectors of life. This book will light a fire to spark passionate reflection on the character, competence, connection, and clarity that is needed to be an effective leader in today's world. Dr. Arau's ability to present concepts of leadership that span beyond the music classroom or performance stage is simply brilliant. *Upbeat!* is the perfect tool to energize the leadership movement and provides the framework of best practices that will guide leaders and their organizations towards success."

— Dr. William J. Earvin
Educational Support Manager and Director of the HBCU Collective
Conn-Selmer, Inc. – Division of Education
Founder/CEO, CreativeED, LLC

Upbeat!

MINDSET, MINDFULNESS, AND **LEADERSHIP** IN **MUSIC EDUCATION** AND **BEYOND**

March 1, 2024

To Emily,

Wishing you an abundance
of happiness, joy,
and peace.

MINDSET, MINDFULNESS, AND LEADERSHIP
IN MUSIC EDUCATION AND BEYOND

MATTHEW ARAU

Foreword by
Tim Lautzenheiser

GIA Publications, Inc.

Upbeat! Mindset, Mindfulness, and Leadership in Music Education and Beyond
Matthew Arau

Layout and Design by Martha Chlipala
Copyedited by Bryan Gibson
Graphics by Jeremy Fermin
Upbeat! logo design by Kyle Hollingsworth

Upbeat!® is a registered trademark.
G.E.T.™ is a trademark of Upbeat Global.

G-10550
ISBN: 978-1-62277-630-6

GIA Publications, Inc.

DEDICATION

Upbeat! is dedicated to my wife, Merilee, who has been my rock, inspiration, and support every step of the way in the creation of this book.

I would also like to dedicate this book to all my music teachers, mentors, and students who have encouraged me and taught me so much.

Finally, this book is dedicated to you, the reader. Thank you for your investment of energy, time, and thought in reading *Upbeat! Mindset, Mindfulness, and Leadership in Music Education and Beyond*.

TABLE OF CONTENTS

PART 1: IGNITE!

PART 2: INSPIRE!

PART 3: LEAD!

FOREWORD

Several years ago, I was presenting a workshop for a group of band directors. As every teacher does, I was constantly surveying the class to monitor the level of engagement, participation, and understanding. This particular occasion was my first encounter with Dr. Matthew Arau and—most certainly—it was a wonderfully positive connection from the get-go. His eagerness to embrace the syllabus content was fueled with a unique intellectual curiosity (an educator's dream-come-true)! When the class ended, Dr. Arau came forward, introduced himself, and asked if he could have some one-on-one time to explore several of the concepts shared during the workshop. Little did I know it was the beginning of a much-treasured lifelong friendship.

You are about to launch on a journey of self-reflection. Of the many benefits gifted to us via this remarkable book, the most important is Dr. Arau's gentle guidance as he helps us take stock of our own present moment posture in life and, more importantly, what we can do to bring us closer to achieving our personal and professional goals. His user-friendly writing style opens a pathway of introspection while giving us multiple options to advance every aspect of our daily habits.

Some books we read; some books we study. *Upbeat!* is a fantastic "read" and an eye-opening "study." You will find yourself racing to get to the next portal of wisdom, then screeching to a halt as you stop to consider how a given concept is applicable to (not only) *what* you do but *how* you do *what* you do and—above all—the all-important reason of *why* it is part of your decision-making. Such thought-provocation has the wherewithal to open our minds, our hearts, and our souls; ultimately, it makes us better people.

Throughout these pages, Dr. Arau strategically plants seeds of inquiry that trigger us to take stock of our mental and emotional processes. "I've never looked at it from that perspective, that's fascinating," was one of my frequent responses as I wrapped my mind around the many philosophical viewpoints Dr. Arau brought to the stage of understanding. Each paragraph is filled with positive value to be planted, nurtured, and harvested by the reader.

Having consumed a library of volumes delving into the endless landscape of attitude development, I often wonder if the authors are merely prescribing some worthy ideas *or* if the creators of the texts are writing from a posture of knowing and being. Rest assured, Dr. Matthew Arau "walks his talk." He has "been to the well." He has dedicated his efforts and energies to serving others via his (seemingly) endless array of talents and skills. Simply put, Matthew is the real deal.

It is a privilege and an honor to share this extraordinary tome with you. It is not a one-time read but rather a reference manual you will "mine" again and again . . . and again. A deafening "BRAVO!" is extended to Dr. Matthew Arau. As is always the case, his contribution makes the world a better place for all of us.

— Dr. Tim Lautzenheiser

PRELUDE

Sweat beaded on my forehead as I raced to the Delta Airlines counter to find a return flight home even though I had just landed. I felt a mixture of shock, disbelief, and fear. Over the course of the past three hours, the world as I knew it had been turned upside down.

That morning I had woken up with anticipation for a big day ahead. I had been heading to Parkersburg, West Virginia, to conduct a district honor band and lead professional development on the topic of Upbeat! Leadership and rehearsal techniques. This event had been in the making for two years and William, the band director who had invited me, was understandably looking forward to seeing all his planning and preparation come to fruition.

That morning, I phoned William to ask a question I had never before asked anyone: "Is it safe where you are?" The date was March 12, 2020, and although COVID-19 was spreading rapidly from state to state, on this day West Virginia was the only state in the country that had zero reported cases. William responded, "All clear. We are all set to go."

I boarded the commuter plane at the airport in Appleton, Wisconsin, at 12:30 p.m. for a 1:00 p.m. departure with a lot of excitement and a little trepidation. I settled into my window seat, readying myself for takeoff, and as I looked out the window at the ground crew prepping the plane, my mind wandered to the importance of music making and the gift of playing in an ensemble. Even while the dark shadow of the pandemic was moving across the United States and around the world, the music these honor band students would play and that this audience would hear would be a beacon of light. I posted on my Facebook page about heading east to conduct this middle school honor band, and within minutes the reactions from band directors and composers began flowing in: "Really?!" "For real?!" "Lucky! My honor band just got shut down." "Wow! This must be the last honor band in America."

I smiled and felt grateful to have this opportunity while so many other events and performances had been canceled. I was bound and determined and almost felt invincible. I was going to continue courageously and valiantly making music until the very last second, and at the same time, I hoped the time would *never* come when we would have to stop creating music together in person.

My flight plan took me from Appleton to Detroit, where I'd connect with another flight to Columbus, Ohio. From there, my host would meet me and we'd drive the two-and-a-half hours to Parkersburg. After landing in Detroit, I made my way to the next gate, all the while looking at the large television screens mounted everywhere. They were broadcasting one news report after another about the dangers and threat of COVID-19.

I landed in Columbus, Ohio, at 5:00 p.m., called my wife Merilee, and headed to the carousel to grab my luggage. While I was on the phone and reaching for my bag, I received a text from William, asking me to give him a call right away, so I said goodbye to Merilee and got him on the line. I could immediately tell by the sound of his voice that something was wrong. He said, "I had hoped to tell you this in person, but our superintendent just issued an order canceling all large group activities and we have to cancel the honor band. I am so sorry." He said that I was welcome to spend a few days in Parkersburg at the hotel they had arranged for my visit. I responded that it would be best if I could find a return flight.

I quickly called the airline service line, which was usually answered by a service agent within minutes. This time, however, the computerized voice said that the wait time was over twelve hours! So I sprinted back up the stairs and ran to the check-in line with my bags, hoping that there was still a flight back home that evening. The agent said, "Wow! You just made it. A flight leaves in just over thirty minutes." He weighed my bag, called the gate, and told the gate agent that I was coming. I made it through security and to the gate within minutes of the plane door being closed.

I then flew from Columbus back to Detroit, then on to Appleton. The planes were packed with people in similar situations heading to conferences and events only to discover that they had been canceled. Many of the passengers wore face masks and everyone was nervously wiping all the surfaces down with alcohol wipes. As the reality of the situation sank in, I thought about how tragic and sad it was that an invisible virus had the power to keep us apart and to disrupt so many things, including our ability to make music together. Never in my life could I have imagined that music could be canceled. After first departing Appleton at 1:00 p.m., I landed back where I had started at 9:00 p.m. Just over eight hours of travel had seemed like an eternity and weighed heavily on me. It felt as if I had walked through a portal, and on the other side, nothing would ever be the same again.

In the days that followed, schools closed to in-person instruction and the teaching of music changed drastically. That was the beginning of the COVID-19 shutdown and the realization that this was serious. Lawrence University, where I teach, closed its doors to in-person teaching the following week and music educators across the United States and around the world had to quickly adapt, modify, and innovate to successfully continue teaching music to their students.

INTRODUCTION

The global pandemic starting in 2020 shook us to the core. As educators, we felt disoriented and disillusioned as concerts, trips, music banquets, and graduations were canceled while in-person teaching (if we were lucky enough) was altered to a physically distanced space where masks hid our facial expressions and hampered non-verbal communication. Those of us who moved to virtual instruction mourned the loss of being truly together, and we had to quickly learn how to teach on platforms like Zoom, Google Meet, and Microsoft Teams that, while helpful, could not replace the in-person experience.

But we found our way.

Often through tears and heartache, we found our way because at the other end of our computer screens were students that needed us. Yes, many of the students kept their video cameras off and it hurt not to see who we were teaching, but still we persisted because we knew the precious time together in music class mattered.

As educators, we are caring idealists who went into this noble profession to make a positive difference in the lives of students. We spend each day focused on encouraging, guiding, teaching, comforting, challenging, and coaching our students, and more often than not, we do not give this same care and attention to ourselves. If we are not careful, though, we can burn ourselves out and damage our health. We cannot continue to pour from an empty cup. Remember that our students also need us to be at our best and to model a sense of balance in our lives. Although we selflessly invest many hours beyond the school day into our students, selflessness should not mean that we work ourselves to the bone until we are all dried up.

We cannot give what we don't have. Spiritual teacher Pema Chödrön writes, "Compassion for others begins with kindness to ourselves."[1] If we want compassion and kindness to be central to our classrooms, we need to begin with extending compassion and kindness to ourselves. Likewise, if we want our students to learn with a growth mindset, we must apply the same standard to ourselves. If we want a vibrant and positive classroom, we need to *be* vibrant and positive. If we want to empower our students to be leaders, we need to begin with leading from within.

It's okay to feel down and depleted. I have certainly been there. Being a teacher is hard work and it can be emotionally draining at times. There are days when we are so exhausted that we keep our eyes on the clock, waiting for the sound of the final bell, looking forward with anticipation to going home and collapsing on the couch. Am I right? Some of us may have even considered throwing in the towel a time or two. But in the end, that spark inside, while it may have dimmed, has not gone out. We stay for our students. We stay for the joy of the "Aha!" moment when a concept finally clicks for a student. We stay for that heroic feeling when a beginning clarinetist first makes it over the break without squeaking, or when a student who struggles to match pitch with their instrument or voice finally gets it. We stay for the student who feels that they can safely be who they are when they are with us.

Where does our spark come from? How do we find it? How do we ignite that spark? How does our spark light a flame? How can we fan the flame so that it burns brightly?

As young children we felt the spark of music when we sang, when we danced, and when we made music with instruments. We felt music resonate throughout our body. Making and creating music was fun and joyful, and as our spark grew, we spent more time with music growing our skills and craft. We performed and shared our music with others and decided to follow music down the path that it led us. Music was the vehicle that led to adventures, travel, and friendships. The ensembles we played in became our second family and social circle.

A pull inside of us called us to share music—to experience, create, and perform together—and we decided that, in addition to performing music, we wanted to teach music. This higher calling to serve, to contribute, and to give back gave purpose to our decision to become music educators.

For many of us, our inner flame burns brightest when we teach music and witness students falling in love with music making and becoming aware of their own progress through personal and group practice.

Remember when you were hired for your first music teaching position? How good that felt? Do you remember the enthusiasm, the freshness, the inner drive to take the music program from wherever it was to a higher level? There may have been just twenty kids in the ensemble, but you were bound and determined to give those twenty students the greatest experience learning music. You were even certain that you could double the size of the ensemble within the year.

When we began our careers, our flame burned brightly because all things seemed possible, and we were focused on what could be. We were future-oriented in our thinking. When we focused on the future at that time, we made decisions and took actions in alignment with where we wanted to head. We let our dream for a brighter future guide us.

Wherever you are in your career, look within and search for that feeling, that spark you had when you started out on this music education adventure. Reuniting with that original feeling will serve you today. You kept the light on when many others would have turned the light off. When many would have thrown in the towel and walked away, you persevered and modeled resilience, creativity, and innovation. When confronted with struggle and challenge, instead of throwing your hands up, you wrung your hands together and said, "Let's get to work."

● ● ●

What does "upbeat" mean? Well, in addition to meaning "a positive outlook," our upbeat is how we choose to start our day, our class, or a piece of music. Just like the conductor prepares the ensemble to play the first note with a preparatory upbeat gesture, we also prepare for the decisions, actions, and interactions in our mind. Every day, no matter how challenging, is an opportunity to choose our upbeat—our attitude and our intention—with which we embrace the moment. Our thoughts and attitude are the upbeat to our actions and behaviors, and we have the power and freedom to intentionally choose our thoughts and our attitudes. *What* we choose to focus on affects how we perceive our circumstances and impacts the people in our lives.

My purpose for writing *Upbeat!* is to inspire you, guide you, and lift you up. While providing hands-on and immediately applicable ideas and strategies, my intention is to affirm how important you are and establish that *what* you do, *why* you do it, and *how* you do it matters. While I wrote *Upbeat!* with the music educator in mind, the principles, concepts, and strategies in this book can apply to everyone. I have taught these ideas to students of all ages and from all disciplines, teachers in every field, and professionals from every walk of life, and although many of the stories come from my life in music, the messages are universal.

Upbeat! is for those courageous music teachers who have struggled and faced immeasurable challenges and yet have charged forth and persevered. This is for the teacher who dove headfirst into the music education profession with light in their eyes and a dream to make a difference on the front line, sharing the mystery and joy of music with students of all ages. This is for the teacher who has been teaching for over twenty years and continues to evolve and adapt. This is for the teacher who has taught for over ten years and is just catching their stride. This is for the teacher in their first decade of teaching who came out of college with vigor and excitement, inspired by their former teachers and a desire to pave their own way. This is for the university student who has a vision of how they want to teach music and sees a future of endless possibilities. This book is also for our students, since what we do as music educators is inextricably linked to their learning, growth, and well-being.

This book is also a reminder of why what we do as music teachers is so vitally important. You will read ideas, strategies, and stories to help lift you up in the dark times and to keep you moving steadfastly towards the light. In our journey together, you will discover that you are in control of your destiny and that you can choose your mindset and mindfully create music classrooms that don't just survive but actually *thrive*.

Teachers and students around the world have been impacted by these Upbeat! concepts, leading to changes in how they live, learn, and lead. It is my desire that this book also ignites a spark within you to inspire you and your students as you reach higher with more enthusiasm, gratitude, and energy. I wrote this book for you, and it is also my hope that, in addition to considering and integrating what is written here, you will also share these ideas with others.

When I teach students leadership, I begin with the message that the students get to play two roles. First, they are learners; they get to absorb, soak up the message, reflect on it, and grow. Second, they are messengers; they get the responsibility of sharing what they learn with others. I hope you will also approach this material as both a learner and a messenger so that together we can share this message and create positive change, both locally and globally, through music, mindset, mindfulness, culture, and leadership.

Upbeat! is divided into three parts:

- **Part 1: IGNITE!** ignites the spark and lights the flame for you to choose your upbeat, to live with the Power of G.E.T., to supercharge your morning, and to sustain your upbeat all day through refilling your cup with self-care strategies so that you can be at your best every day as you share the superpower of music.

- **Part 2: INSPIRE!** brings the power of the upbeat into your classroom, with a focus on elevating mindset, integrating mindfulness, and creating an upbeat culture.

- **Part 3: LEAD!** activates the 4 C's of Upbeat Leadership to empower your students to lead from within so that they can inspire and encourage others to achieve their full potential.

Each chapter concludes with the following:

- **VIGNETTE:** Every chapter includes a vignette from a music educator who shares a true story of how an Upbeat! concept has affected them and their students.
- **APPLICATION:** This section provides suggested strategies for you to apply the content and ideas to your personal and teaching life.
- **JOURNAL:** Take time to pause, reflect, and dig deeper to integrate what you have read into your being.
- **QUOTES:** Discover powerful quotes that add meaning and strengthen the chapter's message.

Before you begin Chapter 1, take a moment to set your intention for how you will approach reading this book. Ask yourself: Why am I excited to get started? What do I hope to gain? Am I open to new possibilities? Set an intention that allows you to get the most out of our time together. My intention is to transform your life and your students' lives for the better by helping you tap into unknown reservoirs of possibility already within you. What is your intention?

Let's begin by rediscovering your own light, beauty, and promise so that you can inspire your students and get the most out of each and every day.

ENDNOTE

1. Pema Chödrön, *Start Where You Are: A Guide to Compassionate Living* (Boulder, CO: Shambhala, 2018), 4.

PART 1: IGNITE!

Chapter 1

CHOOSE YOUR UPBEAT

The upbeat is the preparation for any event.[1]
— Alan Gilbert

You finally fall asleep and, seemingly right at that moment, your alarm clock goes off. Annoyed, you quickly press the snooze button, hoping to get just ten more minutes of rest. Eventually, you groggily get out of bed, exhausted, sore, and cranky, and you think to yourself that it's just another day. Raining, as a matter of fact. You manage to get ready for school, racing around the house trying not to forget anything you need. On your drive, you think about how you wish you could have gotten more sleep. You arrive at school, hoping to find a reserve of energy to make it through the day. And then as class starts and the students walk into your classroom, you notice that the coffee doesn't seem to be kicking in and the students are wound up more than usual. The emails haven't stopped since you announced changes to your grading policy and your administration is breathing down your neck. You wish you could just be home and crawl back into bed and go back to sleep.

Have you ever had a day like this?

What if instead you could live days from beginning to end that were filled with vibrancy, where you felt truly present? Imagine waking up each morning with boundless enthusiasm, springing out of bed with energy and anticipation for what the day will bring, intent on creating the best day ever. You take in some deep breaths and reflect on how lucky you are to be alive and to have this day. You recognize that each and every day is a gift and an opportunity to learn and experience new things. You approach each moment with wonder and curiosity, marveling at the beauty of nature and the various sounds that you hear as you begin your morning routine. You look forward to seeing your students and you recognize how fortunate you are to get to teach music and elevate the quality of students' lives through what you teach and role-model. Yes, this is a good day. Embrace it. You've got this!

Now, let's get real. How often does this happen to us? Our lives are demanding, hectic, and, at times, chaotic. We have pressures that consume us, like family, school, finances, cars that break down, conductor scores to learn, lessons to plan, and just plain ol' life.

Have you noticed that when we focus on what we love about what we do, we feel more energized and motivated, but when we focus on what we don't enjoy, we can end up wallowing in negativity, pessimism, and yes, even despair and defeat? What we think about and focus on definitely has a dramatic effect on our mood and feelings, and we have much more control and agency than we realize.

Is there a relationship between what we think about, our mindset, and music making? A few years ago, I asked myself this question and then stumbled across an article in *The New York Times* from April 6, 2012, called "The Maestro's Mojo" by Daniel J. Wakin on the topic of conducting. The answer to my question jumped out at me. In a discussion about conducting gestures, Alan Gilbert, former conductor of the New York Philharmonic said, "The upbeat is the preparation for any event."[2] I understood the power of the upbeat in music, but now it could be applied to *any event*?! I reflected on how much power and information there truly is in the conducting upbeat—the preparatory beat. Imagining the initial entrance to a piece of music, consider the impact of the breath—the quality of the inhale, the facial expression, the tenor of the eyes, the gentleness or force in the arms, and the speed and size of the gesture. The conductor must hear and visualize the sound they want to create in their mind before it happens. The upbeat anticipates but also motivates the sound that arises.

Our upbeat is our preparatory beat, the conducting gesture that prepares the musicians before sound begins. That beat contains all the information needed to know how the music will sound. The energy with which the baton or fingertips leave the plane shows the articulation and energy that the front of the note receives. The time that it takes from the beginning of the upbeat to the beginning of the downbeat determines the tempo of the piece. The size of the gesture shows the volume or dynamic. The emotion and feeling of the sound are also communicated in the gesture of the upbeat. The conductor hears the music in their head, raises their baton upward, and then lowers it to return to the same location in space from which it began. When the baton touches this place in space, the musicians play and the musical piece begins. The musicians and conductor even sync up their breathing, inhaling on the upbeat and exhaling on the downbeat.

Just as conductors choose their upbeat gesture and the meaning behind it, we can also choose our upbeat—our attitude, thoughts, and what we choose to focus on. We can choose to focus on what is wrong or we can choose to focus on what we want to create. Just as conductors communicate and signal so much important information in the gesture of an upbeat, our mind transmits so much energy through our attitude and thoughts. Our personal upbeat impacts our thoughts, influences our feelings, and impacts our actions and behavior. How we choose to conduct ourselves not only determines our future but makes a difference in the lives of others. **When we realize that we are, in fact, the conductors and composers of our lives, our own lives become more fulfilling, and our students reap the benefits through the clarity of our example.**

Our Thoughts Are the Upbeats to Our Actions

What I have come to realize is our thoughts are the upbeat to our actions, the downbeats. Our attitude is the upbeat to any situation or event. And most importantly, we have the power to choose our thoughts and our attitude. You decide on the *what* and *where* of your focus. Choose to focus on what you *get* to do and what you *can* do rather than on what you *can't* do. Focus on what you enjoy rather than on what you don't enjoy. Focus on the goodness in others rather than what annoys you. When we intentionally choose our upbeat, we transform how we live, teach, and thrive each day.

Viktor Frankl, an Auschwitz survivor of the Holocaust of World War II, taught us this important lesson in *Man's Search for Meaning*: "Everything can be taken from a man but one thing: the last of the human freedoms—to choose one's attitude in any given set of circumstances, to choose one's own way."[3]

The attitude we choose to roll out of bed with in the morning is the upbeat to our day. Our attitude when we arrive at school in the morning is the upbeat to our day at school. The forethought and work we do to prepare for each music class is the upbeat to the class. How we greet and welcome students into our music room is the upbeat to that class. The way the band, choir, and orchestra take the stage is the upbeat to their concert. The way the marching band takes the field is the upbeat to their performance. Beyond music, the upbeat applies to every walk of life. For example, in football, the throw is the upbeat and the catch is the downbeat. In basketball, the shot is the upbeat, the swish is the downbeat. In track-and-field relays, the handoff of the baton is the upbeat and the catch is the downbeat.

Sometimes it may feel that we don't get to choose our upbeat, that we are like the silver ball in a pinball game, aimlessly ricocheting to and fro, directionless. The good news is we don't have to live that way. We can take control of our lives by setting our intention and choosing where we direct our attention and focus. Just as music is played one beat at a time, our lives are lived one beat at a time. **One decision to be intentional about the upbeat to the many moments of our day ultimately ignites the spark that leads to positive change.**

Extending the metaphor of the upbeat, we can see how preparation leads to each event repeatedly throughout the day. We may prepare a meal in the kitchen prior to eating it. In the process of preparation, we set an intention for what we want to make, affected by several factors.

- What are we in the mood to eat?
- What food do we have in the house to choose from?
- What will be healthy and nourishing for our body so we can have more energy and be productive?
- What combination of food feels good?
- How much should we make based on how hungry we are and how many people will be eating?
- How much time do we have to make the meal?

Perhaps we set an intention to prepare a tasty, healthy meal in fifteen minutes because we are on a tight schedule. After we prepare the meal, we may prepare the table by setting out a plate, glass, and silverware. Now we are ready to eat. Thinking about what we want to make is the upbeat to the slicing, dicing, pouring, cooking, and mixing of the food. The making of the meal is the upbeat to setting the table. Lifting the food up to our mouth is the upbeat to the first bite. By breaking down our actions into meaningful steps like this, we see how important the upbeat is.

Every day is filled with upbeats leading to downbeats—your thoughts followed by your intentional actions. In music each beat leads to the next beat; in many cases the beat we arrive on becomes the upbeat to the next beat. Likewise, eating a meal can serve as the physical preparation, or the upbeat, to give you the energy for the next task or action of your day.

Our attitude greatly impacts the decisions we make and how we respond to others. Strive to live each day and approach every situation with a positive, upbeat attitude, not just because you will feel better but also because you will be sharper, more creative, more vibrant, solution-oriented, and more aware of the value and positive attributes of others. In his book *The 7 Habits of Highly Effective People*, Stephen R. Covey writes, "All people see the world, not as it is, but as they are," explaining how our perception changes the lens through which we see and interact with the world.[4] With an upbeat attitude, you will look for the goodness in others and therefore tend to treat others with kindness, respect, dignity, and compassion. **Visualize who you would like to become and then let your aspiration guide your decisions in the present.**

Upbeat People

We probably all have at least one "upbeat" person in our lives. When I reflect on upbeat people in my life, I am reminded of Tom Kowalski, one of the counselors at the middle school where I taught band over twenty years ago. At that time in my career, I remember moving very fast and always being in a hurry. I am sure it was related to the fact that I had over three hundred students in the band program, seven classes a day, and only four-minute passing periods. The counseling office was across the hall from the entrance to the band room, so there were many occasions when, while racing up to the front office or to the restroom during a short break between classes, I would encounter Tom walking towards me. Imagine me, laser focused on my destination and Tom, relaxed and upbeat, waving and saying, "Hi, Matthew! How's it going?" His vibrant energy and body language communicated his excitement to see me and that this was a great day. Tom would stop me in my tracks, and I would pause and respond in kind, "Hi, Tom! I'm doing great. How are you?"

Now, as one of only two counselors for the nearly seven hundred middle school students, Tom's job was just as demanding as mine. However, this did not interfere with his ability to lead from the heart and lift others up. It is remarkable how one person can truly make a difference in the lives of so many by the energy that they choose to bring to situations and relationships. Who are the upbeat people in your life? Are you an upbeat person for someone you know?

Focus *On* Purpose and *With* Purpose

How is it that some choose to dwell on what is wrong while others find a way to focus on the sun amidst the shadows? Diving into research in the fields of neuroscience and positive psychology, I have been fascinated by the following discoveries that may shed some light on this question.

On average, our brain takes in eleven million bits of information per second, but we are only conscious of forty bits of information.[5] What if we could choose which bits we focus on? The remarkable truth is, we can!

The average person thinks approximately 65,000 thoughts per day, but 95 percent of those thoughts are the same thoughts that we thought yesterday, the day before that, and the day before that.[6] First of all, that is a massive amount of thinking, and, secondly, what are we spending our time thinking about? Most of our thinking is actually done at an unconscious and subconscious level and has become a habitual automatic response. However, we can intentionally create new habits of thought that serve us and others better by rewiring our brain through consistent practice.

We tend to worry about the future, but on average, 85 percent of what we worry about never happens.[7] What are worries that you have had that either turned out to be nothing or that led to experiences where you grew and learned from?

How we respond is greatly up to us and has much less to do with the circumstances, good or bad, in which we find ourselves. While 50 percent is brain wiring, only 10 percent is circumstances, and 40 percent is our choice.[8] In his 2011 TED Talk "The Happy Secret to Better Work," Shawn Achor noted, "It is not necessarily the reality that shapes us but the lens through which your brain views the world shapes your reality. And if we change the lens, we can change your happiness and your outcomes."[9] How does this relate to your life? Have you ever changed your attitude and then noticed your perception of reality changed?

In his book *The Power of a Positive Team*, author Jon Gordon reports on research from the Heart Math Institute, which found that "when you have a feeling in your heart, it goes to every cell in your body, then outward—and other people up to 10 feet away can sense feelings transmitted by your heart. You are either broadcasting positive energy or negative energy, apathy or passion, indifference or purpose."[10] As teachers this discovery has profound implications for the impact that our own feelings and energy can have on our students!

We have the freedom to choose where we direct our focus, but unfortunately we tend to let distractions and messaging from others take away that freedom. We are also hardwired to look for danger, threats, and risks as part of our survival mechanism, so it takes concerted effort to notice what is right more than what is wrong. Placing so much attention on what's wrong amplifies what we don't have or what we do have and wish we didn't. What we focus on grows and expands. A 2005 study by the National Science Foundation found that, on average, 80 percent of our thoughts are negative. That means four out of five things that pass through our mind are thoughts of fear, anger, frustration, loneliness, doubt, guilt, or depression.[11] These feelings and emotions are part of being human and are perfectly natural. In fact, some of the greatest music has been inspired by angst, pain, lost love, loss, anger, and fear. Our emotions are our response to a situation, other people, and the human condition. Rather than suppressing unwanted emotions, acknowledge and lean into them. As Marc Brackett writes in *Permission to Feel*, "If you can name it, you can tame it."[12]

The challenge is that when we are consumed with stress, fear, sadness, or anger, the amygdala takes over our brain, sending chemicals like cortisol, adrenaline, and norepinephrine throughout our body. Daniel Goleman, in the book *Emotional Intelligence*, calls this an "amygdala hijack," which kicks into action as part of our fight, flight, or freeze response when we are truly in danger. This stress response narrows our focus, and it can help us get out of harm's way quickly, but if we stay in this state for too long, we find ourselves descending emotionally in a downward spiral. When our amygdala is in control, we are unable to tap into our neocortex and prefrontal cortex, which allow us to see more options, to find solutions, and to see problems and challenges as opportunities.[13]

In contrast, positive emotions, such as joy, pride, gratefulness, and happiness, broaden our focus, allowing us to see more possibilities and creative solutions. In a positive frame of mind, our prefrontal cortex and neocortex are stimulated, flooding our brain with good chemicals, such as dopamine, serotonin, endorphins, and oxytocin, to help reach a higher level in intelligence, physical fitness, energy, and immunity. By intentionally training and wiring our brains to see the positives in others and to see opportunities in challenges, we can activate our growth and development and access the best versions of ourselves. You can practice this by purposefully noticing the good in others, particularly in those that present a greater challenge to you! Let go of your prior experiences and opinions and begin anew with a fresh intention to notice the positives.

As music conductors, we also *choose* where we direct our focus. When we hear a wrong note or rhythm, our ear instinctively notices so that we can work on correcting the mistake. We may also choose to pay particular attention to the balance of the ensemble, making judgments on what voices or instruments should be brought out or turned down in the texture. Alternatively, we may direct our attention towards intonation and determine how pitch needs to be adjusted. In the pursuit of excellence, we also look for positives in the rehearsal to praise and reinforce. We can additionally choose to demonstrate a model phrase through playing our instrument or singing for our students. As educators, we are continually looking for positives to reinforce and areas to critique and improve.

The point is that where we direct our focus determines our perception of reality, and if we make the intentional choice to seek the good in ourselves and the good in others, we will find it. As we look for the positives in others, we may be surprised by what we hadn't noticed before that was right before our very eyes. Through consistent and intentional practice, the upbeat that we choose for our lives will not only lift us up, but it will also lift up our students and everyone else in our lives. **Positivity and negativity are both contagious. Why not choose to spread positivity?**

What Are You Broadcasting?

As music teachers and conductors, the energy that we transmit to our students and ensembles is contagious, which is why becoming self-aware and intentional about how we show up is essential to creating a positive learning environment. Balancing how we feel with what we aspire to communicate is one of the challenges of teaching, because our inner selves affect the external world and our interactions with others. A research study conducted by Dr. Albert Mehrabian in 1967 concluded that when it comes to in-person verbal communication related to attitudes and feelings, we are most impacted by non-verbal and paralinguistic communication (how something is said or the tone of voice) more than the words themselves. The surprising result of this study concluded that the effectiveness of communication, as related to attitudes and feelings, is influenced as follows: 7 percent by the words we use, 38 percent by our tone of voice, and 55 percent by our body language.[14] While this study was limited in scope and applied to very specific situations, these results raise awareness of the diversity of methods and practices that can be used for communication. Have you ever thought that you were communicating clearly to your students only to discover that what you had hoped to convey was misunderstood? Sometimes our facial expressions send a different message than our words, leading to confusion. By teaching with an open and inviting posture, a relaxed face and smile, and enthusiasm in our voice, we can create a welcoming classroom atmosphere.

In her book *Broadcasting Happiness*, former television news broadcaster Michelle Gielan describes the influence that we have on others through what we think, say, and do. Gielan tells her personal story of graduating from college with a dream of becoming a TV news broadcaster. She achieved her goal only to discover that it was not all what she hoped it would be. Starting her career as a news reporter in El Paso, Texas, she moved after a couple years to report the news in Chicago. While conducting interviews there, she was moved by the people living in low-income neighborhoods who, despite adversity, managed to focus on the positive aspects of their lives. In just a couple of years, Gielan was promoted to a coveted CBS news anchor position in New York City. Of course, she was ecstatic, as this was a summit achievement for someone in their late twenties. However, the type of news that she found herself reporting on day in and day out began to wear on her. The news was almost always negative. She realized that the negative slant of the news not only had a negative impact on her own mood and outlook but also on the emotions and thoughts of her viewers.

Rather than continuing to report the news as usual, she made a proposal to the CBS executives to try something new. She asked for permission to report on only positive things for one week, and fortunately CBS agreed. Michelle named this week "Happy Week," a week she filled with stories of gratitude, love, giving, and positive achievements. You can imagine the result: CBS received more positive feedback for Happy Week than it had for all its reporting for the entire year! I wish I could say that this changed news reporting forever; we all know that it did not. CBS returned to business as usual and Michelle left that job to enroll in a graduate program at the University of Pennsylvania, where she researched positive psychology and discovered that broadcasting itself is not limited to reporters; we are all broadcasters![15] Notably, what we broadcast—happiness, anger, sadness, joy, enthusiasm, disappointment—is contagious and can influence how others respond to us.

Gielan shares that we can determine the direction of a conversation by actually leading with a positive statement or question, such as, "What do you *enjoy most* about this piece of music?" or "What are you *looking forward to* the most today?" Gielan calls this a "power lead."[16] I prefer to call it a "positive lead." Regardless of what it is called, leading with positivity can make a significant difference in your communication with administrators, teachers, students, colleagues, friends, and family. Imagine how you can lift your principal's spirits by stopping by their office to ask them what the highlight of their day has been or by simply sharing a recent memorable teaching moment from your classroom.

An analogy that reminds me of the influence I can have on myself and others is the thermometer-thermostat comparison. To know the temperature, I can either look at my phone or look outside at the thermometer on a wall in our backyard. A thermometer simply measures and reports the temperature. I can't do anything to change the weather. Mother Nature does not allow me to have any say in the matter! However, I *can* change the temperature indoors by adjusting a thermostat. In life, we can either choose to accept the emotional weather, like the temperature reading from a thermometer, or we can intentionally choose our attitude and feelings, making a difference like a thermostat, fine-tuning our internal weather forecast.

Choose Your Response

To bring this back to music, I will share an idea I first learned decades ago from choral conductor and author James Jordan at a conducting workshop and then subsequently read about in his book *The Musician's Soul*. When we study music and prepare a score prior to the first rehearsal, we envision and imagine the ideal, pristine sound that we want the ensemble to create. However, the truth is that the first rehearsal rarely matches what we hear internally. Jordan notes that this can cause the conductor to become confrontational with the ensemble because the sound is jarring and incongruent with their vision. A conductor may immediately react emotionally and physically with frustration or even anger. In my early years of teaching, I definitely experienced those feelings. However, when we react with disappointment, we create a confrontational atmosphere in rehearsal. The good news is that if we simply pause for less than a second, breathe, and, instead of reacting with anger, choose to respond with love and openness, we can begin the beautiful process of collaboration. It is as if there are two primary possibilities from which to choose when we are rehearsing an ensemble. We either choose the reaction of anger, frustration, and disappointment or the response of love, support, and hope. When we choose a higher vibing emotion like love, we give ourselves and students grace, establishing a culture of mutual support and a safe space for openness and vulnerability. Jordan describes the feeling he has when he raises his arms up to begin a rehearsal as "embracing the ensemble," a description which has not only changed the way I rehearse but also influenced my relationship with the musicians. I have learned that our upbeat begins long before we actually give the first preparatory beat of a piece. Our upbeat begins in our perception of and attitude towards the musicians in the ensemble.[17]

Learning from Jordan, I now remind myself during every rehearsal that I have the power and *responsibility* to choose my response. How I respond to the musicians' performance impacts the feeling and the direction of the rehearsal. My mental and emotional preparation for the rehearsal, therefore, matters just as much as my musical preparation. Rather than being upset with the mismatch between what I want to hear and what I am actually hearing, I have chosen to teach the students in front of me and appreciate the opportunity to teach and inspire them to work harder, reach higher, and make music together. Choosing to have an upbeat attitude before rehearsal or class begins has made all the difference in how I feel and how the students respond, learn, and achieve. Have you noticed how your own upbeat affects your teaching, rehearsing, and communication with others? Every day brings a new opportunity to choose your upbeat.

Vignette

Mark D. Stice
Director of Bands
Okemos High School, Okemos, Michigan

In the summer of 2019, I was privileged to host Dr. Arau the night before he spoke with student leaders from around Michigan at Okemos High School. We spent most of our time talking about how changing your mindset can help you live an upbeat life. I remember feeling that the spark within my own mind leading into the upcoming school year was not as bright as years past. Because of our conversation, instead of trying to get to the root of my downturn in motivation, I became more curious and motivated to look forward instead of back. The following day, I felt more optimistic and decided to really look at the upcoming school year as a blank slate. I could not have picked a better time to do this because what I heard during Dr. Arau's leadership training with the students unlocked the motivated, enthusiastic, upbeat person within me that had been held back for quite some time.

With thirty of my own leaders present at the leadership training, I knew the tone the leaders set would positively influence the rest of the band. However, it really started with the tone I was setting. As the day went on, my mind began racing with all the times I started rehearsal, instruction, or a greeting with a "don't" statement. Right then, I decided to change just how I spoke with the leaders to address what they should *do*. Immediately, I saw a difference in the students, and it carried throughout the rest of the school year. With this one flip of how I address students, I felt I had the best year of my teaching career as a result.

For me, to be upbeat is to constantly and consistently make a choice of how I will respond in any situation. I can easily choose to show and speak with frustration, anger, or any other way that does not honor the other person. When I have responded in such a way, reaching resolution or reconciliation becomes a more difficult task. However, when I focus on the positive and approach the situation with understanding and compassion, I have found situations resolve with relationships intact much quicker than before. My overall stress level has decreased in every aspect of my life, and I know it's because I make a choice to control my thoughts and focus on being upbeat.

What is more exciting is to see how my students have grabbed onto the upbeat message. After attending both in-person and virtual Upbeat! Leadership Academies, the demonstrations of leadership by my students in and out of the classroom increased. Leaders were taking initiative with their sections in ways that I had not seen before. More and more students were getting together for extra sectionals, there was little to no conflict between students, students left rehearsals with smiles on their faces after reaching for the goals they had set for themselves, and the connections they built could be seen as they passed through the halls of the school. I could hear students using words like "passion," "commitment," "positivity," and "family" when talking with each other. These words come from the mission statement they created during the Upbeat Leadership Academy.

I take an upbeat attitude with me wherever I go, thinking about how my upbeat, the preparation for any event, will determine the success and happiness I feel at the end of the day, and I know many of my students do too.

Application

1. Smile more often. You will feel great and your smile will light up another's day. Smiling stimulates our brains, creating dopamine and raising our energy levels. One study on smiling concluded that those who smile a lot will live up to seven years longer![18]

2. To prime the mind, recall good feelings, memories, and successes. Thinking about positives in the past stimulates you at a physiological level as if you are experiencing those events in the present moment.

3. Practice taking a breath before reacting instantly. This will give you time to process and think clearly and intentionally choose your response.

4. Take time in class to ask students to share successes they have had during the week or during music class.

5. Set an intention to teach music from a place of collaboration.

6. Set an intention to begin class looking forward to possibilities.

Journal Questions

1. How does becoming aware of your power to choose your personal upbeat affect the way you embrace the day?

2. What have you learned from experiences where your leadership came from a negative place rather than from an uplifting attitude?

3. Where do you see yourself five years from now? How do you think your upbeat will impact your journey to get there?

4. Think about a time when you were a thermometer instead of a thermostat. What was the situation? What was the result? How could it have gone differently if you'd had the mindset of a thermostat?

5. Who is your upbeat person? Are you an upbeat person for someone you know?

Quotes

We cannot always control what happens to us, but we can learn to control our interpretation of what happens to us and in so doing learn to be more optimistic and feel better about ourselves.

— Andrew Weil
Spontaneous Happiness, p. 131

Believe that life is worth living, and your belief will help create the fact.

— William James
as quoted in William Chang's
Wisdom for the Soul, p. 92

We don't see things as they are, we see them as we are.

— Anaïs Nin
as quoted in Peter Allman's
Shrink-Proof Your Life, p. 5

Our happiness or unhappiness depends to an important degree on the habit of mind we cultivate.

— Norman Vincent Peale
The Power of Positive Thinking, p. 59

The attitudes you have about yourself determine the attitudes you will have about everything else around you. So if you want to change the way you feel about anything else, you have to start first with the attitudes you have about yourself.

— Shad Helmstetter
What to Say When You Talk to Your Self, p. 140

Always remember, your focus determines your reality.

— George Lucas
as quoted in S. Michele Nevarez's
Emotionally Intelligent Habits, p. 46

Endnotes

1. Daniel J. Wakin, "The Maestro's Mojo," *The New York Times*, April 6, 2012, https://www.nytimes.com/2012/04/08/arts/music/breaking-conductors-down-by-gesture-and-body-part.html.
2. Ibid.
3. Viktor Frankl, *Man's Search for Meaning* (Boston: Beacon Press, 2006), 66.
4. Stephen R. Covey, *The 7 Habits of Highly Effective People: Restoring the Character Ethic* (New York: Fireside, 1990), 277.
5. Christine Porath, *Mastering Civility: A Manifesto for the Workplace* (New York: Grand Central Publishing, 2016), 83. Original source: Manfred Zimmermann, "Neurophysiology of Sensory Systems," in *Fundamentals of Sensory Physiology*, ed. R. F. Schmidt (Berlin: Springer Berlin Heidelberg, 1986), 68–116.

6. Scott Shickler and Jeff Waller, *The 7 Mindsets to Live Your Ultimate Life: An Unexpected Blueprint for an Extraordinary Life* (Hartford, CT: Publish Your Purpose Press, 2019), 85.
7. Robert L. Leahy, *The Worry Cure: Seven Steps to Stop Worry from Stopping You* (New York: Three Rivers Press, 2006), 18.
8. Sonja Lyubomirsky, Kennon M. Sheldon, and David Schkade, "Pursuing Happiness: The Architecture of Sustainable Change," *Review of General Psychology* 9, no. 2 (n.d.), 116.
9. Shawn Achor, "The Happy Secret to Better Work," TED Talk (May 2011), https://www.ted.com/talks/shawn_achor_the_happy_secret_to_better_work.
10. Jon Gordon, *The Power of a Positive Team: Proven Principles and Practices that Make Great Teams Great* (Hoboken, NJ: John Wiley & Sons, 2018), 21.
11. Neringa Antanaityte, "How to Effortlessly Have More Positive Thoughts," TLEX Institute, accessed September 28, 2021, https://tlexinstitute.com/how-to-effortlessly-have-more-positive-thoughts/.
12. Marc Brackett, *Permission to Feel: Unlocking the Power of Emotions to Help Our Kids, Ourselves, and Our Society Thrive* (New York: Celadon Books, 2019), 105.
13. Daniel Goleman, *Emotional Intelligence: Why It Can Matter More than IQ* (New York: Bantam Books, 1995), 13–29.
14. Albert Mehrabian and Susan R. Ferris, "Inference of attitudes from nonverbal communication in two channels," *Journal of Consulting Psychology 31,* no. 3 (1967): 248–252, https://doi.org/10.1037/h0024648.
15. Michelle Gielan, *Broadcasting Happiness: The Science of Igniting and Sustaining Positive Change* (Dallas: BenBella Books, 2015), ix–24.
16. Ibid., 33.
17. James Jordan, *The Musician's Soul: A Journey Examining Spirituality for Performers, Teachers, Composers, Conductors, and Music Educators* (Chicago: GIA Publications, 1999), 109–122.
18. Ernest L. Abel and Michael L. Kruger, "Smile Intensity in Photographs Predicts Longevity," *Psychological Science* 21, no. 4 (2010): 542–544.

Chapter 2

THE POWER OF G.E.T.

There are only two ways to live your life. One is as though nothing is a miracle. The other is as though everything is a miracle.[1]
— Albert Einstein

On September 12, 2020, I woke up around 6:00 a.m. and began my morning routine making green tea, meditating, and stretching. It was a gloomy, drab, and rainy morning—quite chilly for an early September day in Wisconsin. The weather was less than inviting, so instead of heading out to the pool for my morning swim, I picked up my notebook and began to journal. Because it was September 12, I naturally started reflecting on the day before, but I didn't write about September 11, 2020. Instead, my mind traveled back in time to 9/11—September 11, 2001. In the fall of 2001, I was just starting my fifth year of teaching as a middle school band director at Walt Clark Middle School in Loveland, Colorado. I remember arriving at school and hearing the news from my principal that a plane had flown into one of the Twin Towers in

New York City. I quickly walked to my band room and turned on the television mounted on the wall. I was completely unprepared for the image that I saw on the screen.

As the students in my first two classes of sixth grade band entered the room, I motioned for them to quietly sit, and without getting out our instruments, we watched in horror and disbelief. In the first class, we witnessed the first tower crumble in flames and in the second class we saw the second tower fall. I did my best to console my students, but in the moment I truly had no words with which to express myself or explain. After lunch as the first seventh grade band entered the room, they asked, "Can we play our instruments? We are sick and tired of watching the news all day. Can we just play music?" I felt the same way and was glad to be able to focus our attention on creating something beautiful together rather than watching something tragic and unimaginable.

After the students put together their instruments, we had a brief warm-up and then opened our method book to #6, which happened to be a six-measure excerpt of *America* in 3/4 meter in the key of E-flat major. Many know the words to this tune: "My country 'tis of thee, sweet land of liberty, of thee I sing." We must have played that six-measure piece over and over at least thirty times. Those six measures contained all the feeling and meaning that we wanted to find and share. The second seventh grade band had the same experience as the first. Next, the two eighth grade bands followed. The older students also wanted to play music rather than watch the news, so after getting their instruments together and tuning up, we opened our music folders, which coincidentally already had an appropriate piece for the moment, an arrangement of *Amazing Grace*. We poured our heart and soul into the music, and I am not exaggerating when I say we played *Amazing Grace* seven times in a row.

On that day, all of us came to realize the true power of music in a way that we had never felt before. There were no words, but through music we could express our emotions, thoughts, and feelings in ways that words failed. We felt a mixture of shock, terror, and sadness inside, and music provided the outlet for all of us to mourn for the loss of those who lost their lives that fateful day. In addition to trying to be at my best for my students that day, I was equally concerned for the safety of my younger brother, Javier, and his wife, Kelley, who had just moved to New York ten days earlier. My family could not reach them all day, and we were relieved later to find that they were safe.

Writing about this experience and remembering the heroism and bravery of so many shifted my mindset completely from how I felt before I sat down to journal and how I felt after journaling. I found myself grateful to be alive and appreciative for what I do have, and as my writing turned towards making a to-do list for the day, as I had done for many mornings of my life, something shifted in a small but dramatic way.

As my journal reflections evolved into making plans and goals for the day, what would have normally been a long "to-do" list became a "get-to-do" list:

- I get to call Mark.
- I get to email Sarah.
- I get to teach my class on a virtual learning platform.
- I get to attend a faculty meeting.
- I get to teach music.

- I get to play music.
- I get to help people maximize their potential.
- I get to make a difference.
- I get to breathe.
- I get to live.
- I get to smile.
- I get to listen.
- I get to see.
- I get to love.

A spark ignited in my mind as I realized how fortunate I was to be able to do any of those things—that I was fortunate to be breathing, to be alive. I laughed and wrote, "I get to dance in the rain" and "I get to swim." And I did go outside, despite the cold and the rain, and danced and dove into the pool. As I was swimming, I thought about how grateful I was that in the midst of a pandemic I could still stay in touch and communicate with people and teach my students online. Imagine if we didn't have this technology. I kept repeating in my mind all the things I *get* to do and I felt a powerful surge of energy from this new way of thinking.

While I was swimming, I realized, much like Carol Dweck's revelation about the power of "yet" and growth mindset,[2] that I was experiencing the power of "get." "Yet" is such a hopeful word, as in, "We aren't there *yet*." "Yet" implies that eventually we will get there. "Yet" is about the future. When I focus on what I *get* to do, it brings me into the present moment, into the now. The present is the only time where life truly happens, and if we are lost in the past or always thinking about the future, we miss out on the moment we are living in.

This focus reframes anything that I either took for granted or previously looked upon as an inconvenience or a "*have* to do." Most of us pursued a career teaching music because of a combination of love for helping students succeed and a love for teaching the art of music. On the job, however, we quickly became consumed with a mountain of other responsibilities and distractions that kept us away from "the main thing." To keep up with and to prioritize the administrative demands of email, phone calls, social media pages, parent meetings, purchasing, fundraising, organizing, cleaning, and distributing uniforms, we find ourselves making to-do lists, which include everything else that needs to be done outside of our music position as well, such as grocery shopping, going for a run, picking up the kids, attending that meditation seminar, making sack lunches, and driving to ballet classes and sports clubs. Our lists for each day can be overwhelming. It is easy to look at the list of activities in our day as "have to's."

But what if you could change your mindset? Even now as I write this book, I reflect that I *get* to write this sentence with a blue pen in cursive on this lined notebook. I *get* to sip tea from this ceramic mug here on the table next to me. I *get* to breathe fresh air. "Get" inspires me to be grateful for *now*. "Get" sparks enthusiasm for any task or encounter, and "get" reframes experiences as treasured opportunities to grow, to learn, to be challenged, to love, and to enjoy.

• • •

Since that dreary Wisconsin morning, I have worked to build a mental habit of *get*—to replace "have to" with "get to." The words of Max Planck, the 1918 Nobel Prize winner for physics, ring especially true: "When you change the way you look at things, the things you look at change."[3] When I live in a spirit of *get*, I notice a growing number of things and situations to be grateful for. I encourage you to try this. Begin adding the word "get" into your self-talk and even into your teaching and notice the positive impact it makes on you, your students, and your colleagues. There is so much power in this word. When we assign a word to each of the three letters, it acquires an even deeper meaning. In choosing these three words, I thought about how focusing on what I *get* to do makes me feel. Here is the acronym I'd like to share:

G = Gratitude
E = Enthusiasm
T = Treasure

G = Gratitude

Gratitude is the magic potion that shifts our mindset from noticing what is wrong to looking for what is right. When we feel gratitude for the people in our lives and express our thankfulness to them, we lift them up. Have you noticed how it makes someone else feel when you share thanks and appreciation for them? It also makes you feel good to share gratitude, right? Recently, psychologists have discovered how and why gratitude can have a dramatic impact on us and the people around us. Studies show that people's mental and emotional lives improve when psychologists ask what they are grateful for instead of asking them to focus on what has gone wrong in their lives. In a study by Robert Emmons and Robert McCollough on the power of gratitude, a randomly selected group of people wrote down three things they were grateful for in a journal every morning for two weeks. The results showed that those who had followed through on their daily expression of gratitude had gone through a mindset shift that caused them to notice more positive aspects in their lives.[4] This research is just one of many concluding that the practice of gratitude shifts our minds from unwanted or unpleasant emotions to others that are more constructive. Whether we think about gratitude, meditate on gratitude, share our appreciation, practice journaling on gratitude, give thanks, send a thank you card, or express gratitude in another way, we will improve how we feel, and when gratitude is shared, we give a ray of sunshine to someone else.[5] We do not need to wait to feel gratitude in order to find happiness or feel joy. In fact, it is the other way around. When we look for things to be grateful for, we discover joy.

Focusing on what we get to do and being grateful stimulates the positive centers of our brain and diminishes the narrowing and suppressive effects of stress and anxiety on our brains. **When we create a habit of adopting an attitude of gratitude, we become more aware of things that we appreciate. Our field of vision and perception broadens, we appreciate being alive, and we engage wholly to make the most of the day.**

Humans cannot multi-task, and that extends to our feelings and emotions.[6] We can, however, toggle between and amongst emotions.[7] By choosing to focus on gratitude, we can shift from unwanted feelings to what we want to feel more of. **Our choices matter. We can choose to obsess over what we don't have, or we can deeply appreciate what we *do* have. We can focus on everything that is wrong or notice what is *right*.** Although it is easier said than done, we can choose to focus on what we can do rather than on what we can't do. We may even tend to take what we can do for granted until that right or responsibility is taken away from us. We might take our health for granted until we get sick or take our loved ones for granted until they are no longer with us.

When the pandemic forced us into confinement and virtual teaching, we recalled with a greater appreciation all the things that we used to be able to do. We do not need to wait for things to be taken away, however, in order to appreciate them now. When we set an intention to live in a spirit of abundance, we can find fulfillment and gratitude for what we do have. When we feel appreciation and gratitude, no matter the circumstances, we notice that there is still much more to be grateful for.

E = Enthusiasm

The word "enthusiasm" derives from the Greek words for within (*en*), gods (*theos*), and essence (*ousia*). To feel "enthusiasm," therefore, can mean to feel God's essence within us or the spirit within us. No wonder it is such a powerful emotion! This feeling can generate dopamine and stimulate our prefrontal cortex and our senses, allowing us to fully soak in the present with a vibrant awareness. We may find ourselves smiling or laughing as we enjoy the ability to do the most mundane activities, like drinking a glass of water: "I get to drink a glass of clean water!" What a privilege when over two billion people on our planet do not have access to clean drinking water.[8] When we look back at our lives to recall moments when we have felt enthusiasm, those memories and images can further stimulate our brains. However, **we do not need to wait** for a special moment to feel enthusiasm. **We can intentionally choose to make each moment special.** As Brazilian soccer legend Pelé said, "Enthusiasm is everything. It must be taut and vibrating like a guitar string."

Imagine you only had today. How would you change your thoughts or your awareness? With only this moment, you might savor colors, textures, sounds, smells, feelings, and thoughts with greater wonder and amazement. Recall now the experience of finding something fresh and new. Remember what that felt like before routine or familiarity caused your senses and consciousness to go on autopilot. For me, I remember the excitement and enthusiasm I felt at the age of nine when I held my alto saxophone for the very first time and made my first sounds. The saxophone gleamed in its case, and I could not wait to put it together and make my own music. Even though my first sounds were super high squeaks because I had the mouthpiece upside down, I still remember how overjoyed I was to begin my journey as a musician. Can you remember how you felt when you had your first encounter with your instrument or with singing?

I also think back to the nervousness and euphoria of taking my first improvised solo in a concert with my junior high jazz band when I was thirteen. I had recently learned the minor pentatonic scale, and I looked forward to my first public blues-style solo. I remember my heart pounding as the piece was just measures away from where I got to stand up and play. I think I only played five different notes on my first solo, and it was most likely out of time and had a long way to go, but I was in heaven—I had taken my first solo. Do you recall moments of enthusiasm like this in your life?

I also reflect on the depth of emotion and connection to the students and the music I felt when I was a twenty-two-year-old student teacher with the Appleton West High School Wind Ensemble, conducting Percy Grainger's arrangement of *Irish Tune from County Derry*. This was the first piece I had the opportunity to conduct that had a deep level of meaning and expression. Not to say that the theme from *Mission Impossible* (the other piece I got to conduct) isn't a great piece, but I really connected with *Irish Tune*. I found the history and significance of the lyrics of *Danny Boy*, which were added to the original Irish tune, provided feeling, depth, and heart. In the rehearsals, the students and I listened to different versions of the piece and learned the words, discussing how important this piece is to the Irish people and that Danny symbolizes an Irish boy going off to war with the knowledge that he may not return home. The students played with such feeling and heart at the concert, and I was completely drawn into the moment conducting and communicating with the musicians. I noticed tears in students' eyes as they played, and I felt an emotional connection in a way that I had never experienced. The euphoric rush that I felt in those moments elevated my passion for music teaching, and that is why I decided to become a conductor.

We do not need to wait for pinnacle moments like these to feel enthusiasm. We can allow enthusiasm to flow from within for even the smallest tasks that may have become banal or routine. Even though we may have given the downbeat for rehearsals and led our students through warm-ups and fundamentals thousands of times, we can still decide to bring our enthusiastic selves to those moments. Bring a fresh approach to your day by introducing a *new* warm-up or rehearsal strategy. Make one up or add a variation to what you have traditionally done; your students will appreciate the novelty and

.so will you. Have your students sit next to someone in a different section and draw attention to how the listening changes when you sit in different places. Ask students what they notice now that they may not have heard when they were in their prior position. Invite students up front to listen and give comments, or ask a student to conduct part of the piece so that you can just listen. Step off the podium and walk around the room so that you can give individualized feedback. Find ways to change things up or alternate where you focus your attention—from notes, to rhythm, to articulation, to balance, to texture, to intonation, to harmony, to phrasing. Every moment can feel fresh by purposefully changing up the strategy or changing your mindset. In the end, a rehearsal is truly a series of moments connected through time. How are you approaching and savoring those moments? **When we begin to appreciate the little things for the roles they play in adding up to the big things in our lives, our attitude and outlook for each day—and ultimately our life—changes.**

T = Treasure

When I was a child, I loved stories and movies about hunting for hidden treasures. Characters in those tales would risk their lives to find buried treasure of diamonds, gold, and gems. The treasure may have been hidden in a chest in a ship at the bottom of the sea, secretly buried in a field under a great oak tree, or even under a slab of marble in an old cathedral, but it was always out there *somewhere*, eluding searches across years and sometimes centuries.

Unlike hunting for lost treasures, the Power of G.E.T. teaches us that treasure is not some hidden and elusive thing that is difficult and dangerous to discover. The greatest treasure lies within us, in our heart and in the lives we lead. **You are a treasure, and you can choose to treasure every moment and every person that you encounter.**

What if we treated every person, every moment, and every thing as a treasure? What if we looked for the beauty and value within others and appreciated them for what they have to offer the world? Shouldn't we treat ourselves as treasures too? What if we accepted the mission to hunt for the buried treasure in ourselves and in others, even in those with whom we disagree? Although some treasure is buried in plain sight, other times it is just below the surface, and finding it just takes one curious and adventurous person to dig a little deeper and overturn soil, rocks, and stone to find it.

Imagine if you approached every rehearsal with the mindset that you could discover and unlock the treasure of the music and the potential of your students. Imagine seeing every student as a treasure, no matter how well they play or sing. Have you noticed how students respond to your expectations and belief in them? Everyone wants to feel treasured, and as educators we can help our students see the treasure that already lies within them. Treasure the time you have, the things you have, the people you spend time with, and the opportunity to grow and learn, and you will begin to notice the abundance of buried treasure all around you.

The Power of *G.E.T.*™

G = Gratitude
E = Enthusiasm
T = Treasure

Living a G.E.T. Life

Living a G.E.T. life does not mean that we see the world through rose-colored lenses, blind and oblivious to challenges and dangers. What it means is that we will be much more present, aware, and appreciative so that we will find more meaning and purpose in the journey. Even a negative situation can be an opportunity for growth, and at the end of the day we will be able to look back on our experiences with gratitude and thankfulness. Andrew Weil writes in *Spontaneous Happiness*, "We cannot always control what happens to us, but we can learn to control our interpretation of what happens to us and in so doing learn to be more optimistic and feel better about ourselves."[9]

A traditional Chinese story about a farmer and his runaway horse further illustrates this point. The story appears in *The Book of*

Joy by His Holiness the Dalai Lama, Archbishop Desmond Tutu, and Douglas Abrams.

> His neighbors are quick to comment on his bad luck. The farmer responds that no one can know what is good and what is bad. When the horse comes back with a wild stallion, the neighbors are quick to comment, this time talking about the farmer's good luck. Again, the farmer replies that no one can know what is good and what is bad. When the farmer's son breaks his leg trying to tame the wild stallion, the neighbors now are certain of the farmer's bad luck. Again, the farmer says that no one knows. When war breaks out, all the able-bodied young men are conscripted into battle except the farmer's son, who was spared because of his broken leg.[10]

Our lives, like the farmer's life in this story, are filled with struggles, suffering, and pain, but we also get to experience joy, compassion, and love. When we intentionally live each day with a sense of gratitude, a feeling of enthusiasm, and a decision to treasure the opportunities and people in our lives, we will notice abundance rather than scarcity and make a positive difference in the lives of others.

Vignette

Alley Lacasse
Band Director, Belmont High School, Belmont, Massachusetts
Assistant Conductor, Sr. Massachusetts Youth Wind Ensemble,
New England Conservatory Preparatory School, Boston, Massachusetts

"I *get* to wake up every morning and rehearse my band."

Rather than take the everyday school schedule and think about it as a cyclical routine that can often feel daunting, I start each morning with a reminder about how lucky I am to do what I do, which has changed my attitude, energy, and mindset about my job as a high school band director and conductor. I will not pretend that I *only* have good days. I am a human being that deals with stress, deadlines, discipline issues, evaluations, budget, and the everyday email pileup that never seems to stop growing. However, Dr. Arau's approach with the Power of G.E.T. has changed how I calibrate my feelings at the onset of each day. This is a time where I have control over my thoughts and actions. If I am not setting myself up well for the day, that is on me. Dr. Arau's information and training has directly impacted my energy level, enthusiasm for waking up and heading to school, and has put the big picture into perspective. I facilitate the artistic and creative outlet for expression for my students. When you think about it that way, it sends a surge of energy throughout the body! Of course, all parts of the day aren't as magical; this way of thinking, however, allows oneself to persevere and get through the parts of our job as music teachers that challenge us the most.

I have had the distinct privilege of working with Dr. Arau and learning from him on this element of his work with my students. Dr. Arau played an important role in framing part of my virtual teaching in the 2020–2021 school year. In fact, his clinics inspired an idea to team up with a neighboring high school with a similar music program. When I was not able to traditionally rehearse my band due to pandemic health restrictions, I was determined to shift our focus to the culture and community of our band program. I wanted to engage with my students in a positive way, focusing on how we could raise the quality of the culture of our program. I focused on giving the students an outlet to reflect on the *why* of what we do.

When Dr. Arau worked with my students at Belmont High School on our various Zoom/Google Meet calls, he brought all the students through the three key words in the Power of G.E.T. This afforded us the time and space to recognize what we were thankful for, prompted enthusiasm about the music-making process, and helped us treasure each moment while being present and not taking anything for granted. Dr. Arau's approach with recharging the morning routine and focusing on what we *get* to do quickly turned into the language that I was using with my students at the beginning of each rehearsal. This kept the vibe positive and allowed for all of us (students and director) a chance to take stock of how lucky we were. It turns out that taking the time to focus on our gratitude only improves the music making—we are more consciously being creative and artistic. We are not just making beautiful music for a concert; we are making it for ourselves.

One student constantly remarked to me about how the training sessions helped her start her day in a more positive headspace. She is a student who speaks her mind and will never sugarcoat what she is feeling. She was the person who first commented about being grateful to have a list of steps to take to improve her mood and energy level at the beginning of her long day. Giving students the tools to shift their mindset from the negative to positive is one of the major gifts that I took away from this experience.

I am grateful to Dr. Arau for carefully helping me craft a "culture curriculum" for my students. It was a monumental investment of time spent on this subject, and I am certain that this important work has laid the foundation for a strong group of young leaders to prosper. As a community of music educators, let's take the time to treasure what we *get* to do. This type of thinking will further expand from our programs on an individual basis; we will effect major change in the global community of young musicians that we are responsible for molding and shaping before they enter the "real" world. How wonderful it is to focus on gratitude *and* music? They go hand in hand if we remember the former in our rehearsals.

Application

1. Make a G.E.T.-to-do list. Begin each sentence with "I get to."

2. Include the word "get" in your self-talk and when you are speaking with others or teaching. Use the word generously so that you can acquire a comfort level and a new habit of living with a spirit of "get."

3. Create a habit of gratitude by accepting the twenty-one-day challenge of writing a daily list of three things or people you are grateful for. You can do this on your computer, phone, or in a notebook. Review this gratitude journal at the end of each of the three weeks.

4. Share your appreciation and gratitude for someone with them. Don't keep it to yourself; let them know.

5. Set an intention for the day to approach every experience, class, and interaction with a sense of appreciation.

6. Make "get to do" part of the way you and your students talk about the privilege of getting to make music together.

Journal Questions

1. How can you reframe or reconsider how you used to think about your day filled with "have-to's" and replace those same things with "G.E.T. to's"? Consider how gratitude, enthusiasm, and treasure can apply to your day.

2. Reflect on an experience in your own life that shaped or shifted how you think and act in a positive way.

3. Imagine your own music classroom infused with the Power of G.E.T. What does it look, sound, and feel like?

Quotes

Enthusiasm is everything. It must be taut and vibrating like a guitar string.

> — Pelé
> as quoted in G. J. Bajaj's
> *Love Begets Wealth*, p. 184

Learning to live in the present moment is part of the path of joy.

> — Sarah Ban Breathnach
> *Simple Abundance: A Daybook of Comfort and Joy*, January 19

Because attitude affects our feelings and feelings affect what we do and how well we do it, having a good attitude can be the deciding factor in our successes or failures.

> — Shad Helmstetter
> *What to Say When You Talk to Your Self*, p. 137

The world is both wonderful and terrible, beautiful and ugly. At any moment, one can choose to focus on the positive or negative aspects of reality. Without denying the negative, it is possible to practice focusing more on the positive.

> — Andrew Weil
> *Spontaneous Happiness*, p. 154

ENDNOTES

1. Gilbert F. White in Robert E. Hinshaw, *Living With Nature's Extremes: The Life of Gilbert Fowler White* (Boulder, CO: Johnson Books, 2006), 62.
2. Carol S. Dweck, "The Power of Believing that You Can Improve," TEDx, November 2014, https://www.ted.com/talks/carol_dweck_the_power_of_believing_that_you_can_improve.
3. Quote attributed to Max Planck, originally in German, "Wenn Sie die Art und Weise ändern, wie Sie die Dinge betrachten, ändern sich die Dinge, die Sie betrachten."
4. Robert A. Emmons and Michael E. McCollough, "Counting Blessings Versus Burdens: Experimental Studies of Gratitude and Subjective Well-Being in Daily Life," *Journal of Personality and Social Psychology* 84, no. 2 (February 2003): 377–389.
5. Kori D. Miller, "14 Health Benefits of Practicing Gratitude According to Science," Positive Psychology, February 27, 2021, https://positivepsychology.com/benefits-of-gratitude/.
6. Paul Atchley, "You Can't Multitask, So Stop Trying," Harvard Business Review, December 21, 2010, https://hbr.org/2010/12/you-cant-multi-task-so-stop-tr.
7. Chris Adams, "Can People Really Multitask?" ThoughtCo., February 17, 2019, https://www.thoughtco.com/can-people-really-multitask-1206398.
8. "1 in 3 people globally do not have access to safe drinking water – UNICEF, WHO," World Health Organization, June 18, 2019, https://www.who.int/news/item/18-06-2019-1-in-3-people-globally-do-not-have-access-to-safe-drinking-water-unicef-who.
9. Andrew Weil, *Spontaneous Happiness: A New Path to Emotional Well-Being* (New York: Little, Brown and Company, 2011), 131.
10. Dalai Lama and Desmond Tutu with Douglas Abrams, *The Book of Joy: Lasting Happiness in a Changing World* (New York: Avery, 2016), 151–152.

Chapter 3

SUPERCHARGE YOUR MORNING: THE UPBEAT TO YOUR DAY

Each day I acknowledge and accept the responsibility—
not only for my own actions but also for my emotions,
my thoughts, and my attitude.[1]
— Shad Helmstetter

Try to think back to a time in your life when you felt as though you could conquer the world as you woke up and stepped out of bed. It could have been on the morning of your tenth birthday, on a Saturday when adventure awaited, or at sunrise on a winter holiday. The truth is there was a time when the idea of joyfully embracing the day in the morning would not have felt so far-fetched. Just as we can reframe our mind to choose to focus on what we *get* to do, we can also change our habits of thought to change our upbeat to the day—our thoughts and attitude upon waking up. Even if you are skeptical, I encourage you to put the strategies that follow to the test. Over time, I believe you will notice a change in the spring in your step and an increase of joy in your teaching and life. And as we change the trajectory of our morning, we can positively impact our students, colleagues, friends, and family as well.

The time when we transition from sleep to awake plays a critical role for us mentally and emotionally. There is great power in becoming aware of these moments and intentionally taking charge of your thoughts. As we move from a sleep and dream state into wakefulness, we can take advantage of a fresh palette of colors to paint our intention for the day. Remember, you choose your upbeat, and how you wake up may be the most important upbeat of the day. Our initial thoughts and self-talk can play a key role in creating an upward trajectory for our morning. In the previous chapter, we talked about the power of simply changing "have to" to "get to." Here is another powerful example of how changing just one word can drastically improve your day.

Opportunity Clock

For as long as I can remember, I have used an alarm clock to wake me up. When I was a kid, I used the alarm on my clock radio or the alarm on my digital watch, and for about the last fifteen years, I have set the alarm on my smartphone. I had always greeted the grating, jarring sound of the alarm with an internal cry, "No! Please let me sleep a little bit longer!" and the snooze button became a good friend. Can you relate? Then one day I was listening to a motivational CD by Zig Ziglar called *See You at the Top*, where he talks about the power of our words. He said, "And what about that word 'alarm' clock?" Think about it—alarm. The word conjures up danger and fear, and yet that is the word we use to designate the tool that moves us from sleep to being awake. When I heard Ziglar suggest changing the name to "opportunity clock," I laughed out loud and thought, "Yes, why not?"[2] Every day truly is an opportunity, an opportunity to be alive, an opportunity to grow, to serve, to learn, to teach, to make mistakes, to connect, to create, to laugh, and to cry. I began, one morning at a time, to change my habit, thinking of an "opportunity" clock instead of an "alarm." Changing our perception changes our reality. Try it. See how you feel. Persist. If you don't notice a change in how you feel tomorrow, that's okay. You will have *many* more mornings in which to build this new habit!

By taking charge of our morning, rather than delaying the inevitable by pressing the snooze button, we can create momentum and energy from the get-go. Set your phone in another room or far enough away that you have to get out of bed and walk to your phone to turn off the "opportunity" clock. Movement helps to wake you up and to invigorate your senses. Avoid looking at social media, texts, and emails upon waking, and instead focus on getting your mind and body supercharged for the day without distractions from outside sources. One of the first things I recommend is drinking a lot of water to hydrate and splashing cold water on your face to restore energy and vitality. In addition to waking your body up physically, you can create momentum for the day by what you choose to think about.

Sticky Thoughts

The first thoughts we have in the morning set the intention and course for the rest of our day. It is similar to setting the sails and turning the helm of a ship towards its destination. Our subconscious mind is most open to suggestion when we first awake, as our brains operate in the alpha state at around 8–13 Hertz per second. We can take advantage of this transition to train our mind and create habits of thought that allow us to truly supercharge our morning.[3] What we focus on for the first seventeen seconds upon waking turns us in the direction of that thought.[4] If we focus on the dread of waking up, what we are not looking forward to, or any other negative thoughts, what we focus on will lead us in a downward emotional spiral. However, if we deliberately focus on joy, gratitude, comfort, or what we are looking forward to on this day, it will get us off to a good start. That first step matters—a lot.

In many ways our thoughts operate similarly to the algorithms for Pandora or Spotify. When we enter a piece of music or an artist that we enjoy, the app recommends other pieces or artists that are similar, and along the way we might discover new music and artists that we had been unaware of previously. Based on our opening thoughts and intentional focus, we can activate additional similar thoughts. We can begin by appreciating the smallest thing, such as the feel of a pillow underneath our head, and this initial thought of gratitude leads us to notice other things that we are thankful for. Our thoughts can even be "sticky," and as a result, when we direct our focus towards the darkness, we can attract more negative thoughts. The opposite is also true: Focus on the light and we might just find ourselves thinking about positive aspects. Like thoughts can attract and stick onto similar thoughts, which is why it is in our interest to focus on what we want to attract more of into our lives. World-renowned Canadian personal development writer Brian Tracy reinforces this metaphor, writing, "You are a living magnet and you invariably attract into your life the people, ideas, opportunities, and circumstances in harmony with your dominant thoughts."[5]

Begin your day with intentional direction. Set your mind towards joy, gratitude, comfort, or what you are looking forward to, and you will find your mind moves into the positivity realm. When you scan your environment for positive things, you will inevitably discover more. It always begins with the search, and after that you will find what you are looking for. Look for things to be grateful for and you will notice even more to be grateful for. Do this every morning to energize your upbeat with positive energy and, over time, you can re-program your mind to view your alarm going off as an *opportunity*.

Intentionally Compose Your Day in the Morning

You can also spend time in the stillness of the morning to set your intention for the day with positive self-talk and affirmations. Instead of letting the day happen to you, you can take charge by expressing in your mind what kind of day you want to create. What kind of day do you intend to have? What difference will you make? How will you serve others today? By expressing to yourself, aloud or in your mind, the kind of day you want to create, you are taking steps to control the day instead of letting the day control you. Imagine you are a composer who has a musical idea in mind. Your composition process begins first with hearing the music in your mind and is followed by putting the music down on paper or into the computer program. We can do the same with each of our days and intentionally blueprint the feelings and impact we hope to experience and make happen. We, of course, cannot predict everything that will happen, but we can take a moment to set our intention for how we will greet and approach the day.

Visualize the type of rehearsal you want. Visualize the interactions and connections you want to have with your students. Life, however, is unpredictable and there will always be surprises, so you will not be etching in stone every moment of the coming day. However, just as an athlete visualizes their sport—whether making the basket, grabbing the rebound, catching the ball, or scoring the goal—and the musician visualizes their performance of a work before the actual concert, you can intentionally compose your day from the moment you wake up.

In addition to what you think about internally, you can also benefit from journaling in the morning about the day that you would like to create. There is great power in putting your thoughts into writing. I often find that reading a page from an inspirational book or listening to part of a motivational podcast primes my mind with ideas for how I can intentionally embrace the day. Rather than just viewing the morning as the time needed to get ready for work and to get out the door, see the morning as your opportunity to set the stage, choose your upbeat, and create an amazing day.

Embrace the Stillness

Embrace the stillness and the silence whenever possible, for this might be when you can reflect on intention and purpose without distraction. Just like music that is painted on a canvas of silence, your day is composed on a sea of stillness. When it is still, you can find a moment to just breathe, center, and ground yourself before the hustle and bustle of activity takes over. Our emotions are physiologically tied to our breathing, which is why dedicating time to deep breathing is so important. When we are stressed, anxious, or angry, for example, our breathing changes. Notice how your chest and throat tighten when you feel worked up. Your breathing gets fast, shallow, loud, and irregular. This is a physiological response. Our breathing is tied to our emotions.[6] While we can't simply tell ourselves to change our emotions on command—to suddenly just stop being angry or upset, for example—we can focus on slowing and deepening our breathing, which will allow us to gradually change how we feel. When our breathing relaxes, this creates a pathway to a much calmer and peaceful state. Try it. Take a slow deep breath in through your nose and exhale slowly out your nose or mouth and repeat. Notice how much calmer and centered you feel. Andrew Weil, M.D., writes in *Spontaneous Happiness*, "It is much easier to learn to regulate the breath than to will negative moods to end."[7] From a place of serenity, we are more equipped to make rational and intuitive decisions, to be more aware of our surroundings, to be creative, and to be solution-oriented.

Mindful Breathing Techniques

Here are some mindful breathing techniques to incorporate into your morning routine to provide a strong foundation for the rest of the day. These breathing exercises also work well throughout the day and in the classroom with your students. I would recommend trying all of these out over the course of a week, observing how each breath impacts how you feel, and then selecting the ones that work best for you. You may wish to gently close your eyes while focusing on the feel of your inhale and exhale and the rise and fall of your abdomen.

UPBEAT! ◆ Matthew Arau

Focus Breath: Breathe in through the nose for 4 counts and exhale through the nose for 4 counts. Repeat three times. This breath focuses your mind and helps you get in the zone.

Serenity Breath: Breathe in through the nose for 4 counts. Hold for 7 counts. Exhale through the mouth for 8 counts. Repeat four times. This breath works really well to lessen stress and anxiety.

Triangle Breath: Breathe in through the nose for 3 counts. Hold for 3 counts. Exhale through the mouth for 3 counts. Repeat three times. This breath is calming and centering.

Box Breath: Breathe in through the nose for 4 counts. Hold for 4 counts. Exhale through the nose for 4 counts. Hold for 4 counts. Repeat three or four times. This breath is great for grounding and stability.

Renew and Release Breath: While breathing in the nose for 4 counts, think "renew" to refresh, recharge, and reinvigorate. While exhaling out the nose or mouth for 6 counts, think "release" to let go, remove, and detox. Repeat for as long as you like.

Gratitude Breath (Version 1): Focus on something or someone that you are grateful for. Breathe gratitude in through your nose for 4 counts. Exhale stress, anxiety, and anything that you want to release for 8 counts through your mouth. Repeat three times.

Gratitude Breath (Version 2): Focus on something or someone that you are grateful for. Breathe gratitude in through your nose for 4 counts. Exhale out through your mouth what you want to send or give to the world—peace, love, joy, for example—for 8 counts. Repeat three times.

Steps for Meditation

In addition to these mindful breathing techniques, I find great value in meditating every morning. This investment in myself helps set me up for success in my relationships, communication, teaching, and my ability to respond rather than react to challenging situations. I encourage you to give it a try. The benefits to your body and mind are innumerable. In the beginning, you may want to just start off with investing five minutes, but as you practice and become more comfortable you will likely enjoy increasing your time to fifteen or twenty minutes each morning. Here are some steps to get you started with giving meditation a try.

1. Sit comfortably in a chair or cross-legged on the floor with an elevated posture. You may find that sitting on a cushion helps with comfort and posture. You can also lie down while meditating but be sure to lie awake rather than fall asleep!
2. Direct your attention to the physical sensations and sounds of your breath and gently close your eyes.
3. Notice the coolness of the air as it enters your nose and the warmth of your breath as it exits your nose or mouth.

4. Be aware of the movement of the air on the inhale as it expands your abdomen and chest as if blowing up a balloon. Notice that as you ride the wave of your breath, no two breaths are exactly the same. Be curious about your breath.

5. You will notice that thoughts will enter your mind and whisk you away from the awareness of your breathing. Notice your thoughts without judgment, and then return to your awareness of your breath. This may happen again and again, which is perfectly fine and normal.

6. Meditation and mindfulness are practices, and as such we never fully master the ability to quiet our thoughts, just as we will never fully master music or even teaching. Meditation is an opportunity to practice the art of "being" rather than "doing." There will always be room to grow and develop, which is beautiful and exciting.

7. Appreciate the journey and the process. Be confident that 5–20 minutes of sitting in silence with your eyes closed and focusing on your breathing will not just impact you but will also have an impact on everyone that you encounter throughout the day.

In addition to these meditation basics, you may find that you enjoy guided meditations that can be found on YouTube and a variety of apps, like HeadSpace, Waking Up, Chopra Meditation, Ten Percent Happier, Calm, Wim Hof Method, and InsightTimer. These apps also include body scans and daily affirmations to inspire peace and hope. There is no one right way to meditate, and the important thing is to find what works best for you. You are worth the investment of time in yourself.

Preparing for Bumps in the Road

By practicing awareness and mindfulness in the morning, you prepare yourself for the bumps in the road and what lies ahead. We can't wait for the crisis to happen and then hope that we will be able to mindfully respond. We practice so that we are ready for the challenge when it happens.

But hey, sometimes things don't work out as we planned! Have you ever given the preparatory beat to start a piece and the sound that you anticipated and expected to hear did not at all match up with your internal aural image? If this happens enough times, it can be easy to get frustrated. There may be days where you do everything to set yourself up for success. You focus on gratitude as you wake up, you savor and appreciate the aroma of your morning coffee, and you focus not just on what you are looking forward to but also the positive rehearsal climate you plan on creating. Then in the middle of rehearsal just as you are getting into the details that move performances from good to great, the fire alarm goes off and the rehearsal ends abruptly. On those days, you definitely don't get to create that magical moment you had so clearly visualized ahead of time. During times like these, it can be tempting to dismiss all of this "upbeat nonsense." But we can recognize that choosing our upbeat does not mean life will always be a bowl of cherries; it means we get to choose how we respond to whatever life hands us. This is why we supercharge our morning, to be prepared physically and mentally for the challenges of daily life and to create forward momentum. We can choose to get frustrated, or we can turn challenges into teaching and learning moments.

Tune Up the Mind, Body, and Spirit

Just as we tune up our own instrument before playing and just as we spend time tuning up the ensemble before a rehearsal or performance, we can do the same for our most important instrument: our own body, mind, and spirit. When our students tune up as an ensemble at the beginning of each rehearsal, they are able to more accurately and quickly make micro-adjustments to intonation challenges caused by playing together harmonically and melodically. If they don't find the center on at least one pitch before they start, it becomes almost impossible to tune chords or melodies. Our bodies and minds function in the same way. We need to take time each day to fine-tune ourselves so that when we interact with colleagues, family, friends, and students, we can more readily and quickly find alignment and resonance. To tune up your body in the morning, add in some kind of movement and stretching, even if it is just a few leg and back stretches and a short walk around the block. Whether you do yoga, Qigong, or Tai Chi, or you jog, swim, or lift weights, it is not so much the type of exercise that you do but that you are moving and tuning and "toning" up your body. When you exercise your body, you are also exercising your brain, which is one of the reasons we feel more energized and alert mentally after physical movement.

When we invest in our minds, bodies, and spirits, we prepare and strengthen ourselves not only for the challenges that await us but also so that we have more to give. We keep our pitcher full so that we can pour energy into our students and stay fulfilled and replenished ourselves. Not tending to what we need over an extended period of time leads to exhaustion and burnout. In the end, we can only change ourselves—we cannot change others. We can, however, influence others by being fully engaged, present, and invested. And by spending time in the morning to adjust our personal intonation and vibration, we are prepared to make a more positive influence that day.

Vignette

Elizabeth Weismehl, M.M.
General Music and Choir (Grades 1–5)
Avoca West School, Glenview, Illinois

In the spring of 2020, I was perusing a course catalog knowing I needed to find something to help me reimagine how to teach music for the upcoming school year. I happened upon a class being offered for the first time called "Mindfulness for the Music Educator," taught by Dr. Arau. I had never heard of mindfulness. The description sounded intriguing, so I signed up not knowing what to expect. I remember the first Zoom call. Dr. Arau started class by having us share one word that brought us joy, gratitude, or comfort. I remember smiling as I saw the responses—family, friends, nature, music, animals. Before the end of that meeting, I remember feeling a sense of hope for the first time since the pandemic had begun. When I spoke with a colleague after I had finished the class, she said I was the only person she knew that felt prepared for the many unknowns of the upcoming year.

The ideas that I have learned from Dr. Arau have greatly impacted the upbeat to my day, which in turn has impacted those around me. I have found that focusing on my breath during morning meditation and then reading a short reflection helps me set my intention for the day, listen more deeply, and be present in the moment. These practices allow me to think before reacting and to shift my perspective, thus creating the space to be a creative problem solver, whether in the midst of teaching, working with colleagues, or being with family. By focusing on positivity and gratitude upon waking, I welcome the day joyfully and find moments to treasure even—or perhaps *especially*—during challenging times.

Asking students to share something that brings them "joy, gratitude, or comfort" is an example of what Dr. Arau refers to as a "positive lead." This is one of my favorite ways to begin each class and choir rehearsal. I have learned things about the students' lives and interests that I would not have previously learned. This activity also gives students a chance to connect with one another as someone else's answers may resonate with them. It never fails to bring smiles and a sense of happiness into the environment.

When I think of this simple yet powerful opening activity, I often reflect on a rising sixth grader who I'll call Richard. He struggled to fit in and kept mostly to himself. I do not recall seeing him smile much even though I have worked with him since first grade. He rarely participated but would occasionally create a disruption in an effort to fit in and be noticed. Two weeks before we shut down in March of 2020, he was sitting next to me in our community circle. We were doing a singing activity and he joined in the singing. It was a glorious sound—I had never heard him sing—and I asked if he had ever thought about joining choir. He asked me if he should join. Yes! Two days later he had found his singing community. After that when I would ask the students to share something that brought them joy, gratitude, comfort, or something they were looking forward to, his response was always the same. "Choir," he would say with a smile on his face.

Application

1. Set an intention to wake up in the morning to an "opportunity clock" instead of an alarm clock and focus on joy, gratitude, comfort, or what you are looking forward to with eager anticipation in order to create a sticky thought that will attract more thoughts like it.

2. Visualize the day you want to create. Imagine approaching your day with energy and enthusiasm. See yourself making a positive difference in someone's life today and then take action and follow through.

3. Use at least one of the deep breathing techniques once per day. Use the focus breath to center your mind. Use the serenity breath if you are stressed. Use the gratitude breath to shift your mind's focus from an unwanted feeling to a desired positive feeling.

4. Write two positive things you want to remind yourself of first thing every morning for the next month. Why are these important to you? Put them on sticky notes and put them on your bathroom mirror.

5. Plan your morning ahead of time. What are some things you can do to make a morning routine easier for you? (Like setting out running shoes and workout clothes next to the bed or pouring a full glass of water to drink upon waking up.)

Journal Questions

1. What is your intention for the day? How do you intend to make a difference?
2. What are you looking forward to today?
3. How can supercharging your morning create a positive ripple effect for you and your students for the rest of the day?

Quotes

I am not what has happened to me. I am what I choose to become.

— Carl Jung
as quoted in Brené Brown's *Daring Greatly*, p. 80

It is much easier to learn to regulate the breath than to will negative moods to end.

— Andrew Weil
Spontaneous Happiness, p. 146

In all of modern history, no single invention has so perfectly captured the perverse power of the mind to defeat its own best intentions as the snooze button.

— Mel Robbins
Stop Saying You're Fine, p. 9

Another world is not only possible, she is on her way. On a quiet day, I can hear her breathing.

— Arundhati Roy
as quoted in Darby Kathleen Ray's
Theology that Matters, p. 188

ENDNOTES

1. Shad Helmstetter, *What to Say When You Talk to Your Self: Powerful New Techniques to Program Your Potential for Success* (New York: Gallery Books, 1986/2017), 142.
2. Zig Ziglar, *See You at the Top—25th Anniversary Edition* (Niles, IL: Simon & Schuster Audio, 1989), compact disc.
3. Ahmed Safwan, "How the First 20 Minutes of Your Day Can Set You Up for Success," Entrepreneur, July 13, 2017, accessed September 16, 2021, https://www.entrepreneur.com/article/291907; White 1999 in John N. Demos, *Getting Started with Neurofeedback* (Norton Professional Books, 2005), 69, 185.
4. Esther Hicks and Jerry Hicks, *Ask and It Is Given: Learning to Manifest Your Desires* (Carlsbad, CA: Hay House, Inc., 2004), 109.
5. Brian Tracy, *Change Your Thinking, Change Your Life: How to Unlock Your Full Potential for Success and Achievement* (Hoboken, NJ: John Wiley & Sons, 2003), xvii.
6. Andrew Weil, *Spontaneous Happiness: A New Path to Emotional Well-Being* (New York: Little, Brown and Company, 2011), 146.
7. Ibid., 146.

Chapter 4

SUSTAIN YOUR UPBEAT ALL DAY

Self-care is never a selfish act.[1]
— Parker J. Palmer

One of my first cars was a 1986 Toyota Celica. I loved that car, but I made the mistake of ignoring the "check engine" light the morning before taking a drive into the mountains. One warm spring day, I was driving with Merilee in the Rocky Mountains in the Big Thompson Canyon on a day visit to Estes Park. On the downhill return, I noticed smoke billowing from the hood of the car. As there was no place to stop and I did not have a cell phone, I tried coasting down the mountain, hoping to make it back home to Fort Collins. Eventually, I pulled to the side of the road, where I was lucky to find a payphone to call for help. A tow truck showed up and an hour later we dropped off my beloved Celica at the auto repair shop and the tow truck driver drove us home. Soon after, the call came from the mechanic. The engine was unrepairable. My beloved Celica went to the junkyard because I had neglected the warning signs of serious issues.

We need to take care of ourselves so that our own "check engine" light does not turn on. However, if it does, we must heed the warning and take the opportunity to "change the oil and check the fuses" to restore our energy and vitality to be at our best for our students. Our best option is to design our days to include regular maintenance and fueling up so that we can sustain our upbeat all day long.

• • •

Breathe, Just Breathe

"Take a big breath and keep the air supported on your exhale so that you can *sustain* the note for its full value with a resonant tone." Isn't that what we tell our students before they sing or play their instruments? A full breath gives us the air necessary to hold out a tone or phrase for a long period of time.

As in music making, the breath is essential to life. The way we breathe *in* impacts how we breathe *out*. A full breath is necessary to sustain a long tone in music and breathing properly is necessary to sustain a long, healthy, and vibrant life. If we inhale with tension, the exhale will have tension. If we breathe in fully without tension, our exhale will also be relaxed and supported. Music itself also wants to breathe. Just as our heart rate increases on an inhale and decreases on the exhale, music can build to a climax and then relax. A single phrase can follow this pattern, as can an entire piece of music. Music that breathes has moments of space, calm, and reflection. Of course, some music hits the ground with unrelenting energy and never lets up, leaving us breathless.

My hope is that we can find a way to live our lives as music educators like a piece of music that breathes. Unfortunately, we often put our own health and well-being last, causing us to be stressed out and fully spent and depleted at the end of the day. Just as breath gives life to music, breath gives life to us. **Every breath we take is an opportunity to refuel and recharge ourselves.** Too often, however, we figuratively (and sometimes quite literally) forget to breathe.

Although it sounds so simple, taking care of ourselves begins with an awareness of how we breathe. According to James Nestor, author of *Breath: The New Science of a Lost Art*, the average person takes 25,000 breaths per day, breathing in billions of molecules with each breath, for an average length of 3.3 seconds per breath. During the average lifespan, we will take about 670 million total breaths.[2] Just as the quality of the breath is important to the performance of music, the *way* we breathe matters greatly to our health, stress levels, physiology, and mental-emotional states. When we are moving quickly, distracted by the pressure of people vying for our attention, we tend to take shallow breaths through the mouth and breathe with the chest rather than taking in full breaths and filling from the bottom up. At times, we actually stop breathing. Chest breathing activates the sympathetic nervous system, which is part of our fight, flight, or freeze stress response, and if we breathe like this over an extended period of time, the body will become overloaded with adrenaline and cortisol. We can counteract this response by intentionally breathing low into the stomach region, which stimulates the vagus nerve and the parasympathetic nervous system, responsible for calming and centering the mind and body.[3] Leah Lagos, author of *Heart, Mind, Body*, points out that, "When you breathe from your belly, you are actually forcing your lungs to take in more air. This optimizes the amount of oxygen traveling through your bloodstream to your muscles and organs, including the heart and the brain."[4]

Additionally, new research finds that, physiologically, we are designed for optimal performance when breathing in and out of our noses.[5] Breathing in and out the nose naturally expands our abdominal region, engages the diaphragm, and conserves energy. Mouth-breathing, which is how I predominantly breathed until reading about the benefits of breathing through the nose, "can make us more quickly fatigued and sap athletic performance" as well as cause "the body to lose 40 percent more water."[6] I encourage you to shift your style of breathing if you are not a natural nose-breather already. My sleeping, energy, and stress levels have improved significantly since I made the switch. If you have difficulty breathing solely through your nose, begin to engage by inhaling through your nose and breathing out through your mouth with lightly pursed lips.

Our emotions are connected to how we breathe, and changing our breathing habits can in fact change how we feel.[7] We will notice feeling calmer, more centered, and more patient simply by intentionally breathing more deeply. Additionally, research has shown that "the movement of the diaphragm provides an internal massage that assists the heart, even reducing the recurrence of heart attacks."[8] To get even more out of each breath cycle, extend your exhale; in addition to the stimulation of your vagus nerve, this extension also helps to generate acetylcholine—the calm hormone.[9] We can also use our breath to change our perception and response to stress and anxiety. As psychiatrist Fritz Perls advises, "In scariness or anxiety, breathe a little and you'll feel the excitement. Hold your breath a little and you'll get scared again."[10] We can shift our body's response to stress by breathing slowly and deeply, and then we can intentionally use this newly focused energy for greater creativity and productivity. Place reminders in your phone, in your car, in your office, on your computer, and even on your mirrors to remind yourself to breathe deeply. You will notice a positive difference almost immediately when you begin breathing from your diaphragm.

We learn more, process more, retain more, engage more, and care more when we breathe from a calm center. Isn't that what we want for ourselves and our students? One of the obstacles that we talk about as music teachers is we don't have enough time. Focusing on relaxed breathing will slow down time and make the time we do have more valuable. **Just as our upbeat while conducting begins with an inhale, sustaining our upbeat all day begins with how we breathe.** Not only will your health and stress levels improve, but so will your overall attitude and upbeat.

I invite you to briefly reflect on what you just read in this section. Did you find yourself breathing more deeply? Has your breathing slowed? Do you feel different?

Mindful Walking

In addition to focusing your awareness on your breath during mindful breathing exercises or meditation, choose to focus on your breathing while walking—even the walk from your classroom to the restroom, the front office, or the teachers' lounge is an opportunity to breathe mindfully. Being aware of your breath while walking serves as a form of moving meditation. Dedicate five to twenty minutes to a walking meditation, where you direct your focus to your breathing and the feel of your feet and shoes pressing against the ground.

If possible, take a mindful walk in nature to restore your natural connection to wonder and beauty. While walking, tap into all your senses and be more aware of the aromas, scents, and smells. Listen with greater awareness, noticing the sounds around you. Tap into your sense of awe, appreciation, and curiosity and observe details and colors with fresh eyes. Have you noticed how you can walk past the same location hundreds of times and still notice something for the very first time? Even walking the perimeter of the school or around the track (if your school has one) with heightened senses can be renewing and rejuvenating during the day.

You can calm your mind and energize your body simultaneously with the following mindful walking breathing routines.

- Breathe in through your nose for 3 counts at about 1 count per second and exhale out through your nose for 5 counts. Work to exhale more carbon dioxide than the oxygen you inhale. When I take a walk in the morning, I use each of my steps as a count: 3 steps inhaling followed by 5 steps exhaling. I also experiment with this pattern: 4 steps inhaling followed by 6 steps exhaling. Practice these variations until breathing patterns become a habit so that you can enjoy the scenery rather than spending all your time counting in your head as you walk.

- Another mindful walking breathing practice is to inhale through your nose for 5 to 6 seconds or steps and exhale through your nose for 5 to 6 seconds or steps.

The great thing about these breathing practices is that you can do them without anyone noticing. Most of us have adapted habits of shallow stress breathing during our time at work, and it will take conscious, intentional, and consistent attention and reminders to build a new habit. Take a moment, wherever you are right now, and invest in yourself with a few minutes of mindful walking.

Mindful Eating

Make eating well a priority at work and resist the temptation to "wolf your food down" without tasting it as you run off to take care of the next emergency. Treat the time that you *get to* eat as sacred. Tapping into your senses while eating can be stimulating and invigorating, giving you more energy and vitality in the long run. Find a quiet space, if possible, or instead join friends for lively conversation while eating. Begin your meal with gratitude and appreciation and savor every sip and every bite. See your food as a work of art (yes, even that peanut butter and jelly on whole wheat!) and take pleasure in the flavors and aromas. Slowing down to honor the nutrition you put in your body is an important step in making self-care a priority. **We eat mindfully to fill up our cup both literally and figuratively so that we have more to give.**

Reframing your mindset around eating at work may cause you to invest more time in preparing your food at home. Many teachers that I have worked with have found that they started making better food and nutrition choices when they began practicing mindful eating. When we treat eating as a special act, we elevate the importance of what we put into our body. What we eat and drink daily greatly impacts our ability to sustain our upbeat all day. We will be able to maintain our energy and focus throughout the day when we make healthy food choices and treasure every bite.

Mental Nutrition

The nutrition we feed our minds affects us not only mentally and emotionally but also physiologically, making mental nutrition just as important as the food and drink we put in our bellies. Zig Ziglar said, "You are who you are and what you are because of what has gone into your mind. You can change who you are and what you are by changing what goes into your mind."[11] We can choose to replace what we normally feed our minds with positive "supplements" and meaningful *mental meals*. To change habits, we need to replace old patterns with new habits and routines. Instead of spending time scrolling social media or watching the news, replace those habits with reading—books on personal development, biographies of inspiring historical or current figures, or any books that engage you and stretch you. You might even start with a book from the Bibliography and Inspirational Reading List at the end of this book (after you finish reading this book, of course!). Listen to podcasts that help you become the best version of yourself. Watch inspiring videos or movies about courage, music, and overcoming struggles. If you are a religious person, read scripture and spiritual writings. Listen to music that fills you with joy and passion and sing or play music that fills up your tank. Choosing quality mental nutrition primes our minds and bodies to think thoughts that encourage us to be more positive about ourselves and others.

It is easy to become addicted to scrolling through social media and watching the news, but neither is helpful for our psyches or living an upbeat life. Social media, ads, and the news can plant negative messages in our minds and affect what we think and how we feel. While social media can be used sparingly to help us stay in touch with family and friends, a common effect is the tendency to compare our actual lives with the curated and hand-selected snapshots of the lives presented on social media. Comparing our happiness to another's highlight reel can lead to envy and disappointment. Instead, I recommend avoiding social media and the news in the morning before work so that you can be in control of setting your intention and visualizing the day you want to have rather than letting other people's stories or agendas influence your thinking. I also recommend a phone and computer fast for at least an hour before going to bed so that you can prime your mind and body for restful sleep.

When you do get on your phone or computer, open up your torso, straighten your spine, and breathe from your diaphragm to counteract natural tendencies of crunching in your posture and breathing from your chest. Multiple research studies point out that our stress levels elevate when texting or responding to emails, not just because of what information might be exchanged, but also because of how we hold ourselves and how we breathe. One study conducted by Linda Stone, a former executive at Apple and Microsoft, found that 80 percent of people "held their breath or breathed shallowly when responding to a text or email."[12] Another study by Erik Peper of San Francisco State University reported that "when texting, participants tightened their neck and shoulder muscles and breathed shallowly and rapidly. And when you breathe shallowly, you start to trigger anxiety."[13] Since this shallow breathing creates stress, begin by noticing your own breathing tendencies and then create a new habit to intentionally breathe slowly and deeply when on your phone or the computer.

Social Circle

Our lives are enriched by the people we spend time with. Be aware that those you spend time with have an impact on your energy and mindset. Shawn Achor makes the point in his book *Big Potential* that the people we socialize with influence us, and "the key is to seek people who bring out the best in you, not the stress in you." Achor goes on to say, "The more you surround yourself with positive voices, the easier positive change will be to sustain and even amplify." [14] Spend time at school and outside school with a diverse group of people who not only make you feel good about yourself, listen to you, and support you, but also challenge you, push you out of your comfort zone, and bring alternative viewpoints, experiences, cultures, and backgrounds to the table. Our social circles impact our mindsets and personal upbeat. While being compassionate and respectful of others, be intentional about who you invest your time in, because your time is precious, and we are all influenced by others. You may have heard the saying, "You are the average of the five people you spend the most time with," made popular by motivational author and speaker Jim Rohn.[15] I imagine that today that includes those we virtually socialize with as well. Find folks who make you laugh, make you think, and bring out your best self. As your upbeat expands, you will naturally attract more people into your life who are drawn to your positive energy. Establish boundaries as needed and do your best to avoid interacting with people who like to complain a lot and travel down the negative rabbit hole.

Laughter, Smiles, and Hugs

Who doesn't want more laughter, smiles, and hugs in their life?! All of these are essential to a happy and vibrant upbeat life. Because laughter and smiling are contagious, it's easy to do both when we hang out with people who enjoy life and like to have fun. Aside from the fact that laughing feels good, there are many more surprising benefits. Laughter relaxes us, boosts our immune system, releases endorphins, protects our heart, and even burns calories. Laughing with others also helps us feel more connected.[16]

In a TED Talk called "The Hidden Power of Smiling," Ron Gutman shares the results of research showing that smiling a lot can improve your health and "reduce the level of stress-enhancing hormones, [...] increase the level of mood enhancing hormones [...], and reduce blood pressure."[17] A 2005 study conducted in the United Kingdom found that one smile can stimulate your brain at the same level as up to 2,000 chocolate bars or receiving $25,000.[18] Okay, well whether or not you think that is a fair trade, the point is that smiles invigorate us! Giving, receiving, and exchanging smiles benefits everyone, and one study even shared that people that smile a lot live seven years longer on average.[19]

Hugging also provides incredible wellness benefits, including stress and anxiety reduction, immune system boosting, pain reduction, lowers blood pressure, and makes us happier.[20] Whether hugging a significant other, a close friend, or a family member, both of you will feel better after the hug. Consider adding a mindful hug (with permission) into your daily routine.

1. Be fully present with the person you are hugging.
2. Breathe in and out slowly and at the same pace as your partner.
3. Take three mindful breaths together while sharing your energy with each other.
4. Share appreciation and gratitude for each other.

Be generous with smiles, laughter, and hugs, and you will find that your upbeat is energized from sharing with others. Because the good feelings generated will be contagious, you will create an upbeat ripple effect.

The Little Things in Life

What are those little things in life that bring you joy? Perhaps the flowers in your garden, or the cardinal that comes to rest on a tree in your backyard, or the beaming smile on the face of a student who is excited to see you. Perhaps it is the excitement in your classroom that comes from the exploration and performance of music from a variety of cultural backgrounds. Maybe it is the sensation of sipping hot coffee from the perfect mug or looking at the photo of your loved ones on your desk. It may be a collection of thank you cards and notes of gratitude that you collected and placed in a "warm and fuzzy file" for encouragement on a challenging day. If you have pets, your dog or cat may brighten your day with their unconditional love. In addition, you may be energized from watching your cat leap and bound with excitement, from listening to music with a dizzying bass line and frolicking jazz licks, from a great workout, or jumping up and down with a young child.

We often wait for joy to happen in our life, when it already is staring us in the face, right in front of us. We can choose to bring joy into our life and to others by focusing on the goodness in others and the excitement of getting to be together to share ideas and to make music. When we approach every day and every moment noticing the little things in life that bring us joy, we discover we feel happier, more content, and at peace. The great thing about joy is that the sense of joy expands when we share it with others, so share away!

Self-Talk and Setting Your Intention

Become your own upbeat coach. Talk to yourself as if you were coaching someone else to get the most out of each day. Build your confidence with positive "I am" self-talk. First become aware of what you say to yourself throughout the day and catch yourself when you say anything unkind. If you find that you beat yourself up with negative statements such as "I'm lazy" or "I always procrastinate," switch your talk to "I'm a hard worker" and "I plan ahead and get things done on time" to encourage a positive self-image. Your brain will believe whatever you tell it. The great news is you can rewire your brain with positive self-talk to replace the old negative programming with daily repetition.[21]

You can also set intentions and send positive messages to yourself about the different stages of your day. Here are some suggestions.

1. Waking up
    a. "You've got this."
    b. "This is going to be a great day."
    c. "I look forward to making a difference today."
    d. "Thank you for this day."
    e. "I am grateful for being alive."

2. Coffee, tea, and/or breakfast
    a. "I am grateful for this _____."
    b. "I enjoy the energy and nourishment that fills my body and mind from _____."

3. Commute to school
   a. Listen to positive podcasts.
   b. Listen to calm and peaceful music.
   c. Listen to music that energizes and inspires you.
   d. Listen to silence and focus on your breath.
   e. Visualize the day you want to create at school.
   f. Repeat the mantra, "This is going to be a great day."
   g. Set your intention for the morning and the day.

4. Walking into the school building, your office, and/or music room
   a. "Magic happens here daily."
   b. "I look forward to seeing my students."
   c. "We are going to learn and grow so much today."

5. As students enter the room
   a. "I appreciate each and every one of you."
   b. "I am excited about creating a welcoming space for my students."
   c. "I am excited about helping my students discover something new about themselves today."
   d. "I am excited to *get to* make music together."

6. The commute back home
   a. Reflect on what went well, what could be improved, and what you are looking forward to the next day.
   b. Visualize the evening you would like to have.
   c. Set an intention to be fully present for those in your home—even a pet!

7. Before going to bed, ask yourself, "What went well today?" Go on a mental treasure hunt to find the positives and moments of appreciation. Write these down in a journal and include gratitude in your reflections.

8. Before you fall asleep, set an intention for what you want to think about when you first wake up.

Write Your Own Story

Changing your personal story or interpretation of the past can help you face the present. Benjamin Hardy, author of *Personality Isn't Permanent*, writes that transforming one thought pattern can greatly shift how you feel about your past. Instead of thinking that your past happened *to* you, reframe it to recognize that your past happened *for* you.[22] Try to view everything that has happened in your past as a learning experience, a struggle, or an opportunity that has led to who you are today. YOU choose your upbeat. You can also choose how you interpret your past. We are constantly looking for meaning to understand what has happened in the past. By looking for meaning through the lens that everything in your life happened *for* you rather than *to* you, your perception of the past changes. This influences how you feel, act, and respond in the present. Instead of dwelling on the past, look towards your future self and view the present through the lens of "How are my actions serving my future self?"[23] Visualize the best version of yourself and who you aspire to become and act as if you already are that person now. This approach to life is freeing and empowering and puts you in control of choosing your upbeat regardless of what has happened in the past.

The Upbeat to Sleep

There is nothing like getting a good night's sleep! Am I right? When you wake up rested, doesn't the rest of the day go so much better? I wish I could share the *perfect* formula for getting good rest every night, but I am still working on it myself. What I can share is that how we prepare to sleep makes a significant difference on not only how we sleep but also how we feel when we wake up. Here are some things to consider:

1. Winding down one or two hours before going to sleep is helpful. Avoid looking at screens, including your phone, computer, or television before going to bed, as the blue light stimulates our brain into thinking that it should stay awake longer. Avoid eating and drinking anything other than water during this window of time as well.

2. Do anything the night before that can help your morning run more smoothly, such as setting out your clothes and what you will need for school and preparing a lunch.

3. Keep a gratitude journal to write down three things that you are grateful for. Reflect on your day and write about what went well and people or things that you appreciate. Focusing on gratitude prior to going to sleep can also prime your thoughts about what you are grateful for when you wake up and help you supercharge your morning. You can also use this reflective time to set your intentions for the next day.

4. Use some of the mindful breathing techniques shared in Chapter 3 before you get into bed or once you are lying in

bed. The Triangle Breath and Box Breath are excellent for getting into your sleep window. For the Triangle Breath, you breathe in the nose for 3 counts, hold for 3 counts, and exhale out of your mouth for 3 counts and repeat. For the Box Breath, the count is 4, like the sides of a square, as you breathe in through your nose for 4 counts, hold for 4 counts, exhale out the nose for 4 counts, hold for 4 counts, and repeat. My students and I have found that the Triangle Breath works the best for helping you fall back to sleep if you wake up in the middle of the night and have trouble getting to sleep again.

Re-Store

While taking a walk at a nature reserve not long ago, I paused to soak in the beauty and peace. Feeling renewed just listening to the birds, I happened upon a goose nesting on newly laid eggs. What a special and rare sight! I felt restored by simply being in nature's wondrous presence. At that moment, I started playing with the word "restore," dividing the word into different parts.

Where do you go when you open your refrigerator and there is nothing inside? You head to the store to replenish and restock. You *re-turn* to the store when you are running out of food, just like your car needs to *re-turn* to the gas station when it is low on fuel. As teachers, we need to *re-turn* to the store of our passion, our desire, our drive, and our enthusiasm. Where can you find what you need? The store is within you.

To "re-store," take time for YOU. Rest. Relax. Breathe. Reflect on what you have accomplished and how far you have come rather than focusing on everything that didn't happen the way you wished it would have. What we focus on grows and expands. We can certainly find things to bring us down—it's so easy to focus on the negative. But we can choose to shift our mindset to focus on the goodness in our lives.

Give yourself space, grace, permission, and time to "restore" your faith in the value of WHO YOU ARE and WHAT YOU OFFER. "Re-store" your sense of purpose and self-belief. Every day YOU make a difference in the lives of your students. For many, YOU are the reason that they come to school. The community, the sense of family, and the culture of excellence and character that you foster in your music classes—these things matter. **Although it may be hard to see it or feel it at times, you are a guiding light for your students, and they are looking to you to light the way.**

• • •

My wish is that you are inspired to apply many of the ideas and techniques we have discussed in the first four chapters so that you will feel, see, and experience transformative, positive change for yourself and your students. I hope that the ideas shared in Part 1 *ignite* your desire to intentionally choose your upbeat, embrace the Power of G.E.T., supercharge your morning, and sustain your upbeat so that you are fired up throughout the day. Begin by experimenting with some of the ideas that most resonate with you, and notice the impact in your life. Feel free to tailor any of the material in this book to fit you and your lifestyle.

I encourage you to share the information in the preceding chapters with your students. I have found that students resonate with the topics of self-care and personal development just as much as educators and that they are eager to learn more about how to live an upbeat life.

Our upbeat begins with an inhale, a breath. We breathe oxygen into our body to thrive just as a flame draws in oxygen to survive. Through the breath—our upbeat—we give life to our inner flame. Now that our inner flame is ignited, we are ready to inspire. The word "inspiration" comes from the Latin *inspirare*, meaning "to breathe or blow into."[24] So as we take a deep breath and turn the page, let's set our intention for **Part 2: INSPIRE!** so that we can prepare to breathe new life into our music classrooms and raise the level of inspiration for all our students.

Vignette

Lesley Moffat
Author of *I Love My Job, But It's Killing Me* and *Love the Job, Lose the Stress*
Jackson High School Band Director, Mill Creek, Washington

I loved my job but the stress and exhaustion that came with being a high school band director and mother of three who started jazz band at 6:30 every morning, taught all day, had after-school meetings and rehearsals, and evening booster meetings, concerts, games, and fundraisers almost killed me. The drain on my energy made it really hard to stay upbeat all day.

In my efforts to serve my students and community, I was woefully yet unintentionally neglecting my own mental and physical health. The result of putting the needs of others first meant that I didn't have time to do the things that kept my body feeling good and my mind functioning clearly. It was hard to teach my students when I had a hard time focusing or I was distracted by thinking of things I needed to do after class.

Dr. Arau has shared the importance of keeping ourselves mentally and physically fit with a plethora of examples of how we can work new habits into our daily lives. I can't emphasize enough the power in his suggestions. It is through the intentional work we do to keep ourselves in the best mental and physical shape possible that we open up our ability to do our work with more ease and joy and grace and serve our students in a sustainable way.

A big part of sustaining your upbeat all day is creating a classroom where your social and emotional needs (and those of your students) are met.

We music educators teach students to master many complex skills, from the fine-motor skills necessary to play instruments to collaborating with others in an ensemble and so much more. But do we ever teach them how to focus and pay attention? What if we did that *before* we dug into our content and used some of Dr. Arau's breathing techniques to help them recalibrate their brains and bodies so they are in a better frame of mind to learn and create? It's kind of like tuning up our students before we tune up our instruments! Could our students receive what we are about to teach them if we taught them how to relax, focus, and pay attention by practicing that skill with them every day just like we do all the other skills we teach them? And can you imagine how much easier it is to teach when we help ourselves and our students get in a positive mindset before we get into the actual material we want them to learn? *This* is how you sustain your upbeat all day!

SPOILER ALERT: Applying the ideas Dr. Arau shares in this chapter through intentional practice and then sharing these techniques with your students *will* help you create a personal life that is more rewarding and give you the stamina you need to do this important work in a sustainable way.

You spend a lot of time encouraging others to be the best version of themselves. Take the time to encourage yourself to do the same. Dr. Arau's suggestions give you lots of great ideas so you can find a place to start that works for you and grow from there.

As you read this book and think about what it means to you, I speak from personal experience on how powerful it is to take the necessary steps to have sustained and upbeat energy. It takes work, but the results of investing the time in your own foundational habits and thoughts are beyond life-changing. I'm living proof of the possibilities that exist when you tend to your mindset—and you can be too!

Application

1. Take a personal inventory of how you naturally breathe throughout the day. Place reminders to breathe slowly and deeply, ideally in and out of your nose, in your phone and calendar and on sticky notes in strategic places where you will see them. Notice how this breathing slows down your heart rate and helps you stay centered and calm.

2. Carve out five to twenty minutes in your day for a mindful walk, ideally in nature. Don't look at your phone or listen to anything else but your surroundings while walking. Take in all the sights, sounds, and smells with curiosity and enjoyment.

3. For one meal today, without distractions, be fully present and mindfully aware of the taste, look, smell, and feel of what you eat and drink. Savor and appreciate the nourishment.

4. Be aware of the nature of your self-talk and strive to revise how you talk to yourself so that you treat yourself as mindfully as you would treat a close friend who needs your support and care.

Journal Questions

1. How can I be more intentional about my mental nutrition so that I am feeding my mind and spirit with revitalizing and energizing content?

2. I plan to spread joy to others in the following ways.

3. What are three things that I am grateful for today? Why do I feel this appreciation?

4. What steps for my own self-care will I take first so that I am at my best for those that matter most in my life?

Quotes

Our environment, the world in which we live and work, is a mirror of our attitudes and expectations. Your living is determined not so much by what life brings to you as by the attitude you bring to life; not so much by what happens to you as by the way your mind looks at what happens.

— Earl Nightingale
as quoted in Bob Proctors's *The ABCs of Success*, p. 12

We are used to believing that we need to change everything about our lives first, and then we will be happy, or healthy, or whatever it is we think we want to experience. The science of mindsets says we have it backward. Changing our minds can be a catalyst for all the other changes we want to make in our lives.

— Kelly McGonigal
The Upside of Stress, p. 27

Your input determines your outlook. Your outlook determines your output, and your output determines your future.

— Zig Ziglar
as quoted in Tom Ziglar's *Choose to Win*, p. 60

Everything happens for you, not to you.

— Byron Katie
as quoted in Benjamin Hardy's *Personality Isn't Permanent*, p. 223.

Self-care is never a selfish act—it is simply good stewardship of the only gift I have, the gift I was put on earth to offer to others. Anytime we can listen to our true self and give the care it requires, we do it not only for ourselves, but for the many others whose lives we touch.

— Parker J. Palmer
Let Your Life Speak, p. 30

ENDNOTES

1. Parker J. Palmer, *Let Your Life Speak: Listening for the Voice of Vocation* (Hoboken, NJ, John Wiley & Sons, 1999), 30.
2. James Nestor, *Breath: The New Science of a Lost Art* (New York: Riverhead Books, 2020), xxii.
3. Leah Lagos, *Heart, Breath, Mind: Train Your Heart to Conquer Stress and Achieve Success* (Boston: Houghton Mifflin Harcourt, 2020), 67.

4. Ibid., 68.
5. James Nestor, *Breath: The New Science of a Lost Art* (New York: Riverhead Books, 2020), 24.
6. Ibid., 21, 29.
7. Caroline Goyder, *Find Your Voice: The Secret to Talking with Confidence in Any Situation* (London: Vermillion, 2020), 41.
8. Ibid.
9. Ibid., 95.
10. Ibid., 64.
11. Zig Ziglar, "Change What Goes Into Your Mind," Ziglar, accessed September 5, 2021, https://www.ziglar.com/quotes/you-are-what-you-are-and-where-you-are/.
12. Caroline Goyder, *Find Your Voice: The Secret to Talking with Confidence in Any Situation* (London: Vermillion, 2020), 70.
13. Ibid.
14. Shawn Achor, *Big Potential: How Transforming the Pursuit of Success Raises Our Achievement, Happiness, and Well-Being* (New York: Currency, 2018), 74.
15. Scott Shickler and Jeff Waller, *The 7 Mindsets to Live Your Ultimate Life: An Unexpected Blueprint for an Extraordinary Life* (Hartford, CT: Publish Your Purpose Press, 2019), 64.
16. Lawrence Robinson, Melinda Smith, and Jeanne Segal, "Laughter is the Best Medicine," Help Guide, July 2021, https://www.helpguide.org/articles/mental-health/laughter-is-the-best-medicine.htm?pdf=13511.
17. Ron Gutman, "The Hidden Power of Smiling," TED video, filmed March 2011, https://www.ted.com/talks/ron_gutman_the_hidden_power_of_smiling.
18. "One Smile Can Make You Feel a Million Dollars," Scotsman, March 4, 2005, https://www.scotsman.com/health/one-smile-can-make-you-feel-million-dollars-2469850
19. Ernest L. Abel and Michael L. Kruger, "Smile Intensity in Photographs Predicts Longevity," *Psychological Science* 21, no. 4 (2010): 542–544.
20. Erica Cirino, "What Are the Benefits of Hugging?" Healthline, April 11, 2018, https://www.healthline.com/health/hugging-benefits.
21. Shad Helmstetter, *What to Say When You Talk to Your Self* (New York: Gallery Books, 1986/2017), 22.
22. Benjamin Hardy, *Personality Isn't Permanent: Break Free from Self-Limiting Beliefs and Rewrite Your Story* (New York: Portfolio, 2020), 154.
23. Ibid.
24. "Breathing Life Into 'Inspire,'" Merriam-Webster, accessed September 5, 2021, https://www.merriam-webster.com/words-at-play/the-origins-of-inspire.

PART 2: INSPIRE!

Chapter 5

UPBEAT MINDSET

The view you adopt for yourself profoundly affects
the way you lead your life.[1]
— Carol S. Dweck

In the summer of 2014, when I was preparing to move to Wisconsin to become a visiting professor of music at Lawrence University, my former saxophone professor, Steve Jordheim, asked me if I was familiar with "mindset." I thought it was an odd question since the term "mindset" is a common word and expression. I had heard it used in the context of "it's important to have a good or positive mindset," but beyond that I hadn't given it much thought. Steve clarified "mindset" in terms of growth and fixed mindsets. I hadn't heard it described in those terms, so Steve recommended that I read Carol Dweck's book, *Mindset*, and check out her talks.

I dove into the book and those talks, as well as her other research, and I was stunned by what I learned. I felt that I had discovered the Holy Grail for how to unlock our students' potential. Dweck shares that we are all born with a growth mindset—curious, observant, a sponge for learning and growth. Dweck writes, "The growth mindset is the belief that abilities can be cultivated."[2] Dweck teaches that those with a growth mindset believe that intelligence is malleable and can be grown or developed with persistence, effort, and a focus on learning. Furthermore, they look at challenges as opportunities to develop, learn, and grow, as opposed to looking at challenges as opportunities to fail. These challenges can be physical, like learning to walk or play an instrument, or emotional and psychological, like recognizing that we need to become better team players. Someone who learns and leads with a growth mindset accepts that there will be struggle, stumbling, scraped knees, and disappointment, but will continue to seek out new strategies, put in the extra time, and respond to feedback in the pursuit of growth.

We learn to speak and walk by imitating our parents or guardians, and even though we don't succeed on the first try, we continue to get back up and try, try again until we make progress and eventually succeed. As we get older, however, and begin school, we notice that we are judged, which leads us to judge and criticize ourselves and others. We are separated into groups and given labels that correspond to our ability level, such as the slow reading group or the fast reading group. We may be praised for excelling at math, or maybe our grades suggest that math is not for us. Similarly, depending on our initial aptitude, we are encouraged or discouraged from pursuing things like athletics or music.

Because of messages that are shared with us directly or indirectly, we may internalize the idea that if we are not good at something or do not show promise right away that it is not worth pursuing. Accepting the societal message that we have set, predetermined aptitudes, sometimes labeled as "talented" or "not talented," we develop what

Dweck calls a "fixed mindset," meaning that our "qualities are carved in stone" and that we are born with an unchangeable amount of intelligence and talent.[3] Students who develop fixed mindsets will often shy away from challenges. Instead of following the old adage "If at first you don't succeed, try, try again," we think, "If at first I don't succeed, why try at all?"

How do we break this cycle? Dweck's studies demonstrate that the language we use in response to a student's action or achievement can affect their mindset. In her 1998 study of a group of fifth grade students, one group was praised for how smart they were when they finished a series of problems, and the other group was praised for their effort and how hard they worked.[4] When given the choice for the next round of completing a more difficult set of problems or an easier one, the group that was praised for being smart chose the easier problems and those praised for their effort chose the more challenging path. In the third round, all the students were given more challenging problems, and many of the students that had been praised for their intelligence "*lost* their confidence in their ability and their enjoyment in the task as soon as they began to struggle with the problem."[5] In contrast, the students who had been praised for their effort remained happily engaged in the process. Interestingly, in the final round, the students were given easier problems that matched the level of the first round. On average, the students that had been praised for their intelligence did worse than they had in round one, because they had lost their confidence, and the students praised for effort performed at a higher level because they were focused on the process of growing and learning.

The research and studies on growth mindset have profound implications for us as music educators. Whether students enter our classrooms with a fixed or growth mindset, the way we communicate and teach can help shift the classroom into a growth mindset that embraces the process of growing. By focusing on effort and the journey, rather than labeling students as good or bad, smart or not-so-smart, talented or untalented, we can highlight their progress and stimulate a growth mindset. Wouldn't you love for your students to believe that they have unlimited potential and can thrive on challenges? The self-belief that students have regarding their potential to grow is their upbeat to the process of learning. Equally important, how we feel about our own students' potential is our upbeat to the climate we create in our classroom. Let's find out how to create not only a growth mindset classroom but also an upbeat mindset classroom.

Step by S.T.E.P. Growth

When we have an upbeat mindset, we are excited and look forward to learning, growth, and challenges. We accept that wherever we are today is just a starting point and does not predetermine how far we will be able to venture. Learning and developing skills takes daily practice, and mastery does not happen in a day, but it does begin with the first step. Lao Tzu wisely taught this principle 2,500 years ago in the sixty-fourth verse of the *Tao Te Ching*:

A tree that fills a man's embrace grows from a seedling.
A tower nine stories high starts with one brick.
A journey of a thousand miles begins with a single step.[6]

To capture how important that very first step is, picture a toddler learning to walk. Imagine them trying to take their very first step.

What happens? They fall! But the greatest thing happens next— they get back up and try again. Do they succeed on the second try? No! They fall again and they get back up and try again. What an inspiration to us all! The toddler continues to fall, get back up, and try again. Normally there is someone nearby cheering them on and supporting them on this journey. We don't give up on the toddler after their first try or say, "Well, I guess they just aren't cut out to be a walker." After days and days of trying, the toddler does toddle and continues to get better at it daily until they have mastered walking. Yes, "A journey of a thousand miles begins with a single step," and the journey may also be filled with falling down and getting back up and continuing on. We encourage the effort and the persistence because we *know* they can do it. As our students get older and they don't succeed at first, they are not usually given that same level of encouragement and instead are often discouraged from continuing to try.

One of my greatest challenges in junior high band was learning to tap my foot to the beat of the metronome rather than to the rhythm of the music. In order to overcome this challenge, I wrote in the counting and drew down and up arrows on every beat to show what my foot should be doing. I practiced slowly and sang my music while tapping my foot. After untold hours of practice, I was finally able to tap my foot to the beat while playing complex syncopated rhythms, but it was hard work. Challenge students to wrestle with their mindset by having them write about something they were unable to do or understand and what it took to learn what they now know. Through examining their learning processes, students will be able to see that not succeeding at something on the first few tries does not predict their ultimate success and potential.

As music educators, we can help our students believe in themselves again and let them know that making mistakes and not succeeding at first is just part of the normal process of developing musical skills. We can show the pathway towards developing musical skills and break the seemingly insurmountable journey down into approachable, single steps.

The pathway to developing an upbeat mindset classroom is to remember it is also about taking that first STEP. Let's think of S.T.E.P. as an acronym for:

Strategies

Time

Effort

Process

Strategies

What works for some students will not work for all. When a student is not progressing, it is important that, as educators, we consider using a different strategy or method of communicating information. Try to prepare multiple approaches to teaching a concept rather than just one tried-and-true method. As an example, for a student working out the technique on a sixteenth-note passage, we could suggest a combination of any of the strategies listed on the following page. What works well for one student may not work as well for a different student and vice versa. The number of strategies we can come up with is only limited by our creativity. Try out as many strategies as needed until something clicks so that the way you are teaching does in fact spark learning in that student. In addition to the ideas below, feel free to add more strategies of your own.

1. Slow the passage down to half speed and gradually speed up the tempo with a metronome as the technique improves.

2. Slow the passage down and just focus on the fingerings.

3. Then send air through the instrument and tongue the proper articulations without creating a tone in a practice called "toneless wind."

4. After following Steps 2 and 3, play the passage as written slowly and gradually speed it up with the use of a metronome until the goal tempo is achieved.

5. Change up the rhythm of the passage so that the notes are played long-short, long-short, as in a dotted eighth note followed by a sixteenth note.

6. Alternatively, change up the rhythm of the passage so that the notes are played short-long, short-long, as in a sixteenth note followed by a dotted eighth note.

7. After following Steps 5 and 6, play the passage again as written to compare and notice the improvement. This exercise can be started off slowly and then gradually sped up.

8. Ask the students to sing the phrase and then finger and sing before playing it with their instruments.

9. Play the passage backwards slowly, and then play the passage forward. This is particularly challenging, but fun and surprisingly helpful, so plan for this extra time in your lessons.

10. Group the sixteenth-note passage into five-note groupings as in 1 e + a 2, then 2 e + a 3, and so forth. Then combine the segments into a whole.

Your students are sure to welcome new approaches when you encourage an openness to change and provide that all-important reassurance that it is perfectly normal to *not* get it right the first time. They may also really enjoy the possibilities these new strategies provide for their progress.

Time

Everyone learns at a different rate, and putting in more time allows the knowledge or action to sink in and be mapped in the brain and in muscle memory. Students may not see the progress after a practice session, but after a good night's sleep, they may notice the improvement the next day. Our brains often take time to soak in the information and integrate it, and sleeping is when this often happens. What can feel like a plateau could instead be a deepening of understanding that does not appear on the surface until after dedicating even more time to practice. When a student does not show immediate improvement or grasp the new knowledge, be patient and give it more time.

Effort

Staying focused with energy and intention is an important part of the process. Thomas Edison purportedly claimed that his success came from 1 percent inspiration and 99 percent perspiration. Praise students for the effort they put in rather than how smart, intelligent, or talented they are. If a student succeeds right away, raise the bar so that they can take on a higher level of challenge. Take time to notice and acknowledge the hard work that students put into improving and learning. The words "yet" or "not yet" can be used effectively in our praise language, as in "You are close, but you are not there yet."[7]

If a student says that they can't play or do something, encourage them to add the word "yet." "Yet" holds promise that although the student has not risen to the goal level of achievement, with continued effort they will be able to achieve and learn what is necessary.

Process

Focus on the journey and the daily work and growth rather than on the outcome. If we make it about the daily wins, the stepping stones to success, then we can be at our best in the moment. Celebrate being on the path and on the journey so that the process is enjoyable. Every day and every rehearsal is an opportunity to learn and get better. If we make it all about the concert, the ratings at the festival, or the rankings at a marching band competition, we strip away the joy and reward of learning and being in the present. It is motivating to have long-term goals, but when the goals cloud our effort or focus on the now, we are less productive.

Our thoughts are the upbeat to our actions, and our actions define us. We can think positively all day, but if the thoughts don't lead to change, they never gain the momentum to make a difference. Confronting a fixed mindset does not always happen easily, particularly if it requires stepping outside of our comfort zone. We must push ourselves to say "no" to the self-doubt and self-protection that wants us to avoid taking any risks. We have to set challenges for ourselves and then through sheer willpower get after it. When the change or the mountain seems too high to scale, we get intimidated by the magnitude and often find ourselves giving up before even taking the *first step* towards accomplishing a goal.

Reaching for a big goal needs to be broken down into individual, achievable steps. Otherwise, we will likely never even start walking on the trail to get there. Achieving success can be likened to the process of learning a ten-minute marching band show. You wouldn't start off instruction by showing your students a video of the entire show with drill and music and then expect them to be able to march the entire show! You would likely start with teaching the steps from set one to set two. And that move may include sixteen marching steps to get there. You would then ask your students to calculate the length of each step for an even step size by pointing to the halfway mark that would take eight steps. Then they would break that down in half to see where they need to be in four steps. Next, they would cut that in half to two steps and then cut that in half to mark the distance for their very first step. Learning an entire marching show that may include seventy drill pages and over a thousand steps of varying sizes begins with taking just one step. In order to make our big goals feel realistic and achievable, plot out the steps to get there over time, beginning with one step, one change, one direction change. Once you take the first step, each step after that becomes much easier. However, the upbeat—attitude and mindset—that students bring to that very first step matters greatly and can have a significant impact on the outcome and whether or not they enjoy the challenge.

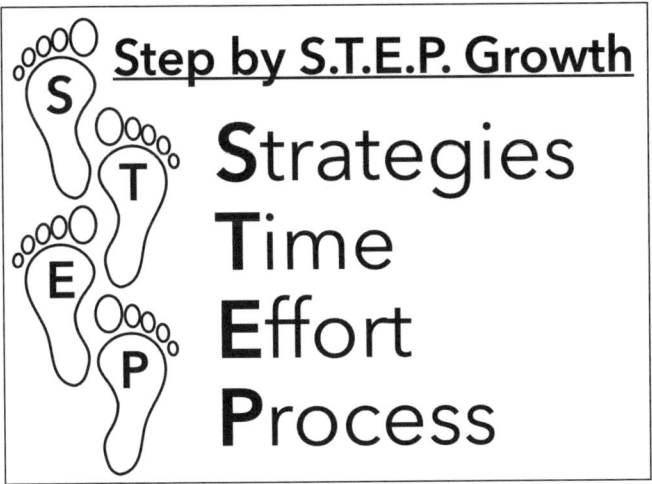

Step by S.T.E.P. Growth

S **S**trategies

T **T**ime

E **E**ffort

P **P**rocess

Teacher Mindsets

Although our students arrive in our music classes with a mixed bag of growth and fixed mindsets, we can intentionally get to work on changing mindsets by shifting our language and how we praise and critique our students' performance in rehearsal and after the concert. The first step is to look within and then accept and wrestle with our own mindset. Developing our own growth mindset is easier said than done since we are products of our environment, society, and circumstances. We will notice that we have deeply rooted beliefs and biases that subtly, or even dramatically, affect how and what we communicate. Reflect on any diminishing messages that you may have heard in your life, which might have sounded like one of the following lines.

- "You are not enough."
- "You aren't good at math."
- "You don't have a good ear."
- "Stick to reading music. Improvisation is not your thing."
- "Do you really want to stick out from the crowd?"
- "Have courage but not too much courage to leave the pack."

In many ways, the story about crabs in a bucket rings true with how others have tried to limit our own potential. When one crab is put in a bucket, it will do everything it can to jump out and escape back into the ocean, but apparently when two or more crabs are put into a bucket, the one that tries to escape will inevitably be pulled back down by the others.

The more we are aware of our mindsets about different things, the greater our ability to flip the switch. Begin with taking a moment to reflect or journal about your personal mindset journey. Consider the following questions.

1. In what areas of your life do you have mostly a growth mindset? Possible topics could include music, athletics, math, reading, relationships, teaching, learning, or communication.
2. In what area of your life have you developed mostly a fixed mindset?
3. What is an example of a fixed mindset that you have overcome? What was the process for this shift?
4. Can you identify the opposite as well? An area where you used to have a growth mindset but have since stopped envisioning growth and adopted a more fixed mindset?

Be sure to ponder these questions non-judgmentally and recognize that we all have fixed mindsets in some areas to a certain extent. One of mine to this day is skydiving, because I think, "What if I fail!?" I view that experience through the lens of only two possible outcomes: (1) fear, exhilaration, and then relief, and that adrenaline rush of conquering a fear, or (2) fear, exhilaration, and death.

Of course, not all fixed mindsets are that extreme. We may have a deeply rooted belief that we could never excel in math or that piano or bassoon are out of our reach. There may be certain musical scores that we think we don't have enough "talent" to learn and conduct. We may have a fear or a fixed mindset about jazz improvisation because we have never done it or been successful with it. We may also have a fixed mindset about public speaking or sports.

We may also hold beliefs about the innate ability of our own students that get in the way of full and equal investment in the progress of each student. **In the pursuit of creating an upbeat mindset music room or ensemble, the most important mindset to tend to and develop is our own, because our belief can either put a lid on our students' potential or break through the ceiling on achievement.**

Fleas in a Jar

I am reminded of a story from my childhood that involves a Chihuahua, some fleas, and a jar. When I was a kid growing up in Sacramento, California, I could not wait for our neighbors to go on vacation. Whenever they left for a few days or more, they would ask one of the Arau children to take care of their dog, Petey. Now, Petey had a vicious streak, and there were many days when I would be biking down our street and Petey would come flying out of my neighbor's home, barking up a storm, chasing after me and trying to nip at my heels. There was something about bikes that really got Petey going. Petey had a fiery personality that contrasted with his small size. A tan Chihuahua, he couldn't have weighed more than ten pounds, but he made up for it with his vicious snarl, ferocious bark, and breakneck speed.

Even though Petey frightened me by chasing me on my bike, I still hoped that my neighbors would ask me to take care of Petey while they were away, not because I loved their dog but because my neighbors had television! I was raised without a TV, so any opportunity to watch shows was a rare, exhilarating moment. I came up with an effective strategy to calm Petey down so that I could safely "veg out" on their big brown leather couch and watch any show that happened to be playing. The couch rested on top of a one-inch-thick brown shag carpet. This is notable because danger lurked within the carpet. Living in the carpet was a boatload of fleas, no doubt brought into the house by Petey. I know, gross, right? But getting my legs bit up by fleas was the risk I was willing to take to be able to watch TV! So, what does this have to do with a growth mindset?

Well, it turns out that we can learn a lot about how our mindset affects our students from fleas in their natural habitat. Whether outdoors or in shag carpet, fleas naturally have a vertical leap of around thirty-six inches. That is incredible if you consider the ratio of the size of the flea versus the height of the jump! But if you take two fleas and put them in a six-inch jar, punch some holes in the lid so they can breathe, and then seal the lid, something will change. In the beginning, the fleas will attempt to leap as normal, but when they do they smash into the lid. They keep trying to leap high but eventually they realize that they can't jump more than six inches because of the lid that has been placed over them. So, now they jump just below six inches. If they stay in the jar long enough, when they are freed, amazingly they continue to only jump just below six inches. But the real kicker is that if those two fleas get together and make baby fleas, they teach their babies to also jump just below six inches![8]

No, I never did try out this experiment, and yes, I did get plenty of flea bites while taking care of Petey. I find that the metaphor of the fleas has much to teach us about how our mindsets can hold sway over how our students view their ability to learn and grow. **So many of the voices that our students hear while growing up are lid-lowering. Our music rooms can serve as a force of positive encouragement that raises and ultimately removes the lid on potential.**

Ten Strategies to Develop an Upbeat Mindset Classroom

The beautiful thing about mindsets is that they are not set in stone and can be changed. Here are ten steps to shift from a fixed mindset to a growth mindset in your classroom. In keeping with the theme of this book, let's call it an "upbeat mindset."

1. Share with students what fixed and upbeat mindsets are. The act of identifying and noticing how our own mindsets affect our thoughts, feelings, and behavior can lead to a desire to make a change. Be open about your own fixed mindsets and how it is natural to hold onto a combination of fixed and upbeat mindsets, but that it is possible to shift from a fixed to an upbeat mindset.

2. Teach your students that the brain is a muscle and that it is strengthened by training, just like our body grows stronger from doing daily sit-ups and push-ups. Share the importance of thoughtful repetition and deliberate practice to create disciplined habits, increasing the agility of your physical and mental systems. Getting better at anything takes patience, perseverance, effort, and time. Perhaps even more importantly, it takes desire and a passion to improve.

3. Remove the mystique that surrounds the word "talent" and share examples that show how achieving lasting success or mastery requires serious work. Share stories of your own struggles and challenges that you faced in becoming a musician and music educator to open up pathways for connection and trust, and talk about what you did to persevere and demonstrate resilience.

4. Show an open and accepting posture through your body language and speak with an authentic and encouraging tone to demonstrate your belief in your students. Students pick up on the silent messages that your presence, mood, and body language communicate, so being more aware of what you are communicating non-verbally is critical. Relax the tension in your face and feel free to smile and laugh more often.

5. Avoid comparing students to each other and instead recognize the growth of the group as a whole. Remember to be specific when highlighting individual progress. Don't

just praise the most advanced players; praise effort and improvement in musicians, regardless of their current level of achievement. In *Big Potential*, author and happiness advocate Shawn Achor writes, "When you tell someone that they are 'better' than someone else, that by definition means that someone else is 'worse.' Moreover, by telling someone they are 'better' or 'the best,' you are placing an unconscious, implicit limit on your expectation for what that other person can achieve. Also, if we are striving only to be better than someone else, doesn't that set our expectations for ourselves too low? It tells us that as soon as we are just a little bit better than another person, we can stop trying, even if it means stopping short of our potential."[9] When you maintain focus on individual and group improvement and progress, you are not measuring a student's work against the achievement of fellow classmates. To create this healthy environment, encourage students to cheer on each other's effort and growth. Use language that unites rather than divides, such as *together*, *we*, and *let's*, as in "Let's play at measure 33." Create the sense of collaboration and community as much as possible rather than separating the teacher and student with *I* and *you* language.

6. Whenever possible, model on an instrument, sing, play a recording, or use movement and gestures to demonstrate how you want the music to sound and be shaped. Provide an aural and mental representation of the goal to which the students can aspire. Showing what is possible is more

important than obsessing over what is wrong. Empower a student to demonstrate to the other students when they are achieving the goal or making significant progress.

7. Share your high expectations openly, clearly communicate goals with students, and give students input. Collaborate with students in the creation of these goals so that they participate in the process and have buy-in for where they are headed as individuals and as an ensemble. Draw attention to the progress they have made towards achieving the goals and what needs more work throughout the rehearsal. Engage students in their own development as musicians by sharing the responsibility of evaluating rehearsals and performances with students. Create a sense of autonomy for students by giving them time in rehearsal to discuss in sections what they can improve. Every student in the section can offer input. Give students the opportunity to step out, listen, and offer support and advice to their peers. Empower students to take the next step to improve the music in sectionals and at-home practice.

8. In your communication with your students, focus more on the process rather than the product. Yes, the concert matters and the goal of producing an outstanding performance motivates and drives us forward, but the recognition of the smaller daily achievements reinforces habits of success. Drop in the word "yet" more often. "We are not there *yet*. We still have much to do to get to where we need to be, but we are definitely making progress." A more specific

example might be, "We haven't achieved rhythmic clarity at measure 43 *yet*, and we will keep working at it until we do." A sculptor does not create their marble sculpture in a day. They consistently, over time, chip away at the block with rapt attention to detail. Focus more on the vision of what is possible and what can be created. Avoid using the word "can't" in rehearsals, and if it is unavoidable, add "yet": "We can't play over the break *yet*." The word "yet" is hopeful, and it implies the expectation that the group will develop the skill to achieve the goal.

9. In addition to the word "yet," turn to the Power of G.E.T. and emphasize what the students and you *get to do* in every rehearsal. The Power of G.E.T. makes gratitude and appreciation for getting to be together, learning, and creating music a centerpiece of your upbeat music classroom. Remind students to focus on what they are *grateful* for, to approach every moment with *enthusiasm*, and to *treasure* the opportunity to be part of something that can inspire, move, and literally change lives.

10. Be specific with praise and feedback. Avoid generalities such as "That was good" or "That was bad." Provide details on what went well and what should continue in addition to what areas went poorly and need to be improved. Provide solutions and strategies for students to address deficiencies. Here are some examples:

- Instead of saying, "You are rushing," say "Relax into the beat."
- Instead of saying, "You are flat," say "Raise the pitch" or "Listen and adjust to remove the beats in the sound."
- Instead of saying, "Flutes or sopranos you are too loud," say "Get your sound inside the lowest voice."
- Use the word "when" rather than the word "if," as in, "I am looking forward to *when* we can all play the sixteenth-note passage at measures 14–19"
- Instead of saying "Good job," be specific, as in "Excellent improvement in maintaining pitch center through the phrase," or "Great progress in separating the staccato notes."
- Instead of saying, "That was not good" or "That was bad," be specific about what needs to be improved, as in, "We need to match pitch on the tonic of the chord, lower the pitch of the major third, and raise the perfect fifth just slightly to make the chord ring and resonate."
- Paint a vision of what can be. For example, "The entrance was together, but our release lacked clarity. Let's release with an inhale on count 4 so that we enter silence with sensitivity."

Practice using these ten strategies to create and sustain the upbeat mindset of your classroom. By applying the Power of G.E.T. and approaching every day with an upbeat mindset, your students will notice the difference and soon they will integrate what you teach and model into their musicianship and their lives in and outside of school.

The Promise of an Upbeat Mindset Classroom

When students choose an upbeat mindset, they look at reaching beyond their own comfort zone with an attitude of, "Yes, I am going to go for it. I am going to step out into the unknown." Students then have the courage to face a challenge and carve a path forward. Every piece of music has its own challenge. It may be rhythms, range, phrasing, dynamics, technique, expression, style, interpretation, intonation, tone, vibrato—there are so many variables. To get better, we have to be willing to step into the unknown, to step into the struggle. No matter what, growth and progress begin with taking that first step. An upbeat mindset classroom fosters enthusiasm for going for it, despite the risk of failure, because falling down is just an opportunity to learn and grow to get better.

An upbeat mindset learning environment does not take away from the pursuit of excellence. In fact, it raises the bar by including every student in the journey. Our upbeat in this case—our beliefs and values related to learning and potential—is essential. Then, through earnestly applying the ten strategies and exuberantly sharing excitement for the learning process, your students will believe in themselves more, engage more, practice more, and feel they are essential contributors to the success of the group. An upbeat mindset classroom demands and expects a lot of effort from the students while being supportive and solution-oriented.

In other classrooms, students may comply with the teacher by simply responding to rules, procedures, and demands. But compliance does not mean intrinsic motivation. When a student is compliant, they do the task but without enthusiasm or joy. In an upbeat mindset classroom, when students get excited about a project, they put their whole heart into it. With a higher level of personal commitment and investment, students will be more aware, focused, attuned, self-correcting, and motivated. Encourage your students to use upbeat growth mindset language that focuses on self-belief, progress, improvement, as well as *yet* and *get* in your classroom. This will also impact their internal dialogue, leading your students to not only take on challenges more readily but also respond to adversity, struggle, and failure with resilience.

Envision your students being thrilled by a challenge just like the young students in Carol Dweck's research who responded to working on puzzles with the statement, "I love a challenge!"[10] What if an administrator had to ask your students to stop running in the hallways during passing period and the students responded that they were running to music class because they could not wait to get there? What if your students could not wait to arrive and did not want to leave when class ended?

As the teacher believes more in their students, the students believe more in themselves. The magic really starts happening when the students begin to truly believe in each other—encouraging, supporting, and cheering on the progress of their peers and offering advice and alternative strategies for students that are struggling. This is the ripple effect that is created from that one pebble thrown into the lake or that one spark that lights the kindling and grows into a giant bonfire. This is the promise of an upbeat mindset classroom.

Bring It!

Having an upbeat mindset does not mean we will always achieve our goals, make our dream a reality, and reach the summit every time.

In fact, we will likely fail more often than we succeed. But what it does mean is that we will try, we will go for it, and we will not be swayed or discouraged by the nay-sayers. If we want it, we will go after it, piece by piece, step by step, moment to moment, day to day. An upbeat mindset teaches us that we will survive when we step out of our comfort zone because we have done it before and learned from the experience.

An upbeat mindset does not mean that life will be smooth sailing from here on out. In fact, it is in the choppy waves and gale-force winds where we become a better sailor. With an upbeat mindset, we call out to the thunder and the dark clouds, saying, "Bring it! Is this the best you got?!" We may careen, pitch to the side, and even capsize, but we will recover and get back up and charge forth relentlessly. An upbeat mindset reminds us that struggle is part of the voyage of life. We may be afraid and fear the unknown, but we will not cower and hide from challenge. We will embrace it and stare it in the eye and say to ourselves, "You've got this."

Vignette

Jayson Gerth
Band Director
Southeast Polk High School, Pleasant Hill, Iowa

Studying Carol Dweck's work on growth mindset completely changed my perspective on how I welcomed students coming into high school from eighth grade. In my school district, lesson and rehearsal schedules did not align well enough for me to spend much meaningful time at our junior high school.

Because of this, I did not get to know the incoming students well and had to rely heavily on our junior high band director for input about students' playing abilities.

For several years, I also asked the junior high director about student personalities, work habits, and perceived potential. However, after reading about the power of "yet" in Dweck's work, I realized I relied on the opinion of my junior high school director too much and formed fixed impressions of the incoming class. His opinions and experiences, both good and not-so-good but offered in the spirit of helpfulness, colored my perceptions of students before I met them and before they met me.

Once I began limiting the input to objective measures of musical development, I found there were sometimes significant differences between how I and the junior high director perceived and experienced students. For some students, the transition between grades, buildings, or teachers can be a resetting point. Once I stopped viewing the student transition from eighth to ninth grade from a "fixed" mindset perspective, my eyes were opened.

One former student, I'll call her Stevie, immediately comes to mind. I knew she entered high school as a mediocre player, and I could sense a defensiveness accompanied by a bit of a chip on her shoulder. She stuck with the band through high school though and graduated as a section leader. Over time, she turned out to be one of those students who challenged me to be a better teacher and pushed her section and the band to be better overall. When she graduated, she told me in the kindest, most profound letter I've ever received from a student that band had changed her life, and she credited her success and passing grades in high school to her time in my class.

Stevie was one of those kids that the junior high teacher had never said anything about, but much later he told me how shocked (and happy) he was that she ended up as she did. She was always getting into trouble in junior high and nearly quit band before high school. I'm sure that had he told me about his experiences with her early on, I would have likely seen her much differently from day one rather than getting to know her and work with her from a fresh perspective. A fixed mindset could have changed the course of her time in high school and our band program, and all those students she helped and inspired would have been worse off as a result.

Application

1. Make or purchase posters with positive upbeat mindset messages and place them around your classroom.
2. Set your intention in the morning to believe in the unlimited potential of each of your students.
3. Reflect on progress made in each rehearsal and chart a course forward based on stepping stones rather than large leaps.
4. Set students up for success by building on what they do well and stretching them just beyond their comfort zone.

5. Challenge yourself to take on a new hobby or learn a new skill that you have shied away from. Feel what it feels like to be a beginner again.

Journal Questions

1. In what areas do I have more of a fixed mindset?
2. In what areas do I have more of a growth mindset?
3. Recall a shift in your life from a fixed mindset to a growth mindset. What happened leading up to this change? How can you apply what you learned to new situations?
4. How does your mindset affect the culture, productivity, engagement, and achievement of your music program?
5. Recall a student who surpassed your expectations. How did that feel?

Quotes

Take the first step in faith. You don't have to see the whole staircase, just take the first step.

> — Dr. Martin Luther King, Jr.
> as quoted in Scott Shickler and Jeff
> Waller's *The 7 Mindsets to Live Your
> Ultimate Life*, p. 110

Your belief will drive your behavior. The thought "I don't think I can" often arises out of "I don't think I am." You will never be more than how you see yourself.

> — John C. Maxwell
> *Intentional Living*, p. 68

*The view you adopt for yourself profoundly affects the way
you lead your life. It can determine whether you become
the person you want to be and whether you accomplish the
things you value.*

> — Carol S. Dweck
> *Mindset*, p. 6

*Whether you believe you can do a thing or not,
you are right.*

> — Henry Ford
> as quoted in *The Reader's Digest*,
> Vol. 51, p. 64

*I have learned that success is to be measured not so much
by the position that one has reached in life as by the
obstacles which he has overcome while trying to succeed.*

> — Booker T. Washington
> *Up from Slavery*, p. 19

*When we plant a rose seed in the earth, we notice that it is
small, but we do not criticize it as "rootless and stemless."
We treat it as a seed, giving it the water and nourishment
required of a seed. When it first shoots up out of the earth,
we don't condemn it as immature and underdeveloped;
nor do we criticize the buds for not being open when they*

appear. We stand in wonder at the process taking place and give the plant the care it needs at each stage of its development. The rose is a rose from the time it is a seed to the time it dies. Within it, at all times, it contains its whole potential. It seems to be constantly in the process of change; yet at each stage, at each moment, it is perfectly all right as it is.

— W. Timothy Gallwey
The Inner Game of Tennis, p. 21

ENDNOTES

1. Carol S. Dweck, *Mindset: Changing the Way You Think to Fulfil Your Potential* (London: Robinson, 2012/2017), 6.
2. Ibid., 16.
3. Ibid., 6.
4. Carol S. Dweck, "The Perils and Promises of Praise," *Educational Leadership* 65, no. 2 (October 2007): 34–39.
5. Ibid., 36.
6. Wayne Dyer, *Change Your Thoughts—Change Your Life: Living the Wisdom of the Tao* (Carlsbad, CA: Hay House, 2007), 302.
7. Carol S. Dweck, "The Power of Believing that You Can Improve," TEDx, November 2014, https://www.ted.com/talks/carol_dweck_the_power_of_believing_that_you_can_improve.
8. Steve Harvey with Jeffrey Johnson, *Act Like a Success, Think Like a Success: Discovering Your Gift and the Way to Life's Riches* (New York: HarperCollins, 2014), 41–43.
9. Shawn Achor, *Big Potential: How Transforming the Pursuit of Success Raises Our Achievement, Happiness, and Well-Being* (New York: Currency, 2018), 120.
10. Carol S. Dweck, *Mindset: Changing the Way You Think to Fulfil Your Potential* (London: Robinson, 2012/2017), 3.

Chapter 6

MINDFULNESS IN THE CLASSROOM

You must live in the present, launch yourself on every wave,
find eternity in each moment.[1]
— Henry David Thoreau

Imagine the elegance of the beginning of a professional orchestra or band rehearsal. The musicians arrive and find their place, set up the music on their stand, and then warm up at their leisure. At some point, either from the direction of the conductor or the principal oboe, clarinet, or tuba, a single tuning note is played. The musicians listen intently waiting for the sound to stabilize at either A440 or A442 hertz B-flat, A, and/or F. Then gently, the musicians begin to enter on the same note, trying to match and blend with the initial single note that is still sounding. The musicians are careful not to play too loudly so as not to cover up the sound of the tuning note.

The instrumentalists listen for any dissonance between their sound and the tuning note, adjusting their instrument or embouchure to raise or lower the pitch until they can create stillness—a sense of oneness. This is the beginning of the tuning process—focusing on just one note—but this is not the end of tuning. The musicians will listen alertly throughout the rehearsal to each other, blending, balancing, matching, and making rapid micro-adjustments to play in tune with their section and the entire ensemble. One's ears must always be alert to the ever-changing soundscape. When the ensemble is in tune, the tone of the ensemble achieves a rich resonance. When the ensemble is not in tune, it can irritate the ears like the sound of fingernails on a chalkboard. The musicians must be able to heighten their awareness to listen to themselves while simultaneously listening to everyone around them. To do so requires self-understanding, compromise, and awareness of their ever-changing role in the complete collage of sounds. This is fine-tuning an ensemble.

But what about the individuals behind the instruments? What about the conductor holding the baton? How do they tune themselves? How does the individual achieve a level of fine-tuning of their most important instrument—their mind, body, and spirit? How can we tune ourselves with the same level of care and intention that we tune up our ensembles? Incorporating mindfulness into our classrooms provides a pathway for tuning the mind, heart, and body for both ourselves and our students. The practice of mindfulness prioritizes the importance of tuning oneself to heighten awareness, appreciation, and mental, emotional, and spiritual well-being. Mindfulness is about becoming more aware of what we're thinking, feeling, sensing, and doing while navigating through our daily events and situations. One of the leading experts of mindfulness, Jon Kabat-Zinn, writes in *Wherever You Go, There You Are*, "Mindfulness means paying attention in a particular way: on purpose, in the present moment, and nonjudgmentally."[2] Integrating mindfulness into our teaching acknowledges that who we are and *who* we teach matters just as much as *what* we teach. Most often, we focus on the *what*; mindfulness creates the space to honor the *whole student* beyond the instrument they play or their voice range. **Practicing mindfulness is an act of self-compassion, and by integrating mindfulness into the classroom we extend that compassion to our students.**

We only have so much time for each class that we teach and for each rehearsal. Wouldn't it be great if we could increase our students' focus, awareness, and attention so that learning and engagement would rise? What if we could ask students to tap into their own feelings and emotions and use those to express themselves through the music they perform? What if we could lessen stress and anxiety for ourselves and our students so that our moments together could focus on creating community, beautiful music, and a culture of compassion and excellence? Through the practice of mindfulness in our classroom, we can.

Integrating Mindfulness into the Classroom

To consider the importance of mindfulness in our music classrooms, it can be helpful to consider its opposite: mindlessness. Just going through the motions of a conducting pattern or going through a warm-up routine without intention, investment, awareness, and purpose robs our students of a vibrant and meaningful experience. We all have times when we check out mentally or let our minds wander, and when this happens we miss out on being fully present with our students and the music. When students practice, rehearse, or perform without listening deeply or being fully present, they miss out on the opportunity to grow and experience the magical musical moment. Essentially, time is wasted because students were not fully invested or engaged, and their minds were most likely elsewhere.

In order to create the moment, we must *be* in the moment. Mindfulness practitioner, teacher, teacher educator, and scientist Patricia Jennings writes, "Mindfulness is 'fullness of mind,' because you bring your full, undivided attention to the present moment."[3] Think about that phrase, "fullness of mind." Isn't that what we want for our students in every rehearsal? In many ways, you probably already are including mindful elements in your rehearsals. When you ask your students to listen intently to a particular voice or instrument, you are integrating a mindful practice. When you ask your students to take a deep breath to calm down before a solo or performance, you are inviting mindfulness into your students' lives. When you ask students to imagine the ideal performance in their mind's eye and inner ear, you are engaging in mindful practice. And when you teach with gratitude and compassion, you are teaching mindfully. When you take a split-second to pause before reacting emotionally to a student who presses your buttons, you are responding mindfully. If your mind wanders while teaching and you notice it and direct yourself back to the present moment, you are practicing mindfulness. And when you or your students become completely absorbed into the beauty of playing, composing, improvising, or listening to music, you are experiencing mindfulness.

Silence and Stillness

What steps can we take to introduce mindfulness into our classroom? To begin with, we can honor silence. Sound rises from a bed of silence, just as thoughts originate in silence. Silence is to music as the blank canvas is to a painting.

Take a moment to reflect on how rare silence is in our lives today. There are the constant whirrs, chimes, beeps, buzzes, and alarms of technology and electronic gadgets—the drones, honking, and clanging of traffic and construction. In the hallways of the schools, there are the sounds of lockers slamming, doors opening and closing, and droves of people milling about, talking, shouting, and laughing. There is the rush and the sense of urgency between classes as students hurry to get from one end of the school to the music hall. In the music room, there is the sound of the hustle and bustle as students get their instruments out and begin warming up on their own and the chatter among friends excited for their favorite class of the day. The bell rings and then it is time for the rehearsal to begin.

Who knows well the racket of this last paragraph? We are so used to the constant barrage of noise that it has actually become part of our comfort zone. In fact, many people choose to walk around much of the day with earbuds or headphones on so that they can listen to something every possible moment in order to avoid interactions with others and the discomfort of silence. Have you noticed your own discomfort with silence and just *being* with your thoughts? This is nothing new. Even during the Renaissance, influential French mathematician and philosopher Blaise Pascal stated in 1654 that "All of humanity's problems stem from man's inability to sit quietly in a room alone."[4] Instead, as Ryan Holiday shares in his book *Stillness Is the Key*, much of our creativity, original thought, and deep personal reflection comes from a place of stillness.[5]

Music education fortunately provides the arena to engage with stillness in ways that modern life may not. World-renowned pianist and conductor Daniel Barenboim, in *Music Quickens Time*, writes about the important but often overlooked role that silence plays in music.

Sound is not independent—it does not exist by itself, but has a permanent, constant and unavoidable relationship to silence. In this context the first note is not the beginning but comes out of the silence that precedes it. If sound stands in relation to silence, what kind of relationship is it? Does sound dominate silence, or does silence dominate sound? After careful observation, we notice that the relationship between sound and silence is the equivalent of the relationship between a physical object and the force of gravity. An object that is lifted from the ground demands a certain amount of energy to keep it at the height to which it has been raised. Unless one provides additional energy, the object will fall to the ground, obeying the laws of gravity. In much the same way, unless sound is sustained, it is driven to silence.[6]

We have the opportunity to establish moments and space for stillness and silence in our music room so that our students, through the contrast, can be much more focused, aware, and present when playing or singing music. Music evolves in and out of silence, and our rehearsals can honor silence in the same way. Stillness precedes movement, and silence precedes sound, yet movement comes to rest in stillness, and music concludes in silence. Before you begin rehearsing or performing a piece, treasure the stillness and the silence as essential to the music itself. **Allow for moments of stillness and silence in your classroom, through investing in mindful breathing, quiet introspection, and the savoring of the resonance of the music during a rest, after a fermata, or at the beginning and end of a piece of music.**

Mindful Breathing

Breathing is key to any instrumental or vocal performance and rehearsal. This is why we devote time in rehearsals to teach breathing exercises so that our students will fill their lungs up fully and sustain and support their tone with excellent breath support. Tubists Patrick Sheridan and Sam Pilafian developed the "Breathing Gym" to teach multiple techniques, strategies, and habits of musician breathing.[7] Along these lines, some bands and choirs even employ PVC pipes or breathing tubes to enhance the students' breathing.

In addition to breathing designed to produce and sustain a resonant, supported, full tone, mindful breathing further heightens focus and mental awareness. The same breathing exercises that you can use to center and ground yourself as a teacher in Chapter 3 also work for your students. In the large ensemble setting, when done as a group, those methods serve to calm, center, and ground students so that they can perform to their potential.

If you feel like your music program has gotten a bit stagnant and needs an infusion of energy and motivation, then breathe new life into your ensembles with the practice of mindfulness. It will do wonders for you and your students. Your students will come to love the centering and calming effects of the various relaxing breaths, and you will find that every aspect of your rehearsal elevates—focus, engagement, classroom management, motivation, and a sense of togetherness. "When we breathe together, we come in together" is a common saying among directors when we want to align musical entrances. When your group mindfully breathes together, it aligns all the musicians psychologically and physiologically. Research has shown that moving together in sync creates a sense of connection and community.[8] This can explain why moving together in marching band or dancing brings people together and fosters cooperation and belonging. Breathing together in sync also creates the sense of community, connectedness, and unity that is essential for a successful music ensemble. Just as mindful breathing serves our well-being, mindful breathing builds trust in ensembles and will help students decompress and feel better. Don't be surprised when they start asking you to include more mindful breathing in your rehearsals and music classes!

By including a gratitude breath at the beginning and/or end of each rehearsal, we can cultivate a habit of gratitude. Ask your students to think of someone or something that they appreciate. It might be a pet, a friend, a family member, their instrument, music, or a memory. Breathe in your nose for four counts while focusing on what you are grateful for and exhale any stress, anxiety, or toxic negativity out your mouth for eight counts. Just release and let it go. It works well to repeat this three times. You may find that it will boost the mood of the players to ask for volunteers to share out what brings them gratitude.

Instead of asking students to stop talking during rehearsal, lead them through the focus breath, breathing in the nose for 4 counts and out the nose for 4 counts for three or four times in a row. This breath will center, calm, and focus your students, and the bonus is that it is impossible to talk when you are breathing through your nose. This is a great way to refocus students in a positive way, to direct them to where you want them to be, fully present and ready to make music, as opposed to focusing elsewhere. When we ask students to "stop talking," it can create a confrontational rather than collaborative climate. Of course, there are times when it just needs to be said, but

I believe that, in the end, you and your students will instead prefer engaging with the focus breath for a few moments. I use the focus breath at the beginning of rehearsal as needed to heighten awareness in the rehearsal and after transitions prior to working on another piece or retuning the group. You might like to refer to the Application section at the end of this chapter for additional breathing patterns that can be used with your students in rehearsal and class.

Beginning a rehearsal with mindful breathing and a focus on gratitude primes the mind for its optimal state for learning, collaborating, creating, and music making. Incorporating mindful practices elevates self-awareness and allows us to fully tap into our feelings and emotions to then fully express meaning through our instruments. Directing our bodies to breathe deeply and our minds to focus on gratitude also calms nerves and anxiety, setting us up to be fully in the moment musically. When we are stressed and our heart rate is elevated, our breathing gets tight, shallow, and pinched off. But when we are calm, our breathing is relaxed and flows, which is optimal for producing a beautiful tone and phrasing.

Through daily mindful conditioning, we are also teaching our students life-long skills for managing, coping with, and avoiding performance anxiety. They will be able to transform nervousness to a calm, focused intensity. Taking a mindful, focused breath as an ensemble before playing a challenging piece at a concert is a great way to prepare students for a high-level performance. **We spend so much time on the technique of "getting the music right," yet we should also spend time on developing habits that will heighten our performance from the inside out.** You can empower your students to lead the ensemble through mindful breathing practices to increase ownership and buy-in. Older students can also mentor younger students on these breathing habits and techniques. Developing breathing habits specific to developing great tone and air support serves an equally important purpose as mindful breathing techniques that help center the mind, heighten awareness, and relax the nerves.

Body Scan

The goal of mindfulness is to be fully aware in the present moment. Since being a musician requires that we use our body to produce sound, becoming more aware of our bodies and physiology is important for us to tap into that next level. Leading your students through body scans is a great way to bring attention to how their bodies feel and move, which can then lead to increased awareness during singing and while playing their instruments. In addition to guiding the ensemble through a deep breathing exercise, take them also through a body scan, drawing awareness to the top of the head and moving down the face, noticing any tension in the eyes or the jaw. Release tension as the scan moves down to the neck, the shoulders, the chest, the arms, and the fingers, observing without judgment and working your way down the legs to the feet and toes. This exercise also reinforces good posture and effective breathing habits, and it works best when the students keep their eyes closed, drawing their attention inward.

Incorporating mindful breathing and a body scan prepares students mentally and physically to listen deeply with a heightened focus for the entire rehearsal. Wind conductor Craig Kirchhoff shared with me at a conducting symposium early in my teaching career that the beginning of a rehearsal should be designed to *sensitize* the ensemble rather than to just warm them up. Sensitizing means raising the level of musical awareness and acclimating the ensemble to the nuances of your conducting. The idea of a warm-up can take on a repetitive, mundane meaning, whereas *sensitizing* seems more purposeful and artistic. That idea has stuck with me, opening the door for me to realize that we are not just warming up our instruments and voices, but we are preparing and sensitizing our *entire being* for the musical experience, including the mind, body, ears, heart, and spirit. Therefore, taking time to center, focus, and ground the musicians becomes essential to sensitizing the ensemble.

Practicing Mindfulness in Music

Mindfulness is a practice and as such it is never mastered. We practice mindfulness by heightening awareness of the present moment by engaging all our senses. As mindful musicians, practice can begin with the act of taking our instruments out of their cases. Invite your students to see the instrument's beauty, its shine and shimmer. Notice the design and craftsmanship and breathe in gratitude for what this instrument allows you to do—to create sounds that expresses your feelings and emotions and allows you to communicate with an audience heart to heart. While assembling your instrument, notice its feel, its weight, the smoothness, or the roughness. Instead of going through the motions on autopilot, soak up the experience as if you are putting your instrument together for the first time. Observe how you feel while assembling your instrument. Notice your emotions as a witness and avoid judging your emotions as good or bad. Just notice.

Before playing the first note on your instrument, get centered and find stillness and silence. Treat the first note as a special moment in which your breath adds beauty to the space you are in.

Be aware of your breath. Notice the expansion from down low and the movement of your chest filling up with air. And then notice the feeling of the exhale through your instrument or through your voice if you are singing.

When you are mindful, you notice and observe with wonder and curiosity acts and behaviors that may have become automatic or almost involuntary. By focusing on your breath, your mind gets centered and is primed to listen more deeply and to notice your physiology, emotions, and state of mind.

Your goal is to be so in the moment that you embrace the present wholeheartedly. This may feel unnatural or uncomfortable at first, because we are used to having our focus and mind wander. Even when you are singing or playing an instrument, you may be thinking about something that just happened or about the future. For instance, "I wonder what's for lunch." When your thoughts wander, you can consciously redirect your mind back to your breath, the color of your tone, or the feel of your articulation. Redirecting attention back to the present moment while singing or playing music is similar to how one redirects their attention to their breath while meditating. Focus will come and go but mindfulness teaches us the skill of returning back to the now, and with repeated practice this ability to be completely immersed in the act of making music will become a habit.

Be in Tune

I often think of the pursuit of pure intonation as the ultimate mindfulness act. When two or more musicians perform on pitch-producing instruments, they must be incredibly alert to the sound of the other, making infinitesimally small adjustments or large adjustments in pitch, depending on the situation. For example, what an audience perceives at a professional symphony orchestra performance as a beautifully in-tune performance is, in reality, filled with the quickest, almost imperceptible adjustments as the musicians listen intently and deeply to one another, making pitch adjustments and compromises throughout a performance. In contrast to equal temperament tuning on the piano where the tuning can only be adjusted by a piano tuner, in pure or just intonation, the role of each note changes as keys and harmonies change, necessitating a shift in the pitch by the musicians to make the waves between the notes stand still and to create an in-tune, resonant performance. Not only do musicians need to be aware of the various pitch tendencies on their instruments, but they need to be able to anticipate and quickly respond to the other musicians around them. **Striving for pure intonation is truly an act of compassion, respect, and love that requires a deep level of listening and awareness.**

As I described in the opening to this chapter, zeroing in on getting one note in tune is just the beginning—the start of the process of playing in tune. We should treat the tuning process as sacred, for it is in the act of matching pitch to one player or tone that we experience what it is like to transform from being many to being one. It is in the pursuit of oneness that we get centered and grounded and raise our awareness of being in the present moment. We can return to oneness and unity throughout the rehearsal just as we return to noticing our breath while meditating. We may tune the ensemble before each piece to bring us back to that centered and focused space.

Mindfulness guides us to be more in tune with ourselves, and it also helps us to be more in tune with other people, and it is this awareness, changing the way we interact, respond, and work with

others, which is critical in a music ensemble. As a conductor, we should be able to sense the vibe of the ensemble and make adjustments based on what we sense. If the group seems distracted, you may decide to use the focus breath, or you may change your lesson plan and rehearse a higher energy piece to harness your students' energy into music. Communication matters from director to musician, but communication verbally and non-verbally amongst the musicians is key as well. Mindfulness practices help the ensemble members to be more self-aware about the impact and influence their communication has on others. When we are grounded, we can pause before reacting and choose a response fitting to the person and the situation in that unique moment.

Mindful Listening

A mindful musician strives to be in touch with their whole being—mentally, emotionally, physically, and spiritually. Our decision to listen more deeply to ourselves and the musicians around us connects us sonorously and spiritually. **We don't listen intently to one another just for the sake of the music. We listen to one another so that we can practice the same level of respect, compassion, collaboration, and compromise outside of rehearsal connecting in harmony to one another.**

When we simply tell students to listen without being specific about where to listen or what to listen for, our students may direct their focus in infinite directions. By focusing our students' listening to a particular voice, the act of listening itself becomes more intentional and meaningful. In addition to focusing on a particular voice or instrument, you can narrow the focus to particular musical elements, such as articulation, phrasing, dynamics, energy, tone, intonation, expression, and emotion. When conducting a large ensemble, I recommend teaching the following five levels of listening. In rehearsal, you can then let students know what level to focus on at a particular time. Notice how the corresponding sounds of the ensemble literally shift as you change from one level of listening to the next. Invite some students up front so they can also experience the difference that is made when musicians alter the way they are listening.

The Five Levels of Listening

1. Listen to yourself.
2. Listen to someone playing/singing the same part as you within your section.
3. Listen to someone playing/singing a different part within your section.
4. Listen to someone playing/singing the same part as you but in a different section.
5. Listen to someone playing/singing a different part in a different section.

Outside of rehearsal, we often find that our lives are go, go, go, do, do, do, deadline after deadline, and we do not invest the time to pause, get still, enter the silence, breathe deeply, and allow our inner-selves—our true selves—to rise to the surface. Music gives us the opportunity to listen to ourselves and others so that we can bring this practice to our lives outside of rehearsal. Music teaches us how to listen and respond rather than react. Our ability to respond as musicians quickens with more experience and the development of our musicianship. Through practice, both students and teachers can practice and develop their mindful listening, which will help create a positive culture as well as build better ensemble skills in music class.

Be Intentional

Practice setting an intention as an ensemble for each phase of rehearsal so that eventually individuals feel prepared to set their own intention for the work to be done. Here are some examples for setting an intention.

- I will be more aware of how my tone blends with the other musicians in my section.
- I will watch the conductor with enthusiasm while making music today.
- I will pay more attention to the space between my notes in the staccato, marcato, and accent articulations.
- I will play with my whole heart rather than just going through the motions of playing the correct notes and rhythms.
- I will be more fully aware of the feelings that the music evokes in me during rehearsal.
- I will make every minute count in rehearsal because I know that rehearsal time is precious and limited.
- I will bring my best self to rehearsal so that I can add positive energy and help move the group towards an expressive and excellent performance.

In addition to setting intentions as an ensemble and as individuals, you may want to set your own personal intentions, such as:

- I will be more expressive with my gestures, facial expressions, and tap into my emotional side today rather than only approaching the rehearsal from my more natural, analytical mind.
- I will look for improvement in individual students and highlight growth in this rehearsal.
- I will look for opportunities to empower students by asking questions about what they think and inviting them to listen or conduct from the front of the room.
- I will breathe mindfully during the rehearsal so that I am able to be more thoughtful in my responses rather than reactive.
- I will express appreciation and gratitude more often in rehearsal.

Setting an intention and visualizing the music in our mind in advance prepares us mentally to be fully invested and present for when we play our instruments or sing. Athletes often use the technique of setting intention and visualization, and the same benefits apply to musicians. Research shows that when we visualize, the result is equal to the actual act of doing it. Our brains do not differentiate between "seeing" an action in our minds and actually doing it physically.[9] When we see and hear the performance in our minds, we are in effect seeing the sculpture within the block of marble. Imagining an ideal performance and practicing visualization techniques are aspects of mindful practice. Ask students to not only visualize the performance but also hear it and *feel* it as if they are actually experiencing it. Visualizing works even better if the students have memorized the music or can at least create a "soundtrack" in their mind. Looking within and embracing the power of the mind is an important aspect of mindfulness practice. Rehearsals are the time to collaboratively chip away at the block of marble until the shared vision that was in our mind and heart becomes a finished sculpture.

Transitions between the warm-up and repertoire and between pieces in a rehearsal are often moments when the group can lose the focus that comes out of silence. I have found that we can be intentional about how we handle these transitions. The ensemble needs to know your expectations ahead of time, so communicate how you want transitions to be handled. I prefer a focused, silent transition, so I teach the habit of breathing in and out of your nose while preparing for the next step in a rehearsal. If the ensemble treats every transition as an opportunity to talk, the group loses the sensitivity and intention established by the initial warm-up provided. Just like rests in music, the spaces between activities in a rehearsal should be embraced as opportunities to begin thinking about the following piece. I realize this is a personal decision, and you may find with the age group that you teach or the length of a rehearsal that encouraging students to talk and/or play in transitions between pieces energizes your students. Whichever way you choose to handle transitions, it is important to return to a calm, focused center before beginning the next element of the rehearsal, and this is where the focus breath works perfectly.

Feeling and Emotion in Rehearsal

By increasing our internal awareness, we are able to look within, examine what we feel, and then label our emotions. Emotions are neither good nor bad; they just are, and we can tap into our full range of emotional experience to heighten our connection to and our communication of the music. Rather than letting our emotions control us, we can harness our emotions to our advantage as music makers. The good news is, as Patricia Jennings shares, "Mindfulness can help us be more aware of our emotional state and how it is affecting the emotional climate of our classroom."[10]

Take a moment to reflect on the joy, excitement, and passion you experienced as a young musician. For many, this feeling motivated us to keep at it and work harder on music that was a stretch technically but touched us deeply. As music educators, we must keep that spark, that reason for doing what we do, in the forefront of our mind. Remember that while we may have taught a concept over a hundred times, this could be the very first time for the students in front of us. Even when rehearsing a passage and removing all the bumps that interfere with the projection of the composer's intent, we can tap into the meaning, feeling, and passion of the music. **Ask your students how the music makes *them* feel and then discuss what can be done technically to show that feeling. Instead of waiting until the day before the concert to put on the final touches of expression, make the goal of expression and emotional investment central to the rehearsal.** Yes, as technique improves, the ability to be expressive also grows, but the emotional commitment *throughout* the rehearsal process, including those first rehearsals, elevates everyone's motivation and inspiration to dig in deeper. If the students are not ready to emote or connect with the emotion of the piece in the early stages of the rehearsal process because they are ultra-focused on the notes and rhythms, play a recording so they can hear and feel what the music has the potential to express. Students can also find a connection through hearing the meaning of the piece in the composer's program notes.

Priming the Mind

In addition to the level of technique and skill, so much of our success or failure as musicians is affected by the thoughts going through our minds while we sing or play an instrument. Mindfulness practice draws our awareness towards the internal dialogue. When we become aware of what we say to ourselves, we can evaluate whether our thoughts are serving us and the music. Every musician has experienced self-doubt or anxiety about the difficulty of a musical passage at one point or another. I sure have. Do any of these statements sound familiar to you or your students?

- "Here comes the hard part. Don't screw up."
- "My solo is coming up. I am nervous because everyone will be listening to me."
- "Here comes that high note. Please don't frack."
- "I don't think I'm good enough."

Our self-talk can either help us or hurt us. I first became aware of the influence that our self-talk has when I read *The Inner Game of Music* by Barry Green and W. Timothy Gallwey as an undergraduate college student. Green and Gallwey describe the inner dialogue as Self 1 and Self 2. Self 1 is our ego and expresses doubt and fear, whereas

Self 2 is absorbed in the music, the feeling, and the artistry. They write that even though Self 1 may talk to us about our weaknesses, we don't need to talk back. They advise:

> We can choose. In fact, there are a wide variety of choices open to us. We can choose to focus on various aspects of the music. We can listen to the sounds, watch ourselves as we are playing, sense the way in which our body is involved in the making of music, or monitor our feelings. Whichever of these or a dozen other choices we make, we are consciously choosing to focus on something that is happening right now, in the present moment. When we are present in this way (focusing on something that is happening right now), Self 2 has the opportunity to emerge and express itself.[11]

Our role as educators can include guiding and assisting our students to become more conscious of their self-talk and to practice programming the mind to share supportive and encouraging dialogue that will help keep them in a state of "relaxed concentration," where they are "alert, relaxed, responsive, and focused."[12] You can practice this for yourself by reading silently or saying positive affirmations out loud in the form of "I am" statements.

- "I am expressive."
- "I am musical."
- "I am confident because I am prepared."
- "I am flexible and able to adapt and respond in the moment."

Saying these affirmations out loud, with conviction and belief, gives your mind an alternative pathway to create a new habit of self-talk. It will make a difference to teach this method to your students.

In addition to becoming more aware of our thoughts, we can also take action to choose thoughts that will lead us to success. Let's say that you or your students have a pattern of thinking "Don't mess up! Don't mess up!" right before the most challenging spot. What is most likely to happen: a smooth performance or messing up? Whatever the mind focuses on can become a reality. By thinking about *not* messing up, our minds actually start thinking about all the possible things that could go wrong, directing us to make a mistake. This happens in golf all the time. If you're hitting the ball near a hazard, you're more likely to hit it into the hazard because you're thinking about it. It happens in cycling too. Pros stress to amateurs to always put their eyes where they want to go rather than where they *don't* want to go.

Daily mindfulness practice in rehearsal can help with this common psychological challenge. Attaching imagery, metaphors, stories, and feelings to the music provides an alternative to the judgmental and analytical side of our mind that is trying to protect us from making a mistake. Great art is not created from trying to avoid making a mistake; great art comes from inspiration, courage, and taking risks. **We can prime the mind ahead of the performance by breathing deeply, visualizing an expressive performance, and focusing on making beauty instead of perfection.** If we have prepared and practiced achieving a pattern of excellence in rehearsal, then when it counts, we will experience the sensation of flow or the feeling of being in the zone.

Mindfulness Beyond the Rehearsal

Students will be able to transfer the practice of mindfulness in rehearsal to their lives outside of music, becoming much more aware in their interactions with friends, teachers, and family members. When we advocate for music, we often list life skills learned and taught in music, inducing discipline, dedication, teamwork, leadership, and creativity. Mindfulness can also be added to this list, and your students will feel the benefits in their life, in music, and beyond. Encourage your students to practice mindfulness throughout the day so that being fully present, engaged, and "in the now" is not just reserved for music class, rehearsals, and performance.

In addition to calling on any of the mindful breathing techniques for calming, focusing, centering, sleeping, and heightening awareness any time of day, students can redirect their mind and heart to be fully present in infinite ways. Here are some examples:

- When a friend is speaking, listen attentively with the intent to understand rather than to respond.
- Notice the beauty of nature that is all around, utilizing all your senses.
- Feel and express gratitude more often.
- Acknowledge and honor your emotions and how you are feeling without judgment.
- Mindfully eat and drink without being distracted by your phone. Be present.
- Mindfully wash your hands and notice the temperature and feel of the water and soap on your hands.

- Mindfully walk and notice your breathing and the feel of the soles of your shoes on the ground.
- When you notice your mind wandering, kindly redirect your attention to the present moment.
- When someone says something that upsets you, pause to take a mindful breath to gather your thoughts before responding. One slow deep breath can lower your blood pressure and allow you to be more thoughtful and empathetic.
- Keep a gratitude journal and write down three things that you are grateful for every morning or at night before you go to sleep.

When educators infuse mindfulness into their classrooms and beyond, they also feel the positive effects on their minds, bodies, and hearts. Simply by leading the students through a renew-release breath, a gratitude breath, or a focus breath, the entire feeling in the room will change and any stress that you and your students may have been feeling dissipates so that you can be at your best in the present moment for your students. Mindful practices make us more aware of our thoughts, help us to manage our emotions, and empower us to choose the thoughts that will serve us best. In essence, mindfulness creates the space that allows us to choose our upbeat.

Vignette

Adam Miller

Band Director

Jeffersonville High School, Jeffersonville, Indiana

One of my most cherished memories as a band director is the very first visit Dr. Matthew Arau made to Jeffersonville. The spring of 2015 was a landmark beginning of an incredible journey for our students and myself. Little did we know that under the leadership of Dr. Arau we would play a small part in planting the seeds of what would evolve into the 4 C's of leadership, the incredible Upbeat Leadership curriculum, and a focus on musicianship mindfulness.

Many believe that mindfulness is something to do on your own or something that may or may not work depending on your personal beliefs. In many conversations and collaborations with Dr. Arau, I came to realize the real hard science and data behind the power of mindfulness. Mindfulness moved from being something on the fringe of our leadership discussions to a key rehearsal skill that we develop every day. The guidance of Dr. Arau has led to full integration of Upbeat and mindfulness as daily rehearsal tools:

• Every class is started by a **student-led** three-minute Qigong (body movement and breathing regulation) session. Depending on the day, each student leader might choose to visualize or focus on a certain aspect of mindfulness or a current band topic. None of our band classes are started by a teacher. Each one starts with a different student leading Qigong each day.

- Focus Breathing: If rehearsal hits a frustration wall, we take a moment to do a variety of focused breaths to regain control of our minds. This occurs almost daily.
- Musicianship Mindfulness Curriculum consists of thirteen weeks of once-a-week mindfulness assignments that students complete. This helps them with their own mindfulness journey while focusing on how mindfulness can help their performance skills. These assignments are designed to treat mindfulness as a skill that musicians can learn to enhance their performance abilities. Students work through lessons that give them specific exercises and reflections that give them real-world techniques to implement in their daily practice and performance.

Here are samples of how our students feel about mindfulness and Upbeat tools in our curriculum:

- "I relate this exercise to music by focusing on what is going on at that moment. It will help me not drift away and think about other things."
- "I feel more ready for rehearsal after we complete the mindfulness techniques."
- "You can use this exercise to help break down pieces of the music you are struggling on to work on it more efficiently."

- "I tend to struggle with being focused in different fields, so this really helped me for other things as well as for band."

The mistake I made at first was believing that activities such as mindfulness would "steal" time away from the "real" rehearsal. The pressure to have the next concert or contest piece ready drove many of our decisions about rehearsal time. The reality is that mindfulness became a new and indispensable tool in making our rehearsals more effective. Instead of taking time, the three to five minutes of student-led, focused mindfulness instruction has actually saved time. With a more focused rehearsal, our students are more efficient in what they achieve and leave our room with a life skill they wouldn't have had otherwise.

In short, the new upbeat focus of our band program is to support the emotional health of every single student with which we have a connection. As a result, our post-COVID rebuild will be musically stronger and more effective. But, upon reflection, isn't that the focus we should have had all along?

Application

1. Introduce one mindful breathing technique at a time with your students. You and your students may want to gently close your eyes or soften your gaze while breathing mindfully.

    Focus Breath: Breathe in through the nose for 4 counts and exhale through the nose for 4 counts. Repeat three times. This breath focuses your mind and helps you get in the zone.

Serenity Breath: Breathe in through the nose for 4 counts. Hold for 7 counts. Exhale through the mouth for 8 counts. Repeat four times. This breath works really well to lessen stress and anxiety.

Triangle Breath: Breathe in through the nose for 3 counts. Hold for 3 counts. Exhale through the mouth for 3 counts. Repeat three times. This breath is calming and centering.

Box Breath: Breathe in through the nose for 4 counts. Hold for 4 counts. Exhale through the nose for 4 counts. Hold for 4 counts. Repeat three or four times. This breath is great for grounding and stability.

Renew and Release Breath: While breathing in the nose for 4 counts, think "renew" to refresh, recharge, and reinvigorate. While exhaling out the nose or mouth for 6 counts, think "release" to let go, remove, and detox. Repeat for as long as you like.

Gratitude Breath (Version 1): Focus on something or someone that you are grateful for. Breathe gratitude in through your nose for 4 counts. Exhale stress, anxiety, and anything that you want to release for 8 counts through your mouth. Repeat three times.

Gratitude Breath (Version 2): Focus on something or someone that you are grateful for. Breathe gratitude in through your nose for 4 counts. Exhale out through your mouth what you want to send or give to the world—peace, love, joy, for example—for 8 counts. Repeat three times.

As a visual aid use the Hoberman sphere, a plastic ball that can contract and expand, to silently lead students through breathing exercises.

2. Sing or play instruments with a heightened sense of awareness, including sight, sound, smell, touch, taste, emotions and feelings, and thought. Then direct awareness to one sense at a time to practice being fully present.

3. Guide your students through the process of visualizing the performance of a chord, a phrase, or a piece of music in the mind and inner ear prior to playing or singing.

4. Set an intention with input from your students for how they would like to approach a rehearsal, perhaps with a higher level of listening to each other or with more energy and enthusiasm.

Journal Questions

1. How do my feelings and emotions today impact my tone and performance? Are my feelings serving the music?
2. How are my awareness and senses heightened during and following mindful breathing?
3. How does relaxing and deep breathing affect my focus and attention?
4. How do you think practicing mindfulness in music rehearsals affects you outside of music class?
5. Have you noticed a difference in how you respond to challenges or conflict since practicing mindfulness?

Quotes

Between stimulus and response there is a space. In that space lies your freedom and power to choose your response. In those responses lie your growth and your happiness.

> — Stephen R. Covey
> in the foreword to *Lead or Get Off the Pot!* by Pat Croce

The challenge of mindfulness is to be present for your experience as it is rather than immediately jumping in to change it or try to force it to be different.

> — Jon Kabat-Zinn
> *Mindfulness for Beginners*, p. 26

Wherever you are, be all there.

> — Jim Elliot
> as quoted in Elisabeth Elliot's *Through Gates of Splendor*, p. 20

Your life requires your mindful presence in order to live it. Be here now.

> — Akiroq Brost
> as quoted in Hoda Kotb's *This Just Speaks to Me*, p. 89

Mindfulness is the conscious awareness of our current thoughts, feelings, and surroundings—and accepting this awareness with openness and curiosity in a nonjudgmental way.

— Goldie Hawn
10 Mindful Minutes, p. 10

When we mindfully experience the fullness of the present moment, a multitude of possibilities arise spontaneously, without effort. When we widen our perspective, our mind makes connections that we didn't realize existed before.

— Patricia Jennings
Mindfulness for Teachers, p. 185

ENDNOTES

1. Henry David Thoreau, *Walden* (Princeton, NJ: Princeton University Press, 1989), 57.
2. Jon Kabat-Zinn, *Wherever You Go, There You Are: Mindfulness Meditation in Everyday Life* (New York: Hachette Books, 1994/2005), 4.
3. Patricia Jennings, *Mindfulness for Teachers: Simple Skills for Peace and Productivity in the Classroom* (New York: W. W. Norton & Company, 2015), 1.
4. Ryan Holiday, *Stillness is the Key* (New York: Portfolio, 2019), 2.
5. Ibid., 5.
6. Daniel Barenboim, *Music Quickens Time* (London: Verso, 2008), 7.
7. Patrick Sheridan and Sam Pilafian, *Guide to The Breathing Gym* (Mesa, AZ: Focus on Music, 2021).
8. Scott S. Wiltermuth and Chip Heath, "Synchrony and Cooperation," *Psychological Science* 20, no. 1 (January 2009): 1–5.

9. A. Pascual-Leone, D. Nguyet, L. G. Cohen, J. P. Brasil-Neto, A. Cammarota, and M. Hallett, "Modulation of Muscle Responses Evoked by Transcranial Magnetic Stimulation During the Acquisition of New Fine Motor Skills," *Journal of Neurophysiology* (September 1, 1995), https://journals.physiology.org/doi/pdf/10.1152/jn.1995.74.3.1037.

10. Patricia Jennings, *Mindfulness for Teachers: Simple Skills for Peace and Productivity in the Classroom* (New York: W. W. Norton & Company, 2015), 140.

11. Barry Green and W. Timothy Gallwey, *The Inner Game of Music* (New York: Doubleday, 1986), 22.

12. Ibid., 23.

Chapter 7

CREATING AN UPBEAT CULTURE

Culture is the living and breathing essence
of what a team believes, values, and does.[1]
— Jon Gordon

C ulture impacts every aspect of our music program, affecting musical excellence, student leadership, how the students feel, the priorities, acceptable behaviors, standards, expectations, and how the members treat each other. In my observations and research of music programs across the country, culture is a byproduct of what the teachers communicate, how they act, what values are important to them, their priorities, and the focus in their classrooms. Culture impacts how the students feel and it influences their learning, enthusiasm, and level of engagement. The culture of a classroom affects everyone and everything. Daniel Coyle, author of *The Culture Code* writes, "Culture is a set of living relationships working toward a shared goal. It's not something you are. It's something you do."[2] In *Leaders Eat Last*, Simon Sinek further points out that, "If character describes how an individual thinks and acts, then the culture of an organization describes the character of a group of people and how they think and act as a collective."[3] In most cases, culture happens haphazardly rather than by design. We can choose, however, to take steps to create the culture we desire. This chapter will provide you with a pathway forward.

Impact of the Teacher on Culture

Whether we are intentional about taking steps to create a culture for our ensembles and music programs or not, a culture will in fact be created. The reality is that who we are, how we feel and communicate, what we think, and what actions we take are the greatest influences on the culture of our music classrooms. While the members also play a role in culture creation, the leader of a group sets the tone and pace for how the members of the group feel, think, and act.[4] This is a tremendous responsibility, which forces us to take that uncomfortable step of looking in the mirror and taking stock of what we see looking back at us. Our personal upbeat, in this case, affects the downbeat of the culture. Who we are has the greatest impact on the culture itself. **So just as the word "upbeat" begins with the letter U, the culture of your program begins with *you*.**

To reach higher, it is important to begin with an assessment of where you are today so that you have a foundation or benchmark from which to build. Take a moment to answer the following questions:

- How would you describe the culture of your music classroom and ensemble(s)?

- Have you taken the time to step back and reflect on the atmosphere, general vibe, and feeling of the classes and ensembles? If not, take time for this reflection. How would you define these perceptions of the places where you lead?

- What are the values, traditions, activities, and norms?

- When someone visits your classroom, what do they tend to notice and observe? What would they see?

- Is the room clean and organized, or is there random clutter strewn about?

- Are there posters on the wall with musical or motivational messages?

- Are the chairs and music stands in good working order?

- When students enter the room, are they smiling and excited to be there or does their body language communicate apathy or exhaustion?

- When students prepare to rehearse, what does their posture communicate?

- Do students appear to feel comfortable talking with the teacher, or is there an imaginary barrier that pinches off communication?

- Can you sense a feeling of connection and belonging amongst the ensemble members, or, on the contrary, does it feel like "every person for themselves"? Be particularly wary of any sensations that contradict a sense of belonging and suggest a lack of connection. As Simon Sinek explains, "In this kind of weak culture, we veer away from doing 'the right thing' in favor of doing 'the right thing that is right for me.'"[5]

- What are the values, traditions, activities, and norms? If this is your first time considering these aspects, you'll want to revisit this question once you've worked on your vision-mission statements in Chapter 12.

If you could choose just one word to describe the culture of your classroom, what would it be? Try not to overthink this. Just say or write down the first word that comes to your mind. There are infinite possibilities and here are just some that you may have considered.

Belonging
Caring
Community
Compassionate
Encouraging
Excellence
Family
Heart
Inclusive
Joy
Musical
Passion
Pressure-cooker
Pride
Sarcastic
Stressful
Supportive
Tense
Tradition

When we zero in on one word, we can reflect on whether that word aligns with what we desire our culture to be. Is there a difference between what *is* and what you want the culture *to be?* It's perfectly natural and okay if the culture that you want to create is a work in progress. What are the values and priorities that are important to you and that you would like your classroom to reflect? The famous NFL football coach Tony Dungy explains the significance of our personal values in *The Mentor Leader*, writing, "Values tell us and others what is important to us—as leaders, as an organization, and as individuals. They are the rudder that steers the ship. They tell us how to treat other people, both inside and outside the team or organization."[6] Begin with making a list of the values and priorities that matter the most to you. Think broadly about your life and beyond your ensembles. In addition to reflecting on where you spend time, think about the focus and intention you give each priority. For example, if creating a sense of community is a priority, what are the steps that you take daily to reinforce this priority?

Take a look at your list of values and priorities to see if they are in alignment with the one word you selected to describe the culture of your music classroom. If you feel that they are congruent with each other, then work to strengthen that relationship further, and if they seem disconnected, work to align your values and priorities with the culture you want to create. Ideally, the culture of a music program will reflect the values and priorities of the music educator. Just like an individual acts with a particular character, our organization will also act with a general character. **The hard question to answer is: Does your group reflect your personal character, and when it does, are you satisfied with what you see?**

The exciting news is that just as we have the power to choose our own upbeat, we can also choose the upbeat of the culture of our classroom. If we want the culture to be positive and uplifting, we ourselves need to be more positive and uplifting. If we want our culture to embody an upbeat mindset, we need to choose that mindset, model it, and communicate it consistently. If we want to have a culture of gratitude where the expression of appreciation is accepted and encouraged, we need to feel gratitude ourselves and express this feeling regularly to our students. If we want the values of caring, empathy, and compassion to be the foundation of how the students treat each other, we need to set the example. If we expect excellence and want to maintain a high standard, then we need to ensure that we are putting in the disciplined work, effort, and preparation of our scores and lesson plans. We have all witnessed the conductor who asks their students to "watch me," and when the students do look up, the conductor has their head in the score! **While striving to create a culture by design, we need to consciously and consistently model the behavior that matches the values, priorities, and qualities we aim for.** Culture begins with the teacher, but it is impacted by many other factors, including the students, the school, and the community. Highlighting how culture is a driving force in organizations, Jon Gordon writes in *The Power of a Positive Team*, "Culture drives expectations and beliefs. Expectations and beliefs drive behaviors. Behaviors drive habits. And habits create the future."[7]

Inherited Culture

When we begin teaching at a school for the first time, we inherit a culture that was established prior to our arrival. The culture reflects the accepted norms, priorities, values, traditions, standards, and expectations of the former music teacher. If the culture does not sit well with us, there will tend to be a rub or friction between what we want to create and what the students have come to expect. Despite our efforts, students will tend to return to the previously established culture of the inherited music program where they belonged. This is why I suggest not making sudden or drastic changes in the first year, because generally the amount of change that is made will be met by an equal amount of resistance. In your first year at a new school, choose just one or two things that are non-negotiables to focus on. As you make gradual improvements, these changes will be accepted better if your students are involved in the process. Ask them what they value about the inherited culture and be prepared to honor what they share with you. Listening and valuing other points of view and feelings will open a doorway to meaningful conversation and a greater understanding of your own intent and purpose. Those involved will want to know the reason behind any changes, so being up front about the potential benefits of each change is critical to encouraging more collaboration. As you build trust with your students and continue to involve them in the process, you will, over time, be able to shift the culture towards what works best for you *and* your students together.

Impact of Students on Culture

While the culture of the group is most influenced by the leader, students also play a key role in creating the culture. Our students contribute to the culture of our classroom by how they show up, the attitudes they bring, how they treat each other, and by the actions they take. Students do not often consider the influence or impact they can have individually on the feel or even the success of the group. However, when students are valued as co-creators and collaborators in the creation of culture, they will rise to a new level. Invite your students to go through the same reflective process that you went through by making a list of desired values and priorities alongside a list of how they would describe the current culture. Ask them to notice whether their values are in alignment with the culture. Engage them in conversation about what they feel is going well and what could be improved.

Be sure to steer the conversation in the direction of solutions rather than just identifying problems. One way to ensure this happens is to insist that students share an idea for positive change when sharing an aspect of the culture that is not in alignment with their values. When we focus on what we want to create and what we want more of, our minds shift into the realm of possibilities and we are able to more readily reach for the full potential of the culture of our dreams. As students contribute more ideas for how the culture could improve, ask them how they can each proactively participate in being part of the change. We've all likely heard the familiar maxim "Be the change you want to see in the world." And so in music, empower students to take responsibility and *be the change they want to see in the music classroom.* If students want to play more challenging music, they need to practice more. If students want more moments of fun and joy, they need to bring a joyous attitude and create joy rather than waiting for the fun and joy to happen. If students want to make connection and caring more central to the learning experience, they need to make the individual effort to reach out, connect, and demonstrate caring to one another. Instead of complaining or wishing things were different, students can take initiative and be proactive in creating a more positive and upbeat culture.

• • •

I learned this firsthand in 2009, when I was teaching music at Loveland High School in Loveland, Colorado. I had been at that school for five years and we had gone through quite the cultural change since my arrival. Approaching the high point of the marching band season in mid-October, I met the students on a Saturday morning for a visual and musical warm-up prior to loading up the buses for a ninety-minute drive to Arapahoe High School in the Denver area for a marching competition, the Arapahoe Marching Invitational. It was much too cold, 19 degrees Fahrenheit, to warm up outside, so we played our musical warm-ups inside before getting on the buses for the drive to the band festival. I had checked the weather for the day, and it was supposed to warm to the upper 30s. Still cold, but nothing we weren't used to in Colorado.

Unfortunately, the weather prediction was incorrect, and the weather continued to hover around 19 degrees for the remainder of the morning and afternoon. I think the high temperature for the day ended up only reaching 26 degrees. This mattered greatly because there were no indoor warm-up options at Arapahoe High School, so we had to prepare for our marching show outside. While the students played through the warm-up chorale and excerpts of the marching show in large ensemble arcs, I remember students coming up to show me icicles clinging to the open keys on their instruments. The weather was so cold that even though the students pushed their tuning slides and mouthpieces all the way in, the band ended up tuning at A=430 instead of A=440. Band parents passed out hand warmers for the students to keep in their gloves as we waited to walk over to the football stadium. Just as we were about to walk from the warm-up area to the field, a messenger came to tell us that our start time would be delayed by fifteen minutes. It turned out that the field was being cleared of snow. As we were about to start our walk over the second time, the same messenger ran to tell us that our start time would be delayed by another thirty minutes. By the time we actually made it to the field, the students were shivering from the cold. After all the build-up and the delays, though, the students were excited to get to march their show.

Considering how cold it was, the students managed to put on a solid performance, even amidst snow on the field and an impossible situation for quality intonation. Instead of staying for the finals performance, we decided to load up the buses, get warm, and return to Loveland. I felt bad for the students and wondered if I had made the right decision to go to the festival at all.

At home on Sunday and at school on Monday morning, I wondered how the students' attitudes would be at marching band practice that afternoon. I surely wouldn't have blamed them if they were feeling down or upset by how cold the weather had been on Saturday and what a letdown the experience had been. Imagine my surprise when the students showed up to rehearsal fired up and driven to have an incredible rehearsal. Not a single student complained about Saturday; instead, the entire band brought their A-game. They ran back to their drill spots between sets, cheered each other on, and approached every moment with enthusiasm. Instead of using the struggle of Saturday as an excuse, they found even greater resolve and passion and they used the challenge as a springboard to work harder than ever before. The students went on to win the Northern Colorado 4A Marching Band Championship two days later, and the following week they won the 4A Colorado State Marching Band Championship.

That rehearsal on Monday, October 12, became the new benchmark for every future rehearsal. The students created the culture on that day. They showed me how impactful and influential the students are in determining the direction and success of the group. After that, it seemed no challenge was ever too great, and the students developed a rallying cry for inspiration to persevere that they would share for years to come, "Remember Arapahoe! Remember Arapahoe! Remember Arapahoe!"

Culture of Excellence

A positive culture is one in which the teacher has high expectations for each student. Positive teachers don't just see students where they are in the present; they see where the students are headed in the future. How do you define excellence? Note that a culture of excellence begins first with the teacher's personal goals, preparation, standards, and approach to communication and rehearsing. The teacher sets the standard in rehearsal with the attitude they broadcast and by how high they set the bar. The teacher balances high expectations with support and encouragement of their students' efforts. The attitude and actions of the teacher, in turn, influence the attitude and actions of the students.

What does excellence in musicianship and performance look like to you? Aspiring to be the best musician you can be is a worthy goal, important for student growth and development. Whether or not our students continue on to be music teachers or professional musicians, learning the value of consistent practice, working through challenges, and discovering the rewards of perseverance and resilience in the pursuit of excellence teaches our students invaluable life skills.

In addition to excellence in performance and music, how else might we define excellence? Excellence can also describe how we act. These actions and how we treat others can then be measured by the level of empathy, compassion, and respect we bestow on others. A culture of excellence reflects the pursuit of achievement in all aspects of the music program. When we aspire to greatness, we begin with honoring the individual. A group is composed of individuals, and for the group to reach excellence, every member of the group needs to believe that they are recognized, that they matter, and that they are valued. They need to know that contributing at their highest level is essential and that they play a significant role in the success of the group.

In the competitive music ensemble world, we often define excellence based on trophies, rankings, and scores at music competitions and festivals. Having an outside standard to check our progress and performance can be a helpful evaluative tool and can motivate the members of the ensemble to reach higher. How we approach competition, however, can greatly impact the culture of the ensemble. If we make success at competitions the highest goal for the group, we can lose sight of other priorities and values, such as the love of music and pursuing music for life. When the single most important motivating factor is a trophy, what happens to the morale of the group and the meaning of the experience when the group does not win?

We do not need to avoid competition in music, but we should teach and model how to approach competition with a healthy mindset. Influenced by the writings and philosophy of UCLA's former legendary basketball coach John Wooden, I often reminded my students that "success is peace of mind which is a direct result of self-satisfaction in knowing you made the effort to do the best of which you are capable."[8] John Wooden also wrote, "You may be able to fool others, but you can never fool yourself. . . . Less than 100% of your effort toward obtaining your objectives is not success, regardless of how many games were won or lost."[9] Success does not happen because of one miraculous final performance; success happens in the hard work and effort that is put forth in every rehearsal and outside-of-school practice. And regardless of the rankings, if students have given it their all in every moment, they have been successful.

Culture of Heart

Culture is more than messaging, activities, connections, values, norms, and priorities. Culture is also a *feeling* that derives simply from being part of the group. I am reminded of the quote often attributed to Maya Angelou: "I've learned that people will forget what you said, people will forget what you did, but people will never forget how you made them feel." Do your students feel that they belong? Do students feel connected to the group? Do students feel free to express their emotions through the music? When rehearsing music, do not gloss over the emotions and expression in pursuit of "perfection." The emotion and expression should not be an afterthought only tended to after the other musical elements have been addressed. We pursue excellence in rhythm, tone, notes, articulation, dynamics, tempo, phrasing, intonation, balance, and blend, not just to get the performance of a piece "right" and "correct," but so that the performance takes us and the listener to a place where the heart is moved and the mind is consumed with beauty and meaning. We are not only conducting music; we are conducting and transferring our attitude and feelings energetically to our students. The culture of our band will rise when we focus on this purposeful expression. While mistakes need to be corrected and music needs to be played accurately, we can shift our verbal phrasing and physical gestures to paint a picture of what the music *can and should be* rather than continually pointing out what it is not.

Although emotions and feelings connect us to music, we tend to get into our heads when we teach music, over-analyzing, thinking, reacting, worrying, and ultimately losing touch with our hearts. Striving to consciously stay connected to the heart and the meaning of the music can help so that even when we are obsessed with "fixing" the music we don't lose touch with the reason we make, create, and listen to music in the first place.

Students living in an era of social media crave true connections now more than ever, and when we can open our own hearts to the feelings that the music evokes, we are able to share in the experience of expression together. When we close off our own hearts, we shut down the valve that opens the mutual flow of artistic music making. To create a culture of heart, we need to be open to our own vulnerability and go to places that are outside of our comfort zone. At first, it may feel unnatural, and our self-doubt, insecurity, and inner voices may start to speak up, but as we reach beyond and let our true humanity shine, we open the door for our students to walk through and let their own hearts shine forth.

If we really intend to get to know our students, we have to listen to them with genuine empathy. When we take time to hear our students, we learn about their experiences, fears, and desires, and our ensemble music-making experience becomes about making human connections rather than just facilitating the production of sound through instruments. Take the time to pull away from the computer or administrative tasks when a student comes to your office to talk. Those moments can be precious to the student, who likely needs to speak with an adult who cares. While listening to each other when playing or singing is central to an excellent music-making experience, listening to each other when not playing is just as important.

The Three Essential Pillars of Culture

Daniel Coyle, in his book *The Culture Code*, examines the culture of successful and unsuccessful organizations in the context of athletics, business, military, and schools, and identifies the following three essential pillars of culture.

1. Pillar one is safety and security that fosters a sense of belonging.
2. Pillar two is a sense of community built on trust through shared vulnerability.
3. Pillar three is a common purpose and alignment of vision.[10]

According to Coyle, when these three pillars are strong and cared for, the group will be successful. Although music classrooms were not part of his study, we can still learn a lot by applying Coyle's pillars to our profession.

Safety and Security

Without the pillars of safety and security, our students will not be able to thrive. To determine whether the culture of your music classroom needs immediate attention, think carefully about the experience you're providing students. Ask some hard questions, look behind the curtain, and peer underneath the rocks to see if the culture you are building for your classroom honors the safety and security of the *individual members.*

According to Coyle, "Group performance depends on behavior that communicates one powerful overarching idea: we are safe and connected."[11] In addition, he emphasizes that "safety is not mere emotional weather but rather the foundation on which strong culture is built."[12]

Here are some questions for personal reflection on the topic of safety and security:

1. How safe and secure do you feel in your job? How you feel will affect how your students feel.
   a. How is your relationship with your administration and colleagues?
   b. Do you feel that you can be yourself? Or do you have to change in order to fit into someone else's box?
   c. Are you worried about job security, and if so, how does that impact your mental and emotional state at work?

2. How safe and secure do your students feel? You may want to create an anonymous survey to collect responses. You may also want to engage in conversation with your students and let them know how important this is for you. With an open dialogue, students will be more forthcoming about how they feel and the challenges they are facing.
   a. Regardless of the struggles, difficulties, and challenges that students may face at home or in school, is the music

classroom a place where they feel they can be themselves, take risks, and make mistakes without the threat of being humiliated, singled out, ridiculed, or punished?

b. Do students have to keep their guard up out of fear of being made fun of or bullied by other students?

c. Are students' opinions, reflections, feedback, and thoughts valued and encouraged, or is the communication in the music classroom and ensemble only one-directional?

As you think about these questions and identify things to be aware of, come up with solutions and actions that could be taken to increase the feelings of safety and security for you and your students. I agree with Patricia Jennings that "we are responsible for creating the social and emotional tone in our classroom,"[13] and how we treat our students will create a ripple effect, affecting how students engage with each other. Model respect and kindness in all your interactions with students, particularly when critiquing and disciplining. Avoid sarcasm, as it can often be misinterpreted and lead to a culture of sarcasm amongst the students. Establish the classroom expectations for how everyone should be treated at the very beginning and then follow through with consequences and procedures. If a student makes an unkind, inappropriate, or disrespectful remark, let the student know immediately that that type of behavior belongs neither in the music classroom nor anywhere else. In order for our students to feel like they belong to the group, they need to feel that they can be themselves without harm coming to them from other students or the teacher. When a safe classroom is established, students will feel secure with being vulnerable and expressive.

Community of Trust

Creating a community built on trust is the second essential pillar of a successful culture. How do we establish trust with our students and throughout the ensemble? In Chapter 1, we referenced Stephen R. Covey, author of the 1989 book *The 7 Habits of Highly Effective People*, and now we will draw on his son Stephen M. R. Covey's 2006 book, *The Speed of Trust*, to find that, in consonance with our Upbeat! approach, trust is built from a combination of character and competence. Using the metaphor of a tree to effectively link character and competence, Covey, the younger, illustrates the composition as integrity (the roots) and intent (the trunk) for character, while competence is made up of ability (branches) and results (leaves).[14] Integrity comes from being honest and following through on your commitments: Do you do what you say you are going to do? Whether we are motivated to serve others or to serve our own egos, the intent behind our actions also defines our character, which Covey argues is simply not enough. We also need to demonstrate competence in order for trust to be strengthened. In our case as music teachers, our musical skills, teaching techniques, and strategies affect how our students respond to our leadership. And finally, we need to be able to demonstrate results. Do the students improve? Do the ensembles sound good at the performance?

In addition to competence and character, I would like to propose a third "C" that is necessary to build trust: *connection*. From her research on courage and vulnerability for *Daring Greatly*, Brené Brown explains, "We are hardwired for connection—emotionally, physically, and spiritually."[15] And a pathway to create connection is through creating a community where it is safe to be vulnerable, and the modeling of vulnerability begins with the teacher. I believe that to develop a culture founded on trusting relationships, connection is essential. The more connections we create in our relationships with our students, the deeper trust will grow. According to Brown, in order to open the channels of communication and connection, we need to lower our shield and be open to connecting. Interestingly, "we need to feel trust to be vulnerable and we need to be vulnerable in order to trust."[16] By being vulnerable and real, we invite others to share more openly from a place of trust. This, however, requires that we open our hearts and share our authentic selves. We can share personal stories that relate to the music we are rehearsing, talk about something that gets us excited, or even do an activity that we know our students enjoy. Connect the music to a student interest, like sports or gaming, to make you and the music more relatable.

As educators, modeling behavior that demonstrates care, compassion, and empathy in our interactions with students can in turn influence them to relate to each other with more care, compassion, and empathy. I wish I could say that I have always done this well, but there are plenty of times in my career when I did not follow the sage words traditionally attributed to St. Francis of Assisi, later made popular in Stephen R. Covey's *The 7 Habits of Highly Effective People*: "Seek first to understand, then to be understood."[17]

● ● ●

I wish I had practiced more patience and waited to first understand where a student was coming from before jumping to my own conclusions. Years ago while I was rehearsing my high school band in the afternoon, I took some time to go over the schedule for the next couple weeks heading up to our concert. All the students were listening silently as I laid out the zero-period sectional schedule, dress rehearsal, and the evening of the concert events. Suddenly, I heard typing on a laptop computer and, lo and behold, as I looked to my left, I saw one of my students typing away. I had a strict no cell phone policy and had never even considered that someone would get out a laptop and start doing work for another class while I was talking. Infuriated, I walked into the second row and took away the student's laptop, closed it, and brought it to the front of the room. After class, this student was so very upset and in tears. I had completely broken her trust by making an assumption without giving her the benefit of the doubt or at least asking her what she was doing before I made a scene and took away her computer. In my office, she explained, amidst sobbing, that she was merely typing the schedule into her computer calendar. Of course, I felt awful and apologized, but I don't know if I ever fully repaired her trust in me. What I learned from that experience is that trust takes time, effort, and patience and that trust can be eroded quickly when we don't treat trust as sacred.

Common Purpose

The third pillar of a successful culture is a common purpose and an alignment of vision. Being clear about the purpose for your classroom and ensembles gives the members of the group a sense of direction and meaning. This takes us back to the exercise at the beginning of this chapter where you defined the culture of your classroom with one word. Now, with as few words as possible, what is the common purpose for you? Perhaps the purpose is to have an enriching musical experience that teaches students to perform at the highest level while creating an environment that is inclusive, equitable, and supportive of all members of the group.

Next, are your students aware of the purpose? Talk with your students about what they perceive is the broader purpose and vision of your ensembles or classroom. You may decide to create a vision-mission statement with your students to develop the common purpose together. (In Chapter 12, we will go into detail about how to create a vision-mission statement as a class.) The process of discussing the common purpose will reveal whether everyone is on the same page or not. For many students, friendship, pride, and community are their driving motivations for being part of the group, while others may be drawn to the pursuit of achievement and high standard of excellence.

Intentionally creating the culture we want takes reflection, discussion, and thoughtful planning to streamline the effort and collaboration into action. Deciding together the common purpose, values, and direction of the group is just the beginning. In order to gain momentum and sustain culture, we need to be vigilant and persistent with our messaging, behavior, communication, thoughts, and actions. The messaging in the group influences the priorities of the members and the self-talk of the individuals. Invite students to make posters that include the vision statement along with goals and values of your ensembles. Place those posters around the classroom. Make the values integral to the daily experience.

Aside from talking about the common purpose, it is important to model and live this purpose day in and day out. If you and your students decide that excellence is important, then be sure to pursue excellence every day. Likewise, if a caring community is important to you, reinforce the value and act of caring on a daily basis. Step back to reflect if the common purpose is congruent with what is actually happening in the classroom and whether it is reflected in the actual culture.

Action Steps to Integrate Core Values into Classroom Culture

- If gratitude is part of your culture, take the lead by sharing your own gratitude with your students. Make a gratitude wall where students can place notes of gratitude on sticky notes. Invite your older students to make notes of encouragement and appreciation for the younger students. Devote time in rehearsal for students to share out in duets or trios what they feel gratitude for. Taking one minute of class time to devote to fostering a culture of appreciation can energize the rest of the rehearsal and make the day more memorable.

- If pride is part of your culture, provide opportunities for students to express why they are proud to be part of the group. Invite students to make a list on the board or on a shared digital document of reasons they feel pride in the group. Taking time to share stories in or outside of class that highlight pride in the ensemble will reap positive rewards. Moreover, when you take time to let the students know why you are proud of them and why getting to be their teacher is a great source of pride to you, your students will beam with delight.

- If joy is part of your culture, be excited about sharing your own joy and create opportunities for your students to feel joy and express their own joy. Look for moments to celebrate the little things. When a student plays a solo well or shows dramatic improvement, take time to cheer and do a classroom foot shuffle (students shuffle their feet to acknowledge the achievement). After an impressive performance of a piece all the way through in a rehearsal, unabashedly show your joy and pride in your students. Strive to make your classroom a place where students look forward to feeling joy.

• If creativity is an element of your culture, provide space for students to be creative, expressive, and improvise. Invite students to use their imagination and create stories, poems, or artwork that reflect what is happening in the music. Ask students what they think the music expresses and encourage their responses without making them feel they need to respond in a predetermined "in the box" way. Ask students how they think a section of the piece should be interpreted and try it out. Celebrate creative responses in order to encourage more. Step away from the written music and give students space to improvise variations on melodies or improvise using a scale over a drone or groove. Make composing part of the large ensemble experience.

• If community is part of your culture, do more than just say that community is important. Give time in rehearsal or outside of class for students to get to know one another and to support each other. Let students mix up the seating so that they can sit next to someone they don't normally get to play or sing with in a different section. (In Chapter 11, I share more examples of activities designed to increase connection and community.)

- If an upbeat mindset is part of your culture, use language that expresses the belief that each student is capable of achieving success. This will increase your students' confidence. Focus on daily progress while being specific about what needs to still be improved. When given specific praise for forward progress, students become inspired to keep putting in the effort so that they can contribute meaningfully to the success of the group.

- If you would like to reinforce values of diversity, equity, and inclusion, consider creating an equity statement with your students to help maintain your collective resolve. Writing an equity statement together has the added value of dedicating time to analyzing and understanding the repertoire you are working on to see how they reflect the ethos of your classroom. This example from Lexington High School Wind Ensemble in Lexington Massachusetts begins with a strong title and even references when the version was created since the statements can vary to serve different purposes and situations.

Lexington High School Wind Ensemble Equity Statement
"Commitment to Music-Making through the Lens of Diversity, Equity, and Inclusion" v. 4/06/21

The Lexington High School Wind Ensemble is made up of a beautifully diverse community of musicians who are committed and invested to performing music at its highest quality possible while also sharing a deeply rooted investment in each other as contributing members of this organization.

Through our time together we have come to realize that music-making is a transformative enterprise that has the power to entertain, express, and bring voice to the composer, to their intent, and to the musicians. While we have very much appreciated and valued our diverse community, we have also recognized that there are cultures and backgrounds that are not well represented within the makeup of our organization and that much of the repertoire that we rehearse, perform, and invest in lacks the representation from composers of a myriad of different cultural backgrounds, races, genders, and identities. Why is this? Through our continued collaboration and with a tremendous amount of trust, honesty, and transparency, we have been able to listen to and learn from one another in a way that has not only underscored our roles as performers of an artist's work but has also helped to concretize our understanding of the role music has in celebrating and supporting the rich diversity that exists around us.

Through this collaborative reflection, the LHS Wind Ensemble is deeply committed to using music as a vehicle for connecting with each other, our audiences, and the world that we live in. This includes not only the aesthetic qualities of a piece of music, but also the composer's intent, and thereby our own intent as musicians, interpreting and sharing the vision that has been offered by the composer. It is through this deliberate selection of repertoire, coupled with a conscious approach and rehearsal of these works, that we will be able to collaborate, communicate, and discuss the content from a myriad of different perspectives and lenses.

We are faced with an insurmountable amount of social challenges that are expressed in a variety of different media. The arts, being such an expressive and intimate forum, are an impactful medium to encourage conversations around social justice issues such as race or gender as well as the celebration of diverse artists. Here, we are able to contextualize these themes not only within the art itself, but also by relating it directly to our own experiences, observations, and lives in an authentic way, enabling us to discover and realize something so much greater about ourselves, about each other, and about our contributions to the world we live in. Indeed, music has played a centralized role in underlining so many challenges.

We have begun and will continue to uncover our own conscious and unconscious biases, recognize the implications of systemic racism, and consider our own identities within the context of social justice. We realize that this generation has the power to make change, to lead by example, and to move on from where our nation currently stands regarding racial segregation and identity. We must commit to our shared interest and value in equality, the celebration of diversity, and the importance of inclusion in all that we do. To this end, "We All Belong."

Music Class Traditions

As the seed of culture sprouts, roots, and blossoms, encourage and empower students to create traditions that are a natural outgrowth of the culture. Here are some ideas to jumpstart the potential planning you can do.

1. Spirit Days: Designate a theme for each day during the week of a big concert, festival, or competition to create enthusiasm for the upcoming event, like favorite movie character; school colors; band, choir, or orchestra T-shirt; dress up like your favorite piece of music; and many more.

2. Section Gift Bags: At the beginning of the school year or before a big performance, section leaders bring treats or kind notes for each member of the section.

3. Students design a T-shirt for the entire ensemble or for their respective section and everyone signs the back of the shirt.

4. Banquet to celebrate the accomplishments of the group with students and parents.

5. Friday Fun Day: On Fridays the students choose a piece they really like to play during that day's rehearsal.

6. Social gatherings to celebrate growing collaboration beyond the school schedule.

7. A bracelet with one word or a short phrase that has significant meaning to the students.

8. Section posters that include the goals for each section shown prominently on the walls of the classroom.

9. A Gratitude Wall in the music room or music hallway where students post what they are grateful for each week.

10. A volunteer community project to collect donations outside the supermarket for a cause of the students' choice.

11. Giving voice and encouraging music in others, like sing-alongs at the park or at a retirement home.

12. Creating a new banner for the classroom as a visual confirmation of the culture being created together.

13. Visiting music classrooms at another school or hosting them at your school to exchange ideas and see how other music groups work and get along.
14. Service projects that contribute either to the school or the community.
15. Collaborating with another school, perhaps a feeder school, to host younger musicians in rehearsals at your school.

Discipline and Motivation

The culture of the classroom affects the mood, thoughts, behavior, and motivation of the students. In ensembles where the director assumes control and leads with an authoritarian style, motivation tends to be extrinsic. The musicians want to do well to please the teacher or avoid being called out or humiliated. Often, the authoritarian director motivates through intimidation or fear. Students who excel musically are rewarded, while those who don't feel discouraged. This external discipline plays a role in classroom management, and the positive student behavior is more about avoiding any disciplinary action.

The root of the word "discipline" is disciple, which means someone who follows or learns. We either follow another or we are motivated by an inner drive to excel. When our main inspiration comes from within, we are *self-disciplined*. Culture can play an important role in igniting an inner flame that leads to intrinsic motivation and self-discipline.

Our students are motivated by different things, so creating an environment that honors a variety of forms of motivation is important. Many students are motivated by the pursuit of excellence and the sense of pride that comes from belonging to a high-achieving and successful group. Others prioritize the social and team connections. Still, some are drawn to the fun and joyous aspect that can be part of rehearsals but also comes from the extra trips and events outside the school day. **Students are motivated by the prevailing culture.** They are motivated by their peers and the teacher, and when students feel truly connected to the group, they become self-motivated and self-disciplined.

Motivation increases in classrooms that give voice to the students, honor individual differences, and collaboratively create goals for achievement. When students become part of the decision-making process and are given opportunities to grow, develop, and shine, their intrinsic motivation grows, along with self-discipline. Students thrive in a well-supported, caring, and compassionate community where they feel that they matter and make a difference. Teachers can intentionally create a space where students are celebrated for their dedication, work ethic, and teamwork. In the same way that the teacher's values and priorities influence the culture of the classroom, the teacher's own sense of self-discipline, drive, enthusiasm, and motivation exemplify to their students how pursuing one's passion with fire and intensity lights up the room and ignites the inner flame of the entire ensemble.

Sustaining Culture

Deciding what matters most for the culture of your learning environment is key. Keeping it going and growing gives culture roots. The initial image of your ideal culture is the seed. The input, ideas, feedback, and involvement of your students in the process is the planting of the seed and adding soil, water, and mulch. Sunshine and continual watering will hopefully ensure that the seed sprouts roots and grows into a healthy tree. After the initial excitement of creating a vision for the culture we want, we need to set about doing the real work of nurturing the culture daily. Leadership teacher and former middle school band director Cameron Jenkins shared this observation with me in a personal conversation: "Culture is not what you say. It's not what you write. It's what you allow." This is an important reminder to walk our talk even when it is inconvenient or uncomfortable. In music rehearsals, musicians will rise to the standard that is set. If we let the little things go—a late entrance, poor posture, talking, walking in late, poor breathing—we are sending a message about what matters and what we value. If notes and rhythms are repeatedly played incorrectly or an out-of-tune chord is sustained without acknowledgment from us, we are allowing less than excellence. If respect is part of what we want our culture to include, yet we *allow* students to be disrespectful to us or to each other, we send a message that we don't really mean what we say.

The *allowed* behavior speaks volumes, and it essentially becomes *a loud* behavior. This becomes literal in the instance that we decide there should be no talking during rehearsals except at designated times. If we allow a little bit of side conversation, we are communicating that when we say "silent" we actually mean something different. At first, reminding students to remain silent can be tedious and uncomfortable, but holding them to a high standard pays dividends in the long run.

Culture comes down to not only what we allow but what the students themselves allow. Every day, whether by design or by accident, teachers and students create culture together. Students in a recent European-wide study of innovative teaching opened up to new perspectives by "challenging their own assumptions, the hidden and often unconscious ideas, beliefs, and convictions" we all have.[18] Like the students in this study, we can uphold this high standard of exccllence through meeting the challenges that make us better together, building the culture we aim for, and sustaining our upbeat mindset. Approaching culture with a collaborative team spirit makes it about the whole group and not just about the teacher. Check in regularly with students about the culture, ask for feedback, and then make adjustments as needed. Be intentional about creating and sustaining culture, and empower all the members of the group to play a meaningful role so they take pride in the group's mission.

The culture of our classroom not only impacts how our students think, feel, and act, but it also influences recruitment and retention. Students are our best recruiters, and if they feel safe, valued, motivated, and inspired by the direction the group is headed, they will share this with the other students in the school and the feeder-program students as well. People are drawn to excellence, joy, camaraderie, and pride. We are all pulled to be part of something greater than ourselves, so when the culture of the group is inspiring and positive, successful recruitment will be a natural outgrowth of culture. Retention responds to culture as well. Students choose to stay in groups with a positive culture and high standard of excellence. Of course, the opposite is also true; students are not drawn to low energy, unsupportive, and poor-quality music programs. This is why culture matters and makes a significant difference.

Like everything in life, the quality of the culture in our music class begins with our personal upbeat. We can have all the tools, plans, facilities, instruments, and students, but if our upbeat does not radiate what we desire for the culture of our classroom, there will be a disconnect and the culture will be out of alignment. While the students play an integral role in the culture of the music classroom, culture is largely determined by the teacher. How we show up each day matters the most. It all begins with our upbeat, so be intentional about what you want to bring and project to your students, and you will be on the path towards creating the culture you desire by design.

• • •

In **Part 1: IGNITE!** we focused on upbeat strategies for the educator. In **Part 2: INSPIRE!** we transferred skills and techniques into the classroom with a focus on mindset, mindfulness, and culture. Now, in **Part 3: LEAD!** we will take the next step towards further empowering and giving voice to our students through student leadership, creating an environment where students are more motivated, more inspired, and even more engaged. Before turning the page, take a deep breath in and out and set your intention for what you hope to gain and learn in Part 3. Here we go!

Vignette

Jared L. Cassedy
2015 GRAMMY Music Educator Award Winner
K–12 Performing Arts Coordinator
Lexington High School Wind Ensemble Conductor
Lexington Public Schools, Lexington, Massachusetts

"Culture" is such an amorphous term. We use the term in so very many different ways and to define so many different aspects of the organizations we are part of. From the feelings that it elicits, to how it helps us identify the core values and beliefs of the organization, to the foundation it places upon the development of expectations and goals that guide our work—there is no denying that the definition of culture spans so many different landscapes. Within the music program, culture is clearly evident even when it is not directly focused on nor defined. I heard it stated once that the behavior of the organization is the "what" and its culture is the "how" and the "why." In our world of music, perhaps the music is "how" we get to the "why."

As I look at the instrumental ensembles and music programs I have led today and in the past, there is no denying that our work as music educators must be rooted in the "how" and the "why" in order to authentically serve our students; otherwise, we are ignoring the fundamental understanding that the power of human connection is what underscores the strength of our ensembles, which can be so dramatically forged through the process of music-making. As I have continually expressed to my students, we are not just a group of individuals playing instruments at the same time. We must invest in each other as a collective in order to play as one, to play as an ensemble. And this means not only being musically aware but also socially aware of our own contributions to each other, forming personal relationships and capitalizing on our own shared sense of musical passion. Indeed, music is our vehicle for connecting, unabashedly, with one another in one of the most significant enterprises we can ever be part of.

This past year, 2020–2021, we took the time and unrelenting opportunity to dive into the idea of culture within our wind ensemble, giving students the space and agency to consider, share, and further define their own purpose within the ensemble and what our musical experiences together are built upon. We questioned and considered why we love to play music so much, what inspires us to become part of this ensemble, and what we want our music to do for our community. In tandem with our neighboring school district in Belmont, Massachusetts, and their high school band director, Allison Lacasse, we invited Dr. Matthew Arau to collaborate with our programs on developing a culture creation curriculum. The focus of culture is of great importance, as many times it is easier to feel what it means to be a part of something rather than outwardly defining it. That said, the space we all shared enabled us to further clarify and celebrate what kind of culture exists within our programs. Words such as "family," "friendship," "community," "investment," "support," "value," "care," and "compassion" were used. In two school districts with music programs focused on that "perfect performance," on aiming for excellence in all regards, it was clear that this conversation helped to shift mindsets. Process over product, celebrating successes large and small, sharing in moments of gratitude, leading by example, and feeling safe were all things that were emphasized and have been embodied not within a vacuum, but within the context of each rehearsal and each time we are together.

As we continue to reflect and act upon our goals for culture, I encourage us all to consider what it means to belong, to be valued, cared for, and supported. An organization's continued commitment to excellence is more than just getting a job done; it truly transcends its actual outcomes. We must provide space and time for open and honest communication, and we must invest in each person on a myriad of different levels, ensuring that everyone's contributions are valued. We must hold each member to high standards, empowering everyone to reach beyond their own perceived potential, and we must provide an environment that enables trust and safety. Behaviors are the *what*. Music is the *how*. Culture is the *why*.

Application

1. Ask your students to share their responses to questions like: How would you describe the culture of the music ensemble or program? Would you like to make any changes to the culture and why? This conversation can show that the teacher honors and values the students' opinions and feedback in a process that can create more of a community built on trust. Be sure to stress the importance of participating in a culture of treating everyone's input with respect.

2. Make a list of priorities and values for the music ensemble with your students. Next to each word or phrase, add *how* each individual can contribute to making the priorities and values central to the success of the community.

3. Ask your students for feedback on how well the group is creating a sense of safety, security, and belonging and what can be done to make progress in these areas.

4. Ask your students what new traditions they would like to start for the music programs. See earlier in the chapter for some ideas to kick-start the conversation.

Journal Questions

1. Describe the current culture of your music program and contrast that with your ideal culture. What ideas are you considering to begin a cultural transformation?

2. The leader of the group has the most influence on the culture. How can you be more intentional about being the reflection of how you want your music culture to be?

3. As a music educator, there are times when we are more focused on getting the details in the music correct and then there are times when we open up our hearts, emote, and invite a deep level of emotional, musical expression. Think about your mindset in recent rehearsals. Think about what you did and how you felt. Were you catering to the head or to the heart?

Quotes

CULTURE: *from the Latin cultus, which means care.*

— Daniel Coyle
The Culture Code, p. ix

After a while, people see through the talk when it doesn't line up with the walk.

— Tony Dungy
The Mentor Leader, p. 3

Treat a child as though he is already the person he's capable of becoming.

— Haim G. Ginott
as quoted in Judy Arnall's *Discipline Without Distress*, p. 220

Group culture is one of the most powerful forces on the planet.

— Daniel Coyle
The Culture Code, p. xviii

We are responsible for creating the social and emotional tone in our classroom.

— Patricia Jennings
Mindfulness for Teachers, p. 72

ENDNOTES

1. Jon Gordon, *The Power of a Positive Team: Proven Principles and Practices that Make Great Teams Great* (Hoboken, NJ: John Wiley & Sons, 2018), 15.
2. Daniel Coyle, *The Culture Code: The Secrets of Highly Successful Groups* (New York: Bantam Books, 2018), xx.
3. Simon Sinek, *Leaders Eat Last: Why Some Teams Pull Together and Others Don't* (New York: Portfolio, 2014), 163.
4. Gordon, *The Power of a Positive Team*, 17.
5. Simon Sinek, *Leaders Eat Last: Why Some Teams Pull Together and Others Don't* (New York: Portfolio, 2014), 163.
6. Tony Dungy with Nathan Whitaker, *The Mentor Leader: Secrets to Building People and Teams That Win Consistently* (Carol Stream, IL: Tyndale Momentum, 2010), 38.
7. Jon Gordon, *The Power of a Positive Team: Proven Principles and Practices that Make Great Teams Great* (Hoboken, NJ: John Wiley & Sons, 2018), 15.
8. John Wooden and Steve Jamison, *Wooden on Leadership* (New York: McGraw-Hill, 2005), 56.
9. Ibid., 14.
10. Daniel Coyle, *The Culture Code: The Secrets of Highly Successful Groups* (New York: Bantam Books, 2018), xix.
11. Ibid., 15.
12. Ibid., 6.
13. Patricia Jennings, *Mindfulness for Teachers: Simple Skills for Peace and Productivity in the Classroom* (New York: W. W. Norton & Company, 2015), 72.
14. Stephen M. R. Covey with Rebecca Merrill, *The Speed of Trust: The One Thing that Changes Everything* (New York: Free Press, 2006), 56–57.
15. Brené Brown, *Daring Greatly: How the Courage to Be Vulnerable Transforms the Way We Live, Love, Parent, and Lead* (New York: Gotahm Books, 2012), 150.
16. Ibid., 47.
17. Stephen R. Covey, *The 7 Habits of Highly Effective People: Restoring the Character Ethic* (New York: Fireside, 1990), 237.
18. María del Carmen Arau Ribeiro, André Nusselder, Nataša Brouwer, Natália Gomes, and Noel Lopes, "An International Student Workshop on Design Thinking in Time of Corona: Redesigning an International Event as an Online Interactive Learning Experience," in *Innovative Teaching Methods: Practical Teaching in Higher Education*, ed. Lidia Pokrzycka (Lublin: Maria Curie-Sklodowska University Press, 2020), 23.

PART 3: LEAD!

Chapter 8

UPBEAT LEADERSHIP

*Leadership is not an innate, mystical gift; rather, it is a learned
ability to influence the attitudes and behaviors of others.*[1]
— Tony Dungy

Just about everything that could go wrong did go wrong the
year before I became the head band director at Loveland High
School. The percussion instructor had quit on the high school
band between semifinals and finals at the Colorado State Marching
Band Championship in the fall, and then at the semester break in
mid-January, he gave an ultimatum to the high school percussionists:
"You need to choose between staying in my percussion ensemble
(unaffiliated with the school) or band. You can't do both."
Unfortunately, over 80 percent of the percussionists quit the high
school band, and the two directors and the new percussion instructor
had to start a percussion section from scratch with wind players who
volunteered. Then, that winter, both directors decided independently
and simultaneously to leave the high school. One decided to retire,
and the other decided to teach junior high band in another school
district. When they announced to the band students in February that

they would both be leaving, the students thought that this was the end of the band program as they knew it.

When I was hired in the first week of June, there was a culture and leadership crisis. It was definitely a rough first semester, and many of the seniors, upset that they did not get to finish their last year in high school with their beloved directors, took their feelings out on me. I encountered resistance, and students undermined my leadership. There was a lot of tension within the band and fighting within and amongst sections, and I struggled to earn the respect of the senior class. I share this to give context for how I got started teaching leadership. At that time, I did not have a grand vision for how my actions would transform the program or that I would eventually be given the opportunity to teach leadership across the country and around the world. Far from it. I started teaching leadership out of sheer survival. I look back on my challenging first semester as the director of bands and recognize that without the crisis and the struggle, I may not have seen the need to develop a student leadership program, but as is often the case in life, we learn the most from the hardest times.

The second semester had just started, and on a Tuesday in the last week of January 2006, Greg and Brad, two trombonists, a junior and a sophomore, knocked on my office door. I invited them in, and they opened up with, "We are sick and tired of how the seniors are acting, and we'd like to know what you think we can do about it. We trust you and believe in you and our former directors also believed in you." I cannot tell you how much hearing this meant to me, and I felt a wave of relief to hear that it wasn't just me who was struggling with the tension and culture in the band. I thanked them for coming to talk to me, saying, "Let's go ahead and plan a meeting in a couple days after school that is open to any student in the band to talk about forging a direction forward. Let's talk about what kind of band we want to create." Greg and Brad, excited about the idea, helped me advertise the meeting, and on that Thursday about thirty students gathered for the very first of what would become our weekly Leadership Symposium.

At the meeting, I thanked everyone for attending, and I showed an excerpt from a DVD called *Synergy: Leadership Success*, featuring Tim Lautzenheiser talking with a classroom of high school band student leaders about the concept of servant leadership. He shared that student leadership is not about the glory or the resumé or the power to tell others what to do. Leadership is about serving others and leading by example.

You could have heard a pin drop as my students learned an entirely new way of thinking about leadership. This led to a conversation about how we could create a paradigm shift for the ways we viewed the role of the student leader. I asked questions and guided the discussion while one student took notes to share with the students who were unable to attend. Over the first few weeks, here are some of the questions we discussed.

- What kind of band do we want to create?
- What new traditions do we want to start?
- What are our values?
- What is important to us as a band?
- What does it mean to be a servant leader?
- How do we define leadership?
- Can every member of the band be a leader?

- What responsibilities does every individual in the band have to contribute to the whole?

To kick off each Leadership Symposium, we would watch an excerpt from *Leadership Success* or discuss a chapter from books on leadership and personal development. The primary texts that we used in the early days were Stephen R. Covey's *The 7 Habits of Highly Effective People*, John C. Maxwell's *The 21 Irrefutable Laws of Leadership*, Stephen M. R. Covey's *The Speed of Trust*, and John Wooden's *On Leadership*. Students were excited to volunteer to lead the discussion on different topics.

As we talked about different leadership principles, the students were eager to try them out in their own lives. While diving into "Habit 1: Be Proactive" from *The 7 Habits*, the students decided they would test the theory out by making one change: making their bed every day. Students did this for one week, and at the next Symposium many reported that their parents were so impressed with their new behavior that their curfews had been extended!

I also saw the benefits of empowering and giving voice to the students in rehearsals. Before wind ensemble rehearsal started, Pierson, a saxophone section leader, asked if he could address the band. I asked him what he wanted to say, he told me quietly, and I responded, "Sure!" After we warmed up and played through the first piece, Pierson came up to the front of the room and addressed the band to share that he thought we could be doing better, that we could be more focused and respectful in rehearsals, and that if we would take rehearsals more seriously, we could be really good. Students like Pierson taught me that encouragement from a peer can often be more motivational than statements from a teacher.

During the second year of the Leadership Symposium, I knew things were really taking off when I received a phone call at home from the percussion section leader, Johnny. Here is how I remember that conversation.

"Hi, Mr. Arau. This is Johnny."

"Hi, Johnny. How's it going?"

"Great! I'm in the business management section of the Barnes and Noble bookstore."

"Wow! What are you doing there?"

"Well, I was looking around at the leadership books here and I just found one, *Developing the Leader Within You* by John Maxwell, that looks pretty good. Could we buy it for the band leadership library?"

"Sure, Johnny, that sounds great. I'll pick it up this week."

Thanks to Johnny, that was the beginning of creating a band leadership library and a sign that students were excited about developing their leadership skills. By intentionally focusing on leadership, goal setting, peer teaching, personal development, and character, every aspect of the music program was elevated, including our rehearsals, performance level, individual accountability, focus, motivation, fundraising, achievement, commitment, respect, and joy. The meaning of being a student leader transformed from having a title and getting to be in charge to the greater responsibility of leading by example, serving, and lifting others up. Everyone benefitted, whether or not a student held an official position, because the Leadership Symposium was for all students in the band. And when a student decided to audition and apply to become a student leader, they already had the necessary training to help them be successful. After being selected as an official student leader, they continued to have ongoing leadership education and support through the weekly Symposium. Investing in the teaching of student leadership took time, preparation, and effort, but in the end, it was the greatest investment I could have made to transform the culture, positively impact the lives of my students, and elevate the level of the entire music program.

Leading from Within

As music educators, we may not necessarily view ourselves as leaders, but, in fact, we are. We instruct, organize, plan, prepare, influence, teach, encourage, and inspire our students by setting an example. Our students watch, imitate, and learn from us, impacting how they, in turn, think, act, and lead. I have had educators share with me that they don't feel comfortable teaching leadership, and I reassure them that they know a lot more about leadership than they give themselves credit for just from being a music educator and having been a part of multiple organizations in their lifetimes. Because of this experience, educators have had the opportunities to lead and be a part of teams that were led with a multitude of leadership styles.

Leadership takes many forms. There is top-down leadership, which places all the responsibility and power with one person. Traditional models of the maestro and their orchestra have reflected this model, and school ensembles have been led this way for many years. This very efficient way to lead often feels less risky to the leader. As education psychology and motivation theory have evolved, however, we have learned that when the members of a group are given a voice and empowered to be part of the process and delegated responsibilities, their sense of ownership, commitment, and buy-in are elevated. Empowering students to take on additional responsibilities, giving students input and a voice in ensembles, trusting students to lead and serve as role models for their peers, and creating an uplifting community is what Upbeat Leadership is all about. Furthermore, when students are given leadership positions and are properly trained, they become an asset to the ensemble in all respects—musically, culturally, and as role models. Notably, no one is born a leader, contrary to popular wisdom. **Leadership is a skill that can be learned and taught just like any other skill.**

Since actions are motivated by one's thoughts and attitudes, it is important to recognize that leadership comes from within. Rather than focusing on leading others in the beginning, we must first work on developing ourselves. For example, we need to focus on developing our own upbeat mindset so that we can honestly teach from a belief that our students have unlimited potential. If we don't believe that leadership is a skill that can be developed, much like learning to play an instrument, we will have difficulty teaching all our students how to be successful leaders. Mindfulness is another key to successful leadership because being fully present, aware, and centered allows us to consciously direct our focus and choose an appropriate response to every situation. Mindfulness helps you to "know thyself," and this is the initial step towards connecting and getting to know and empathize with the members of the ensemble. Our students will reflect our attitudes and behaviors, which is why it is important for us to model how we want our students to lead. We need to become *who* we want the band, choir, or orchestra to be. Our students will copy our tone of delivery and communication styles. They will even imitate our positive or negative attitudes, which is an incredible responsibility that should not be taken lightly! Booker T. Washington is thought to have said, "There are two ways of exerting one's strength: one is pushing down, the other is pulling up." What kind of leader do you want to be, and what kind of leader do you want your students to be? Even if we were taught by a director who led with a top-down style of leadership, we can make a change and become the type of educator who decides to pull up, push up, or lift up others rather than "pushing down."

Leadership by Design

Whether you are thinking about starting a student leadership program or you want to further develop and improve your leadership program, I recommend reflecting on the following questions:

- Why is student empowerment and leadership important to you?
- What would your ideal student leadership program look like?
- What are the different roles that student leaders would have?
- What qualities, values, and characteristics would you like your student leadership team to have?
- How will your student leadership program positively impact *all* the students in your program?
- How can student leadership positively impact recruitment, retention, culture, and performance?
- How comfortable are you with delegating responsibilities and empowering your students?

Before diving headfirst into creating your student leadership program, take some time to ponder and reflect on these questions. Dream big! Imagine how a deeper collaboration with your students can lead to a more vibrant, productive, and joyful experience. Visualize your students uplifting and encouraging each other, looking for ways that they can serve the program. Our students want to be a part of something bigger than themselves, and when they get to play a more significant role in the success of the group, they are motivated to contribute wholeheartedly.

I remember when I started the Leadership Symposium, we began shifting the role of student leader from one who gives commands to that of a servant leader. When we then expanded the expectations for a student leader, members of my marching band staff were skeptical about my decision to give leadership responsibilities to teenagers. Interestingly, leadership teacher and mentor Tim Lautzenheiser had already cautioned me that I would likely encounter resistance from the adults in the program rather than from the students who were being empowered. And he was right. However, as the positive changes in the program became evident in less than a year, the whole team became united in support of the Leadership Symposium and the expansion of student leadership responsibilities.

I learned that it is important to teach and coach on leadership all year rather than simply relying on a one- or two-day leadership camp. Our music programs will represent what and where we choose to invest our time and energy, and thus by making student leadership an essential component to your students' music education, you will notice a notable difference in the performance, culture, and overall attitude. Have you noticed that when you listen to another group perform at a festival you can tell what the focus areas of the rehearsals leading up to the concert have been? Based on the aspect that is most developed or prominent, we can expect that focus and time were invested in that area. Some groups clearly emphasize rhythm, or notes, or tone, or dynamics, or balance, or blend. Of course, excellent groups integrate all musical elements at a high level, including expression, interpretation, and beauty. We can also see what has been important to the conductor and students based on posture, instrument carriage, eye contact, movement to the music, and how a group enters and leaves the stage.

Beyond this, if student leadership is valued, we will also notice a higher level of engagement, respect, and enthusiasm in the way students behave and interact with each other. A focus on leadership lifts every member of the group towards becoming the best version of themselves, particularly when positive Upbeat Leadership is modeled and taught. Rather than just assuming your most advanced players will naturally become great leaders and letting the chips fall where they may, dedicate the time and energy to teaching Upbeat Leadership by design.

You Don't Need a Title

Leadership is not reserved exclusively for those who lead a political movement or the drum major of the marching band. **Every member of the music program can have the mindset and the heart of a leader when they take personal responsibility for their attitude and actions.** It is important to recognize that most of the qualities of an effective member, participant, or follower are also qualities of an Upbeat Leader, which is why I am a proponent of teaching leadership to *all* students in your program rather than the select few.

It was important to us at my high school that every member of the band, whether they had a leadership title or not, could aspire to think and act like a leader. We also wanted to create a program that focused on lifting rather than putting others down. During one of the first Leadership Symposiums, my students and I collaborated to develop the following definition of leadership.

Leadership is inspiring and encouraging others
to achieve their full potential.

This definition still resonates with me today because you don't need a position or title to inspire or encourage others, and yet, by doing this you are, in fact, being a leader. Students also resonate with this definition. Here is a suggestion for how you can introduce this concept.

Ask your students whether they have ever had a day when they actually received the encouragement they truly needed. Ask them how it felt to receive that encouragement. Then ask them if they have ever been on the other side, in a position to give encouragement to someone in need. Ask how that felt. Then tie it together by asking if it felt equally good and rewarding to receive and give encouragement. Generally, the students agree, which leads to an important discovery: giving and serving others is rewarding to both the receiver *and* the giver. Help students understand that the *decision* to encourage someone and then actually doing it is, in fact, an act of leadership.

What about inspiring others? We can inspire with our words and communication style when we have a strong belief or commitment and confidently share a vision for the future. We can also inspire with our actions. A student who has been struggling with their

UPBEAT! ◆ Matthew Arau

performance but makes the decision to practice every day and shows growth can be inspiring to the other students. A student who struggles with marching technique and stepping off with the correct foot but persistently works to improve and then finally gets it inspires acts of courage. A courageous act could be something as simple as stepping out of one's comfort zone and intentionally talking with and getting to know someone outside of their section or social circle. **The individual has the freedom to choose their upbeat, their thoughts, their response, their attitude, and their subsequent actions and behavior. Leadership is a choice. When we choose to aspire towards growth, service, and excellence, our actions serve the well-being of everyone else in the group.**

The Five Levels of Upbeat Leadership

There are five ascending levels of student leadership. Talk with your students about the associations between these levels and other areas of their lives to spark conversation and to promote moving up to the higher levels.

Level 1: Tell Others What to Do

This is the basic level because it takes the form of giving commands. It is authoritarian and relies on the power of the hierarchy to persuade others to do what you want them to do. This approach will only get you so far, as those you are leading might follow you begrudgingly and could eventually resist or ignore your commands. Although there are appropriate times to be direct and succinct, be sure to speak with an uplifting rather than a "bossy" or demeaning tone.

230

Level 2: Invite Others to Do Something

When we invite others to do something rather than telling them, their response could be even more agreeable. Everyone wants to be treated respectfully, so framing a request as a question or invitation changes the interaction. An example of a question is, "Would you please start at measure 21? We are going to work on the triplet rhythm there." A friendly invitation also works well, as in, "Let's begin at measure 21." Level 2 adds the consideration of mutual respect and cooperation that leads to more agreeable collaboration.

Level 3: Do the Task with Those You Are Leading

Leading by example is key to effective Upbeat Leadership because people will be moved to action more by what you do than by what you say. Never ask someone to do something you won't, wouldn't, or can't do. Do the task, whether that involves marching, playing an instrument, singing, or cleaning up the music room, in collaboration with those you are leading. Recognize that those you lead will rise to the level you model. So, aim high, project a positive attitude, and demonstrate at your absolute best. Level 3 leaders will often do the task alongside their team, acting as a guide and a role model. It takes courage to be a Level 3 Upbeat Leader since demonstrating the task can reveal the leader's own vulnerabilities. Level 3 helps make the leader–team member relationship feel more like a collaboration rather than a hierarchy.

Level 4: Ask Those You Are Leading for Input

As a leader, be aware that it is human nature to need to feel valued, so more than one opinion and voice matters. Rather than assuming you have all the answers, ask your team what is important to them, what their goals are, what they would like to work on, and how you could better serve your team. More importantly, be prepared to act on this input as you make changes. When we ask for input, we end up learning more about what the team members are feeling and what they are or are not comprehending.

Level 5: Empower Others to Lead

Empowering others, as the highest form of Upbeat Leadership, requires trust. Student leaders should not jump to Level 5 until their team members demonstrate that they have the skill and attitude to deal with any leadership responsibility that is delegated to them. By sharing leadership with others, we lift team members up and help grow future leaders.

Educators can also reflect on how the Five Levels of Upbeat Leadership can affect how they choose to teach and lead their students. For example, when a teacher creates and supports a student leadership program, they are exhibiting Level 5 Upbeat Leadership. Inviting a student to conduct a portion of a piece and then stepping back to listen to the rehearsal is an example of Level 5 Upbeat Leadership. It takes a lot of trust, and it also *builds* trust while increasing motivation.

The 5 Levels of *Upbeat* Leadership

LEVEL 5: Empower Others to Lead

LEVEL 4: Ask Those You are Leading for Input

LEVEL 3: Do the Task with Those You are Leading

LEVEL 2: Invite Others to Do Something

LEVEL 1: Tell Others What to Do

Trust

Trust is an essential quality to a successful student leadership program. The educator's pathway towards developing trust with ensemble members begins, like so much we are working on in *Upbeat!*, with developing self-trust. In order to trust another, we need to trust ourselves. Here are some questions for you to consider. Notice that students can also ask these questions of themselves:

- When you set goals for yourself, do you follow through?
- What do you do that makes you believe that you are someone others can count on?
- How frequently do you follow through with what you commit to and do what you say you are going to do?
- To what extent can you trust your skills as a musician, teacher, and conductor?
- Think of examples that show that you can trust yourself to keep private what someone shares with you in confidence.
- How do your actions shout out that personal integrity is an important value for you?

Just like our attitude and mindset, trust comes from within, extending outwards. The next step to build trust is to demonstrate through your words and actions that your students can count on you to be there for them, that you will follow through, and that you will be honest, authentic, and committed to their well-being and growth. Trust takes time to build but only moments to tear down, and humans tend to be wary and cautious before trusting one another.

Another pathway to building trust is to ask for your students' input and ideas to demonstrate that you honor and value what they think and have to say. In rehearsals, ask students questions about what they think about phrasing, balance, dynamics, interpretation, and intonation. When we create a more collaborative space, we remove barriers to trust. Include your students in the process of goal setting—short and long term. At the beginning of the year, ask students how they would like to grow and develop as musicians. Find out what their goals are personally, as a section, and as a group. Ask how you can best serve and support your students to help them stay committed and achieve their short-term and long-term goals.

Getting Started

Upbeat Leadership can be infused into your music program in a variety of ways. You may decide to hold a weekly Leadership Symposium after school or during the lunch hour. Alternatively, you may prefer to weave in a brief five-minute leadership lesson into the occasional rehearsal. You may also want to jump-start your leadership program with an Upbeat Leadership camp or workshop. The concepts of Upbeat Leadership are intended to be tailored to fit what you and your students need.

You can begin the process of developing your student leadership program by extending opportunities for service, such as tightening up loose music stands, straightening up the chairs, or partnering with another student to help with playing their part better. Engage students in a discussion about qualities that every student should strive for as a member of the ensemble. Share that the road to becoming a leader begins with being an excellent member and participant by daily giving one's best. And being prepared, attentive, and engaged demonstrates commitment and dedication. Approach challenges with curiosity, creativity, and a "can do" attitude. Be encouraging and proactively seek out things you can do to help and go the extra mile. Be a solution-finder instead of a blamer who dwells on what is wrong. Be someone who takes action to make the best of any situation. These are qualities and actions of an Upbeat Leader.

The figure on the following page represents how Upbeat Leadership contrasts with other styles of leadership. [2] Notice how the different types of leaders fall on a continuum of expectations and support. The goal is to strive to live and lead in the Upbeat Leadership upper right-hand quadrant.

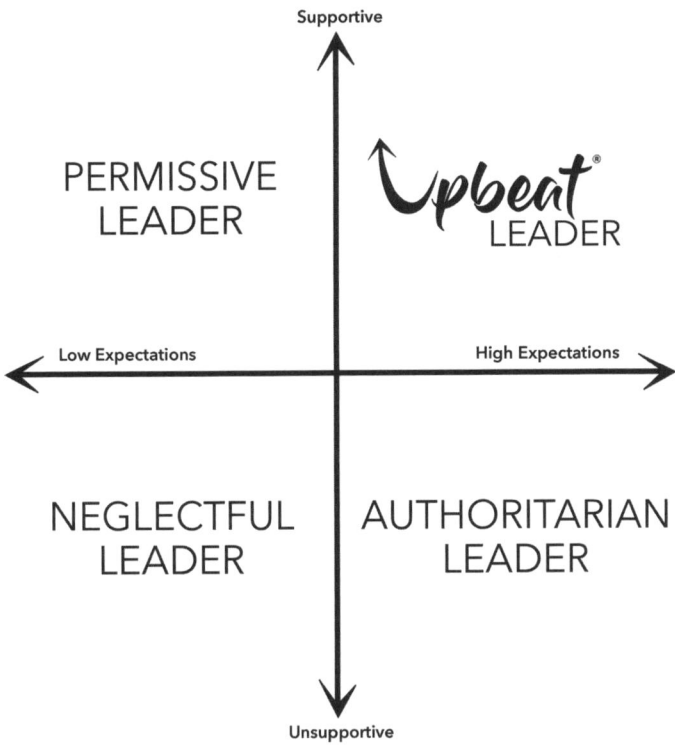

A permissive leader has low expectations and is supportive. They tend to "go with the flow" and not be very motivated. They tend to value being friends with those they lead and are therefore supportive, but they do not push or motivate their teammates to reach higher and improve.

A neglectful leader has low expectations and is unsupportive. They tend to be "checked out" and either don't show up or, when they do, they don't devote energy towards raising the bar or caring for their teammates.

An authoritarian leader has high expectations and is unsupportive. They tend to be highly demanding and act as a "drill sergeant," ordering others around with the intent to raise the bar of performance. The problem with this leader is they do not offer the care, encouragement, and support necessary to create a cooperative and collaborative culture.

An Upbeat Leader has it all—high expectations and supportive behavior. They have a strong belief in those they are leading, and they communicate their high expectations through being encouraging and setting stretch goals together. They show their support by going the extra mile to meet people where they are at, modifying their teaching to help each individual be successful. They are caring, compassionate, and encouraging, and they especially listen deeply to understand.

In the next four chapters, we will get into specifics about how you can model, teach, and develop the 4 C's of Upbeat Leadership in *all* your students and take your music program to new heights.

Vignette

Nate Sletten
Former 7–12 Band Director
TLC Coordinator and Secondary Instructional Support
Lake Mills Community Schools, Lake Mills, Iowa

In May of 2020, I was attending the virtual Iowa Bandmasters Association (IBA) conference. Looking through the conference schedule, I was excited to see a session titled "Care and Compassion for All" by Dr. Matthew Arau. It had been a very tough year with school shutting down, and I was looking for some hope. The session was incredible! And better yet, I was able to stay online and chat with Matthew following the session. After many conversations and phone calls, I was told about an Upbeat Global Leadership Academy for Drum Majors that summer. My student leaders were eager and excited to attend! One of the things I realized in our program is that we had student leadership "positions" without student leadership "training." At the leadership presentation, my students learned ways to improve their skill of conducting and score study, and they were able to learn more about mindset and servant leadership. They came out of the session on fire and passionate to bring this upbeat message to their friends. This all started the "upbeat way" in our band program and school.

I found out that Dr. Arau and his team would be leading a virtual Upbeat Global Leadership Summit that next fall. Lake Mills is a small rural community in north-central Iowa, and there was a need for a leadership program in both the school and in the band room. Many of the yearly honor bands and travel opportunities were canceled that school year, so we decided to offer this leadership summit to our students. With so many busy students, I was not sure how many would sign up for this opportunity. We had over fifty students sign up to be a part of the leadership summit! The students ranged from seventh grade to twelfth grade, and it was incredible to see our very own Upbeat community continuing to grow. I ended up learning so much about our students through the summit, and they had a blast learning more about themselves and the peers around them. Upon reflection, one student wrote, "I didn't even know I could be a leader. I now realize I have choices and I 'get to' make an impact on the students in band and throughout the school."

Whether discussing the Power of G.E.T., the 4 C's of Upbeat Leadership, or simply our breathing, Upbeat Leadership has become a common language for personal and program growth. It wasn't just the seniors or upperclassmen that understood the benefit. Upbeat Leadership was learned by students of all ages in our program. That common language helped us to create a vision, a mission, and a growth mindset when making big decisions and creating small daily habits. Every student and director deserves to see the benefits of applying these ideas.

Application

1. Discus the Five Levels of Upbeat Leadership with your students and ask them to share examples of each level from their own experiences.

2. Collaborate with your students to create a definition of leadership that resonates with everyone and can be applied to your group. Make a list of concrete actions that can be taken to embody your shared definition.

3. Give responsibilities to students that impact a larger group of students, such as making sure that the chairs and stands are put away appropriately at the end of class, so they can experience leadership as service and support of others.

4. Share stories with students that let them see your vulnerable side. This opens pathways of communication and trust.

Journal Questions

1. What are challenges in your music program that you would characterize as leadership challenges? What steps can be taken towards addressing these issues?
2. How do you feel about empowering your students and giving them a stronger voice in your ensemble? Would anything need to change for you to feel more comfortable?
3. How we lead as teachers models to our students how we would like them to lead. What changes, if any, might you make in your personal leadership style, knowing that your students' attitudes and behaviors are often a reflection of your own?

Quotes

Great necessities call forth great leaders.

— First Lady Abigail Adams in
a letter to Thomas Jefferson
as quoted in John W. Gardner's
On Leadership, p. 39

Leadership is unlocking people's potential to become better.

— Bill Bradley
as quoted in Christine Porath's
Mastering Civility, p. 131

*I've come to believe that a leader is anyone who holds her-
or himself accountable for finding potential in people and
processes.*

— Brené Brown
Daring Greatly, p. 185

*As you build your leadership skills, it's important to
remember that why you lead is as important as whom you
lead.*

— Tony Dungy
The Mentor Leader, p. 9

ENDNOTES

1. Tony Dungy with Nathan Whitaker, *The Mentor Leader: Secrets to Building People and Teams That Win Consistently* (Carol Stream, IL: Tyndale Momentum, 2010), xv.
2. Angela Duckworth, *Grit: The Power of Passion and Perseverance* (New York: Scribner, 2016), 212. The leadership graphic is an adaptation of a model for Wise Parenting from Angela Duckworth's *Grit*.

Chapter 9

THE 4 C'S OF UPBEAT LEADERSHIP: CHARACTER

What we know matters but who we are matters more.[1]
— Brené Brown

I n early May 2016, I sprang up wide awake at 4:30 a.m. with an exuberant certainty and said out loud, much to the astonishment and concern of my wife Merilee, who had been sound asleep next to me, "It's 4 C's! It's 4 C's!" I ran downstairs to write them down so that I would not forget. They came to me with such a bang and feeling of inevitability. I had a clear understanding of what they meant and why all 4 C's were essential for success. I knew that the first C had to be *character*, since character must be the foundation for all one does as a leader. Next, in order to lead by example, being highly competent is critical, which makes *competence* the second C. I recognized, however, that character and competence are not enough. We need to be able to connect, communicate, and relate to others in order to influence and bring others along, which is why *connection* is the third C. Lastly, if we don't know where we are headed, if we are direction-less, we cannot lead effectively; we need a clear vision. This is why the fourth C is *clarity*: clarity of both mind and vision.

The 4 C's of Upbeat Leadership are character, competence, connection, and clarity. All four are important on their own and yet developing and strengthening all 4 C's together will make successful leaders.

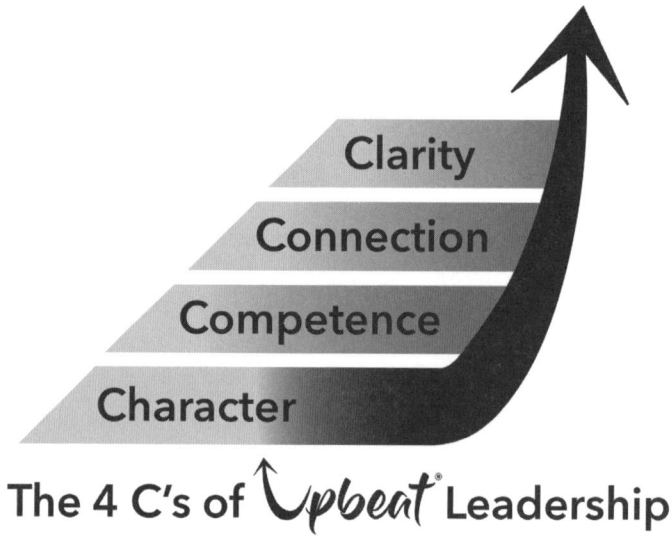

The 4 C's of Upbeat Leadership

The foundation of an Upbeat Leader is their character. It all comes down to character. If we don't have character, nothing else matters. Our character reflects our values, principles, attitudes, thoughts, and how we choose to act on those values. Our character is defined by what we say and do, how we serve, how we contribute, and what we stand for. Leaders with a strong character have integrity. They build trust by following through on what they say they are going to do. They are responsible, reliable, and accountable for their actions. When confronted with different pathways, the decisions we make and actions we take reflect our character. Character is not innate, like your blood type or curly hair. It is not something you are born with. **Character is something you learn, and every day is an opportunity to choose and develop your character.**

Possibly the greatest coach who ever lived, John Wooden, made character central to his coaching. As the coach of UCLA's men's basketball team from 1948 to 1975, Wooden built the "winningest" team in NCAA men's basketball history. From 1964 to 1975, the UCLA Bruins won ten NCAA championships, seven of which were in a row. Over the course of two seasons, the Bruins won eighty-eight straight games. Coach Wooden focused on three primary principles with his players: character, fundamentals, and teamwork. Character was central to his coaching because he felt that he was teaching much more than basketball. Teaching his players to be good people on and off the court, he reminded them regularly, "Be more concerned with your character than your reputation because your character is what you really are, while your reputation is merely what others think you are. . . . The true test of a man's character is what he does when no one is watching."[2] Like John Wooden did with his players, we, as music educators, should make character development an essential part of student leadership training and an expectation in our music programs.

Let your students know not only that how you treat others in a group reflects your own character but also that your actions will influence how your teammates think, feel, and perform. This is a big responsibility, and there will be times when you will fall short of living up to your ideal image, which is okay. What matters is that you learn from your mistakes, ask for forgiveness of others and of yourself, and continue to work at being your best. Past indiscretions or regrettable decisions do not define you. You can change. **Who you**

were yesterday does not determine who you are today or who you can become tomorrow.

• • •

I clearly remember the moment when Michael approached me in my band office at Loveland High School in the winter of 2006 with a burning question. Michael, a junior in high school and one of the trumpet section leaders, said, "Mr. Arau, I'm just one person. What difference can I possibly make?"

Intrigued, I responded, "Well, Michael, what difference do you want to make? What's on your mind?"

He said, "I've noticed that there is a lot of cussing in the band hall and it's starting to bother me. Is there anything I can do?"

Excited by Michael's interest, I asked, "Well, Michael, do you cuss in the band hallway?"

"Well, yeah," Michael said sheepishly.

This was a perfect opportunity to put what we had just started studying and discussing in the Leadership Symposium—"Habit 1: Be Proactive" from Stephen R. Covey's *The 7 Habits of Highly Effective People*—to the test.[3] I challenged Michael, "All right, would you agree that we really can't change other people; we can just focus on changing ourselves?" Michael nodded. "Okay, then let's plan an experiment together. I want you to stop cussing around the band hallway for thirty days and then report back to me what happens." Michael smiled, happy to be part of a secret experiment and committed to taking on this challenge. "This won't be easy," I reminded him. "It will take a lot of commitment and fortitude to follow through, but if you are up to it, go for it. Report back to me in thirty days and let me know how it is going."

Thirty days later, Michael came back with his report. Hoping for the best, I asked, "How did it go?"

"I really can't believe it! I stopped cussing around the band hallway and around my band friends, and the craziest thing happened. My friends have also stopped cussing around me!"

I was ecstatic, as Michael's commitment to change demonstrated that through changing ourselves we truly can impact and influence others in positive ways. For years, I have shared this example of how being proactive about developing our character can elevate our ability to lead successfully. Through Michael's work on himself, he not only strengthened his own character but also became one of the most influential student leaders in the band. Skeptical at first that he could truly make a difference, Michael learned that by reaching higher himself, he also inspired others to do the same. I also learned that when we are intentional and committed to making a change, we can. **Character is not something we are born with. It is something we become.** We can choose our character, and the choices we make matter.

Act with Care

Say the word "character." Now say it slower, "char–act–er." It sounds like "care actor." What does an actor do? They act. When we act with character, we act with care. In other words, to have character, or "care actor," could be to *act with care*, to act thoughtfully and intentionally. When we don't act with care, our behaviors and knee-jerk reactions can occur without thinking and may not emanate from a place of respect or kindness. Our character puts our beliefs into action, and our actions speak louder than our words. **When we act with care, we are conscious of how our actions affect, influence, and**

impact others. We think beyond ourselves and recognize that what we do, say, and think has consequences. We take responsibility and we are accountable for our actions.

Just as culture reflects the character and values of a group, character reflects the beliefs, values, and morals of an individual. Tony Dungy writes, "Make sure that your actions mirror your words. If they don't, there's no surer way to a credibility gap and resulting crisis of confidence for those who follow you."[4] In other words, it's important that we walk the talk. We may believe in a particular value, but if our actions and decisions don't reflect that belief, we lack congruence in our character and in our lives. Breaking an agreement with ourselves hurts our integrity just as much as not living up to an agreement that we made with someone else. Acting with congruence leads to living in harmony and balance within and with others.

We resonate more fully when we act with care, and our character has a ripple effect on those around us. A leader's character influences and is emulated by the character of the members of the group. **Character is the foundation of our Upbeat Leadership qualities and abilities, which is the root of successful student leadership.** When our words and actions are congruent with our values, we are living in alignment and with character, so others can trust that they will be able to count on us to follow through with our commitments.

Every day we have an opportunity to live into our character. We are not born with character. We are taught character, and we choose our character. During the course of a day, we will encounter situations, events, and people that will challenge us and test our character. We can be intentional and fully present when we make decisions, or we can be persuaded to take the easy way. When we are intentional and purposely act with care, even if it takes us on "the road less traveled," we will earn the respect and trust of our ensemble, class, or team.

How we act towards ourselves—the character that we show ourselves—provides a foundation for how we treat others. As an exercise, respond to the following questions.

- Do you think it is important to treat others with kindness?
- Do you think it is important to show compassion to others?
- Even though it can be difficult at times, do you think it is important to find it in our hearts to forgive others?

Okay, so this is where it gets more difficult. We often treat ourselves worse than we would treat a close friend or mentor. How would you respond to these questions?

- Even though you think it is important to treat *others* with kindness, do you often find it difficult to extend the same kindness to yourself?
- Even though you think it is important to show compassion to *others*, do you find it difficult to show compassion to yourself?
- And perhaps the most difficult of all, even though you believe it is important to find the space in your heart to forgive *others*, do you find that the hardest person to forgive is yourself?

I challenge you to become more aware of how you act towards *yourself* with your own self-talk and mindset. Treat yourself with the same character you would share with a loved one or even a stranger. Showing compassion and kindness to others, to paraphrase Pema Chödrön, *does* in fact begin with showing compassion and kindness to ourselves.

Act with Courage

When the temptation to think negatively feels overwhelming, remember that it takes courage to be positive and that courage is contagious. So much of the news media, our conversations, and the attitudes in our daily lives are negative, and it is easy to get sucked into the downward spiral. However, the world does not need more negativity to push us down; we need Upbeat Leaders to lift us up. As the popular saying goes, "Being positive isn't pretending everything is good. It's seeing the good in everything." When we choose to be positive, we can also be more creative, better team players, and solution finders. Acting with courage means that we will often choose the more difficult road, the route with peril, risk, and a high chance of failure. **Standing up for what is right—even when it is not popular—is an act of character and of courage.** Students are often placed in these difficult situations and their character is challenged. It is in the midst of crisis and challenge, however, that true character is revealed.

Just as we can choose our thoughts, response, and attitude in a situation, we can also choose to embody the character that resonates with our value system. Often when we say or do things that don't reflect our best self, it is because of our attitude or personal upbeat. Certainly, we are capable of a full range of behaviors. I know that if I don't sleep well and am hungry and stressed out, I can be a "bear" to be around. It is during times of stress that I may say or do things that don't represent my finest character. Becoming mindful and aware of our personal tendencies can help us avoid making poor decisions. I am sure that we can all relate to being "hangry," hungry and angry at the same time, right? When we are hungry, exhausted, nervous, anxious, or depleted, these challenging times test our character and we get the opportunity to rise above. There will be hurdles to jump over, holes to avoid, and stumps that trip us up. The trick is to not feel defeated by these struggles and failures. Instead, learn from each fall and find ways to manage the emotions to be able get back up again and keep going.

• • •

During the school year, there are emotional ups and downs—periods of time when attitudes and spirits are high and times when the group as a whole lacks energy and drive. How can we intentionally sustain a sense of positive forward movement every day? Some of my high school band students wanted to know if this goal was even possible. They wanted to know what they could do about the students who had a negative attitude and brought down the energy level of other members of the group. This is a tough question, as we cannot change other people; we can only focus on changing ourselves. The addendum to this, however, is that by choosing to have a positive upbeat with the complementing attitude and consequent actions, the positivity rubs off on others, creating a ripple effect.

This conversation with my students first happened in the midst of our second marching band season together. They shared that the band, in general, during and after band camp, was excited and fired up for the marching season, but when school would start a week or two later, the positive attitude in the band would then start to turn negative. Stress and anxiety would go up with the academic and social demands of the new school year, and this would impact their attitudes and feelings during band rehearsals. What could a student leader do in this situation to rekindle the flame of passion that had burned brightly during band camp?

We decided that there are two trains in the band. Before school starts, our mood, energy, and attitudes are running high, when all our time and attention can go to that one thing that we all want to be really good at: marching band. At this point, almost everyone is on the positive train. It's fun to be on the positive train together, and the momentum of progress keeps us on the tracks. When school starts and outside demands increase, it is more difficult to sustain a positive upbeat. That is when some of the students jump from the positive train that is moving one direction and get on the negative train that is going in the opposite direction. Also, in the beginning stages of learning the music and the marching drills, progress occurs in large leaps, but as the refining and polishing process commences, progress is not always as clear and obvious. It takes perseverance and long-term vision to *stay* on the positive train, especially when the work to improve becomes more demanding. The students remarked that, after the first halftime football game performance or first competition with the marching band, students who had been riding the negative train would often rediscover their spark and reboard the positive train.

My students named this period when attitudes descend in a downward spiral "the doldrums." By naming and acknowledging the problem, we were on our way to finding a solution. Upbeat Leaders don't ignore problems and challenges by burying their heads in the sand. In the same manner that downhill skiers anticipate the moguls, trees, and obstacles prior to racing down a mountainside, Upbeat Leaders scan their environments, learn from the past, and look forward to the future with an eye towards potential challenges and struggles. Downhill skiers notice the obstacles and then chart a course to avoid the trees and go around or over the moguls. Upbeat Leaders, when faced with challenges, decide to focus on broadcasting an upbeat attitude, confront the challenges head-on, or even create an alternate pathway for everyone involved.

Regarding those "doldrums," the student leadership team decided that instead of giving in to the lull in motivation and uninspired attitudes, they would increase their own positive energy, excitement, and encouragement by three times to make the band and, in essence, the positive train so much fun that students would have no thoughts or temptations to board the negative train. Even when they did, they would promptly return to where all the fun was happening. Student leaders went out of their way to encourage and cheer on their peers. They reminded each other why they enjoyed being in the marching band. They shared stories of past struggles they had overcome and why it was worth pushing past the doldrums. For the first-year marchers who had never experienced performing at a football game or at a festival or competition, the veteran students inspired and motivated them by telling stories about their favorite memories. Instead of obsessing over the passengers on the negative train, the student leadership team embodied the character and attitude possible on the positive train that they wished for the band as a whole. They modeled a "be who you want the band to be" upbeat mindset, and eventually all of the band was happily boarded on the same positive train, heading in the same direction.

Servant Leadership

Share with your students and show them that an Upbeat Leader leads by example and with character that shines brightly. Be aware that others will either be inspired or turned off by your character, and for your group to be successful, you must strive to lead from the solid foundation of your character, where your mind and spirit are primed to be at their best. Intentionally choose your attitude and upbeat, knowing that your attitude is contagious and will impact the thoughts, motivation, and actions of those you lead. If you or your students find it difficult to get into the right headspace to be able to lead at your best, take a moment to focus intentionally on gratitude and breathe mindfully and strategically. We may not be able to suddenly move across the emotional spectrum from depression to ecstasy, but we can shift from one place to another, where we can then focus on others rather than just on ourselves. Supporting and serving others can help us feel better about ourselves and give us the mental and emotional energy we need to be fully present as we lead wholeheartedly.

Upbeat Leadership is not about what it can do for you, but what it can do for those who look to you. Leading from the solid foundation of character, Upbeat Leaders practice looking for ways to serve and lift others up. This is particularly important for student leaders to understand. They will grow in influence and make a bigger difference when they direct their attention toward supporting others. Being a servant-leader does not mean being a servant, as in waiting for orders to be given. Quite the opposite, servant-leaders are proactive and seek out opportunities to engage, encourage, inspire, support, and positively influence. In the words of former NFL coach Tony Dungy in his book *The Mentor Leader*, "Truly serving others requires putting ourselves and our desires aside while looking for ways and opportunities to do what is best for others."[5] Just as lighting someone else's torch adds to our own flame, helping someone else makes us feel good and ultimately elevates our level of influence.

How we treat others reflects our character, but how do we know how others hope to be treated? We can begin by following the Golden Rule, which encourages us to treat others as we would like to be treated, but we can be even more sensitive to others' needs by asking those we lead how *they* would like to be treated. David Kerpen, author of *The Art of People*, introduces the Platinum Rule— treat others as *they* would like to be treated—to take into account our differences, acknowledging that the way you prefer to be treated may not be in alignment with how someone else would like to be treated.[6] As leaders, strive to serve and support others and be sure to *ask* those you are leading how you can best support *them*.

A Mark of Character

I love learning about word origins. Motivated by writing this chapter on character, I was fascinated to discover that it was not until the seventeenth century that the word "character," as I have been using it in this chapter, began to appear in published writing.

The first uses of the word "character" referred to symbols or marks. The word is first found in Ancient Greek, from the word *charassein*, which means "to sharpen, cut in furrows, or engrave."[7] The mark or symbol that was created was called *kharaktēr*, and it also meant "a defining quality or individual feature." The Greek spelling was later changed to "character" in Latin. Then, in Old French in the late fifteenth century, *caratere* was defined as an "alphabetic letter, graphic symbol standing for a sound or syllable." It wasn't until the 1640s, when an additional definition of character—the "sum of qualities that define a person or thing and distinguish it from another"—was added. And in 1712, the definition was expanded to include the "moral qualities assigned to a person by repute."[8]

While the word "character" can refer to a letter, symbol, or part in a play, it is noteworthy that our character literally leaves a *mark*, making an impression in others' minds. Despite the thousands of years of evolution, the earliest meaning has great significance. Our character makes an *imprint*. People watch and notice how you act, behave, and treat others. Much of the time you lead without being aware of it, because your actions speak louder than your words. **Let your students know not only how important their character is but also that their character leaves a mark and, ultimately, a legacy.**

Character in Music

We can strengthen our character through the study of music, whether listening, singing, or playing. Music rehearsals are an ideal space to draw parallels between leadership, character, and music. While programmatic music may be an easy inroad to connecting life experience with music, the music does not need to tell a literal story in order to provide moments that engage with character principles. Here are some suggestions for how to connect character to music.

- Listening to one another with respect is fundamental to being an excellent performer. We show respect to one another by playing with refined intonation, balance, and appropriate dynamics. We can apply this principle of respectful listening to how we listen and act when not engaged with music.

- We grow in empathy and understanding through the study and playing of music with others. We learn that we are not alone and that striving to match tone, pitch, and dynamics develops our ability to be empathetic outside of music.

- Blending our tones together grows our ability to not only work well with others but to also realize that we are not the center of the universe. Blending tones creates a beautiful color, just as people with diverse opinions and thoughts can work together in harmony to create something new and vibrant.

- The harmonies in music model how we can achieve harmony with others. It takes effort, work, and compromise to make a harmony sing, but it is worth the commitment.

- Taking responsibility for learning our music for the good of the group demonstrates character. When we are accountable for our part, we model the importance of being accountable and build trust with the members of the ensemble. Taking responsibility and following through on our commitments are acts of character.

Vignette

Cameron W. Jenkins

Founder/CEO of Full Potential Leadership

2018 Gulfport School District Teacher of the Year

Bayou View Middle School Band Director, Gulfport, Mississippi

Imagine with me the excitement of hearing your administrators say, "The school district's board of trustees has approved a resolution to seek a $41.2 million bond issue to construct a new high school, and we are building the new state-of-the-art fine arts complex first. We need you to serve on the research team and building committee for this new project."

Fast-forward three years and you are now at the ribbon cutting ceremony of your new building and your administrator says, "Remember, building is spelled with an '-ing.' Our efforts here to keep this space moving forward will not end today. It will require on-going updates, fresh paint, new innovations, and much more. The '-ing' is on-going."

Building is spelled with an "-ing." Those six words were life-changing for me. How much truth did you draw from that statement? As leaders, we are committed to the work of "building" better teams, "building" more efficient systems, and "building" strong character in ourselves and our teams.

This commitment was tested the day our district president approached me at the spring honor band concert to inform me that three of my eighth-grade students were caught in the act of bullying a student because of the student's nationality.

I was embarrassed. Hurt. Disappointed. Yet, I had to push all of that aside to discover how I should help these eighth graders repair their character. What is our next step in the building process?

Each student was required to write a two-page report about what this incident revealed regarding their character's blind spots and how they plan to realign their character to match the culture of our band program. Currently, these three students are serving on the leadership team in our high school band with the character qualities that match our culture of belonging, empathy, and grace.

Reminder, building is spelled with an "-ing." Dr. Matthew Arau understands the power of this on-going work. Character is not "built" overnight nor is the work truly finished. In Upbeat Leadership, character development is a journey and a destination.

In every season of your leadership story, you will serve yourself well to stop and make any necessary repairs, replacements, and renovations to the building of your character. If your roof has flown off, stop and repair it. If your foundation has a crack, stop and replace it. If your views and perspectives are outdated, stop and renovate.

After a real inspection of your character, what improvements do you need to make? What areas of your character are you willing to give a face-lift? How can *Upbeat!* help you get there? Keep "building" my friends.

Application

1. Make a list of five of the character traits that you aspire to live by and embody daily. In the course of a day, refer to your list and be intentional and conscious about acting on those five values. At the end of the day, reflect and evaluate how you did with meeting your character goals.

2. Ask someone you trust how they define your character. Get another view of you.

3. Have a collaborative discussion with your students about values, habits, and traits that they believe a member of the class or ensemble should emulate and demonstrate. When students are given voice to share what character attributes are important to them, it helps everyone aspire to the next level. Feel free to add your own priorities to the list so that it is truly a group effort. Ask questions that push the students to think about why a specific value matters and how it can best be modeled.

4. Reinforce the importance of character in all interactions with your students. When we let inappropriate behavior, words, and actions slide, we send a message that respect and character are not important—as if character only matters when it is convenient.

5. The music we select gives us an opportunity to delve into the topic of character. Intentionally select repertoire that opens up the channel for discussion of meaning, significance, and decisions that have been made that reflect character. Repertoire that tells the story about an historical figure or historical event can serve as a jumping off point for engaging discussions about character and values.

Journal Questions

1. What steps or actions can you begin to take to develop your character to become the best version of yourself?
2. Reflect on how your character is mirrored by your students in your classes. What aspects of yourself do you see present in your students?
3. In what ways does the music and content that you teach and rehearse exemplify or honor admirable character traits?
4. Character is the foundation of leadership. How can you be more intentional about teaching, celebrating, and reinforcing attributes of quality character?

Quotes

The greatness of a man is not in how much wealth he acquires, but in his integrity and his ability to affect those around him positively.

> — Bob Marley
> as quoted in Thomas R. Hoerr's
> *The Formative Five*, p. 73

Integrity alone won't make you a great leader, but without integrity you will never be one.

> — Lolly Daskal
> *The Leadership Gap*, p. 140

Your character is constantly radiating, communicating. From it, in the long run, I come to instinctively trust or distrust you and your efforts with me.

> — Stephen R. Covey
> *The 7 Habits of Highly Effective People*, p. 238

Someone's opinion of you does not have to become your reality.

> — Les Brown
> *The Courage to Live Your Dreams*, p. 155

Everyone makes mistakes, but only a person with integrity owns up to them.

> — Nicole Guillaume
> as quoted in Dr. Purushothaman's *Character Quotes*, p. 116

ENDNOTES

1. Brené Brown, *Daring Greatly: How the Courage to be Vulnerable Transforms the Way We Live, Love, Parent, and Lead* (New York: Gotham Books, 2012), 16.
2. John Wooden, as quoted in Tony Robbins, "The Midnight Workout," Medium, February 15, 2017, https://medium.com/thrive-global/the-midnight-workout-d870c24305b0#:~:text=The%20great%20John%20Wooden%20once%20said%3A%20"Be%20more,what%20he%20does%20when%20no%20one%20is%20watching.

3. Stephen R. Covey, *The 7 Habits of Highly Effective People: Restoring the Character Ethic* (New York: Fireside, 1990), 65–94.

4. Tony Dungy with Nathan Whitaker, *The Mentor Leader: Secrets to Building People and Teams That Win Consistently* (Carol Stream, IL: Tyndale Momentum, 2010), 132.

5. Ibid., 39.

6. David Kerpen, *The Art of People: 11 Simple Skills that Will Get You Everything You Want* (New York: Crown Business, 2016), 96.

7. "The Characteristics of 'Character,'" Merriam Webster online, accessed August 19, 2021, https://www.merriam-webster.com/words-at-play/word-history-of-character-origins#:~:text=Character%20can%20be%20traced%20back%20to%20the%20Greek,meaning%20that%20was%20shared%20by%20the%20Latin%20character%29.

8. "Character," Etymonline, accessed September 5, 2021, https://www.etymonline.com/word/Character.

Chapter 10

THE 4 C'S OF UPBEAT LEADERSHIP: COMPETENCE

When we feel competent and capable, the world is ours.
We boldly set out into the unknown, we adapt and learn readily,
we conquer our fears and meet our challenges, and we experience
heightened levels of confidence, success, and mastery.[1]
— Brendon Burchard

Have you ever had one of those moments when you learned something so enlightening about learning and teaching that you wished you could go back in time and teach those years all over again? Okay, well maybe there are certain things you would not want to do all over again! Perhaps you could take a pass on the new teacher induction meetings or some of the drawn-out faculty meetings, grading, emails, and early mornings. But if you were given the opportunity, you would gladly return to re-do moments when you said something or did something that you regretted. Or maybe you wish you could change the way you thought about a student's ability or that you hadn't let your own hang-ups get in the way of reaching every student. I certainly have many times. And this is why teaching is not just a science; it is also an art. Because we are dealing with thinking, breathing, growing, and emotion-filled human beings, we are going to make mistakes.

• • •

After teaching music for fifteen years in the public schools in Loveland, Colorado, I began my doctoral studies in instrumental conducting and literature at the University of Colorado Boulder. In my first semester in fall 2012, I had a life-changing conversation with a professor from the wind faculty about two brothers I had taught in high school. Both had excelled in academics and music. The older brother was pursuing a double major in mathematics and music performance and was one of the most skilled musicians I had ever taught. I commented to this professor that, while both students were incredibly talented, the younger brother might be even more talented. He stopped me, saying, "Careful how you use that word." Asking which word he meant, he said, "Talent." When I inquired further, he asked if I had ever read *The Talent Code* by Daniel Coyle. I was determined to find out more and two days later became engrossed in the topic. I began to realize that what we label as "talent" is actually the result of much more than innate abilities.

I learned that there are multiple factors that lead to the development of talent, such as a special kind of targeted practice called "deliberate practice," a phrase coined by Anders Ericsson, and that most who achieve mastery or exceptional talent have a burning desire and an outstanding teacher or coach. I learned how the brain learns and how every time we practice a skill or do an action, a nerve fires and myelin is wrapped around a neuron, called an axon, and the more myelin wraps, the faster information travels in the brain.[2] *The Talent Code* did not answer all the questions about nature vs. nurture, but it certainly piqued my interest enough to send me down a rabbit hole on how expertise in any field is attained. After reading every book on the topics of mastery and achievement that I could get my hands on, I came to the conclusion that talent is recognized after hard work—not before—and that talent is better understood as a collection of skills layered upon layers mapped in the brain through deliberate practice. Researcher Anders Ericsson and science writer Robert Pool emphasize this point in *Peak: Secrets from the New Science of Expertise* when they write, "Both willpower and natural talent are traits that people assign to someone after the fact."[3]

I looked back on my teaching career and how my narrow understanding of talent had clouded my view of the clear potential of individual students. I regretted sharing with parents that their child was "talented," because it negated the importance of their child's effort and motivation. I also started thinking about how the word "talent" is used so much in the world of music and athletics, diminishing the hard work that individuals put in to refine their skills. The narrow construct of talent waters down the fact that "every master was once a disaster" and that everyone who has achieved success has struggled, fallen down many times, and gotten back up again.[4] I came to understand that instead of shining a spotlight on talent, we should be glorifying the challenging path that successful people have endured to acquire a high level of skill and competence. The path to excellence is never easy; it is filled with struggles, dead ends, scraped knees, setbacks, and falls. What separates those who achieve a high level of competence from those who don't is their resilience, fortitude, and determination—their attitude and mindset make the difference. It is how they respond to falling and not hitting the mark the first time that determines whether they will continue to grow and develop or whether they will plateau and give up. Nelson Mandela said, "Do not judge me by successes. Judge me by how many times I fell down and got back up again."[5] To achieve competence, we must be willing to get back up after we fall, to continue after our goals. **Achieving a high level of competence has as much or more to do with having an upbeat mindset as it does with having an innate ability.**

Our Upbeat Impacts Competence

A belief in our students' unlimited potential motivates us to never give up on them and to continually find appropriate strategies that will help them improve and develop their skills. This upbeat mindset for education influences how we feel, what we say, how we teach, and how we challenge our students. When we push our students to step outside of their comfort zone to reach higher, we demonstrate that we believe they can achieve at the next level. Motivation comes from the belief that you can succeed. It is the combination of our belief, support, and encouragement that helps motivate our students to set more ambitious goals and to work harder and with more enthusiasm towards growing their level of competence. The belief that competence—skills and abilities—can be learned and taught impacts every aspect of music education, including musicianship, literacy, leadership skills, performing, marching, improvisation, composing, communication, and more. For student leaders, it is important that they continue to develop their competence since leading by example and the ability to demonstrate skills is essential to being an effective and trusted leader.

Additionally, our personal approach to learning and growth affects how our students feel about their own learning process. Whenever possible, we should openly display our joy and excitement for their learning as they develop a higher level of competence with a "can do" attitude. When we further broadcast our own passion for learning itself, we embolden our students to share their purposes, passions, and desires with others as well. Approaching practice, work, and effort with a sense of purpose and goals can motivate everyone to reach for a higher level of achievement.

Our students also learn from seeing how we personally respond to struggle, challenge, and failure. If we draw attention to our flaws and mistakes with a negative attitude, our students will tend to mimic a similar response when they make their own mistakes. Instead, recognize the mistake, learn from it, and continue on the path. Aim to create a culture in which taking risks and stepping outside of the comfort zone is celebrated; this means that we have to be okay with not always hitting the mark. The surest route to growing competence is to learn from mistakes and obstacles. The pathway to becoming excellent in any field—skiing, rock climbing, music, football, art, public speaking, writing—will include a whole lot of stumbles. View struggle and failure as feedback, learn from it, and keep moving towards your goal. An upbeat mindset helps you see possibilities where others would only see problems. As Brendon Burchard writes in *The Charge: Activating the 10 Human Drives that Make You Feel Alive*, successful people "get up faster when knocked down because they take the knockdown as a lesson rather than a defeat."[6] The word "competence" begins with the word "compete," and I like to think that to build our confidence we actually compete with, but not against, ourselves—to learn, grow, improve, and get better than we were the day, the week, or the year before.

Our students will be more motivated to build competence when their efforts are directed towards a meaningful goal. While it is critical to have a strong "why" and purpose to inspire our daily teaching and learning, it is equally important to our students. Share what drives and motivates you, and ask your students what inspires them to persistently work towards improvement. Daniel Coyle shares that an initial spark is necessary to ignite the interest and enthusiasm for putting in the necessary practice and work in order to grow, and that a coach or teacher often provides that spark or encouragement.[7] Leading by example, student leaders can also be the motivating spark for their peers, inspiring others to aspire to a higher level of competence.

Building Habits for Competence

Our competence in any area is connected to our habits, which are created from doing or thinking something repeatedly and consistently over time. While growing up, I did not floss regularly, so the night and morning before any dentist appointment I would floss my teeth with the hope that the dentists would think that I was a "flosser." Since I could never fool them, I would always get a lecture on the importance of flossing regularly. Eventually, I did start flossing more often, but it was definitely not a daily habit. Finally, in my thirties, I decided to work on creating a flossing habit. I set out to floss every night for twenty-one days in a row. After I hit this goal, I had conditioned myself to actually want to floss before going to bed. In fact, I got to the point where I *had* to floss, because if I didn't, my mouth noticed. In essence, I took something that I did *not* enjoy doing, turned it into something that I *wanted* to do, and ultimately it became something that I *needed* to do. Now flossing is automatic because it has become a habit.

Growing our competence or skills in any area follows this same pattern or process. Just as it takes work to create a habit, it takes effort to get better at anything. Raising the bar of competence is essential since leading by example is necessary for successful leadership. Students can't be expected to lead members of their section to march or play well if they can't do exactly that at a high level of competence themselves. Similarly, teachers can't expect to lead their students without studying best practices or expect to rehearse their groups effectively without focused score studying, attentive listening, and advance planning. People will follow what we *do* more than what we *say*, so approach every day as an opportunity for growth. Believing that you can improve and get better is the first step towards improving your skill and ability.

The latest research in developing habits encourages us to focus on making small changes that will lead to massive results. In *Atomic Habits*, author James Clear shares the following analogy.

The impact created by a change in your habits is similar to the effect of shifting the route of an airplane by just a few degrees. Imagine you are flying from Los Angeles to New York City. If a pilot leaving from LAX adjusts the heading just 3.5 degrees south, you will land in Washington, D.C., instead of New York. Such a small change is barely noticeable at takeoff—the nose of the airplane moves just a few feet—but when magnified across the entire United States, you end up hundreds of miles apart.[8]

In the world of music, an example of a small change that can lead to significant results might be altering the way a student inhales before singing or playing their instrument. Shifting from chest breathing to diaphragmatic breathing may seem subtle, but the impact on tone, support, and resonance will be tremendous. Even minor changes in the angle that an instrument is held can greatly improve sound quality. When making minor changes to increase competence, we need to encourage patience, as growth and improvement are not always immediately obvious. In a world of instant gratification, our students may become discouraged since building competence rarely happens overnight. Learning stick-with-it-ness is one of the important principles that students learn through the study of music and leadership. It takes time to become great and, as noted by James Clear's example from nature, "Bamboo can barely be seen for the first five years as it builds extensive root systems underground before exploding ninety feet into the air within six weeks."[9]

During the summer between my eighth and ninth grade years, I decided I wanted to make my highly competitive high school jazz band. My private saxophone instructor, Mark, suggested that I start practicing three hours a day to increase my chances, so I began putting in the extra time. A month into the summer when I saw Mark driving past our home, I waved and he stopped for a moment to talk. I confirmed that I was indeed practicing three hours a day, although I didn't seem to be getting much better. He encouraged me to stick with it, and he promised that eventually I would see and hear the results. He was right. By the end of the summer, I had created a new habit of daily practice, my competence level had grown a lot, and I did get into the high school jazz band.

Just as we have habits of doing things, we also have habits of thinking. According to Scott Shickler and Jeff Waller in *The 7 Mindsets to Live Your Ultimate Life*, "Our mindsets form habits, and our habits tend to drive the results in our lives."[10] We create habits from repeated actions and behavior, yet just because a way of thinking has become routine for us does not mean that it is in our best interest. What we choose to focus on influences our words, actions, habits, and character. In order to grow, we need to become aware of our habits of thought and behavior and reflect on whether these habits are serving us well or whether it is time to develop a new habit. You choose your attitude and thoughts (your upbeat), and your thoughts then determine your feelings, behaviors, and actions. Making a difference and making a change begins with creating a new habit of thought. Your new thought patterns will lead to actions that grow your competence, which in turn will increase your self-confidence and lead you to aiming beyond what you previously had thought was out of your range.

Developing Confidence

Students often say they would like to have more confidence, even asking, "How can I be a more confident leader?" Confidence is actually directly linked to competence so that as competence goes up, confidence goes up. It is difficult to lead with confidence when we doubt our own level of competence. Work on growing competence, and confidence will flourish. Perhaps you want to get better at demonstrating on your instrument. Decide that you are going to make the effort to improve your instrumental technique. Then commit to consistently working on the necessary skills. Start with small achievable steps, such as creating a pure tone on long tones at a variety of dynamics and gradually increasing the tempo of your major and minor scales in order to see improvement. Through persistence and repetition, you will develop new habits and rewire your brain for a higher level of competence. Along the way, ask others for feedback so you can get a clearer assessment of your progress and what to work on next. As your confidence goes up, of course, you will make bolder choices about what you want to improve next. Growing competence is a never-ending cycle, because as we get better we become enthusiastic about going for the next level. **With an upbeat mindset, the possibilities of growing your competence are endless.**

Show your students the following pathway to developing more competence and confidence:

1. **Choice.** Choose something that you want to get better at and do it repeatedly. Break the skill down into small, achievable chunks. As each chunk is mastered, combine chunks until the entire skill is practiced together.

2. **Consistency.** Be consistent. Stick with it. Consistency is key. Developing skill and ability takes time. Get past the "I don't wanna's," fear of failure, and self-doubt. Remember your "why" and motivating sense of purpose to keep going. Celebrate progress and persevere even when you don't quickly achieve the goal of forming a habit. Ask for and be open to feedback.

3. **Competence.** With consistent practice, your competence, built on habits, will increase. By putting in time, effort, and targeted practice, achieving the skill will begin to feel natural and take less concentration.

4. **Confidence.** Choosing to improve, practicing consistently, and growing competence will lead to an increase in confidence. Self-confidence founded on authentic skills will help students demonstrate and role-model skills and leadership at a higher level. The other students' confidence in their leader rises still higher as the student leader's competence rises.

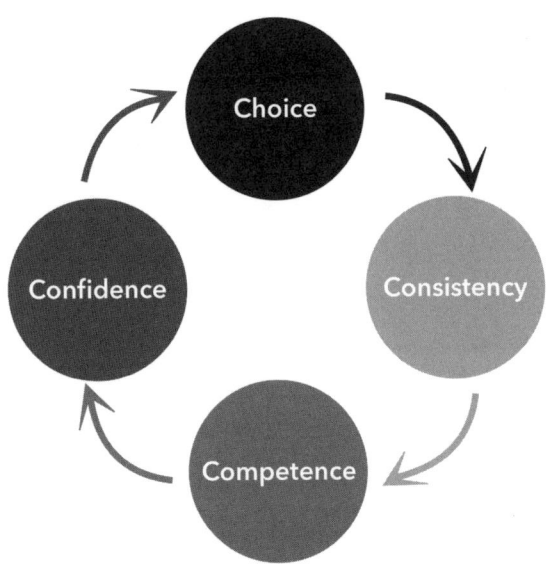

Confidence - Competence Loop

As our competence goes up, our confidence goes up.
The confidence others have in us as leaders also goes up as our own competence grows.

This diagram represents how the sequence functions as a continual loop. When competence and confidence go up, this leads to selecting a goal that is just beyond the newest level of competence. Imagine setting a goal to climb to the summit of an 8,000-foot mountain. It will take effort to get there and your arrival at the top should be celebrated. However, imagine once you arrive at the summit, you look around and see another mountain with a summit at 10,000 feet. Because you have succeeded at getting to the top of the first mountain, you now have the confidence and desire to climb the next highest mountain. After achieving *that* goal, you may even reach for the *next* highest mountain. This cycle can theoretically continue forever. When music and/or leadership are involved, there is no limit or cap on learning and growing. There is always another level to advance to and another summit to climb. With a focus on continual improvement, however, it can be easy to forget to take time to acknowledge and notice progress. Be sure to pause and reflect on how far you have come and celebrate what you have achieved. Brendon Burchard reminds us to *observe* our competence growing so that we can raise our confidence. "We're always onto the next thing before recognizing what we just accomplished. And if we don't recognize what we've accomplished in life—even the small things—then we never *feel* accomplished. We don't feel more competent, capable, and confident today than we did yesterday or the day before."[11]

Mental Hurdles

Here are some mental roadblocks to watch out for that can get in the way of our desire and follow-through in the pursuit of growing competence and confidence.

- Be aware of fixed mindsets that may stop you from taking on new challenges or trying new strategies to improve your competence. Unfortunately, those with a fixed mindset are five times more likely to avoid challenges than those with a growth mindset.[12] Notice any self-doubt, feelings of inadequacy, or self-limiting beliefs that may be holding you back.
- Recognize a fear of failure that may get in the way of trying.
- Notice whether comparison to others causes anxiety and lessens the joy of learning.
- Observe any other self-imposed limitations or limitations imposed by others.

Overcoming Hurdles

Our personal upbeat, thoughts, and attitude play a critical role in our drive to succeed and our eventual achievement. Here are some strategies to help overcome hurdles and those roadblocks to growing our competence.

- Reflect, journal, or talk with a trusted friend about what you have learned and where your competence has developed in the last year. It is common to not take the time to notice how far we have already come when we are looking forward to the future. Focus on your past successes to build the confidence that you will be successful with the present challenge of the moment. Recall overcoming mental roadblocks in the past to prime your mind to do the same in the present.

- While acknowledging the real challenges related to getting better at something, focus on how growing your level of skill will *feel* rather than the possibility of failure. Look forward to the process of getting better through deliberate practice with eager anticipation.
- Focus on the joy of the learning process and how it makes you *feel* to get better for your own sake. Compete with yourself and track your own progress rather than obsessing with the skill level of others.
- Counter negative self-talk with encouraging and affirming statements to yourself, emphasizing a belief in your ability to continually learn, develop, and figure things out. Make a plan that includes bite-sized chunks you can accomplish daily. Even in the process of writing this book, I have been overwhelmed by the magnitude of writing an entire book. The way that I managed that feeling was to focus on consistently writing a little every day.
- Stay connected to your desire to get better and your sense of purpose. Write down your "why" and look at it to remind you of your original intention during the times when you feel like giving up. Jon Gordon writes, "We don't get burned out because of what we do. We get burned out because we forget why we do it. Remember your why and you won't lose your energy along the way."[13]

Practicing

Anything we decide we want to learn, improve upon, or master takes practice. Demonstrate and discuss with your students the following proven and effective strategies for growing competence. Since practicing is essential to getting better at our performance skills and leadership ability, daily practice is much better than practicing once a week. Consider a skill or area of leadership that you want to develop and then make a plan to go after it consistently. Mentally prepare for the challenges ahead by anticipating what could get in the way, distractions or temptations that may occur, and struggles that may throw you off course. See yourself successfully avoiding, dealing with, or picking yourself back up when you fall down. Imagine and take time to visualize achieving the end goal.

It is important that you have a model in your mind for what you would like to successfully do. Listening to the highest-level musicians on your instrument is key to developing an ideal image of tone or even the performance of a piece of music. Watching outstanding marchers helps imprint excellence in your mind. Anders Ericsson clarifies how integral visualization is to successful practicing and achievement: "In any area, not just musical performance, the relationship between skill and mental representations is a virtuous circle: the more skilled you become, the better your mental representations are, and the better your mental representations are, the more effectively you can practice to hone your skill."[14] The clearer and more defined that our image is in our ears and minds, the more effective we will be at chipping away at the stone until the sculpture within is revealed.

Notice the similarity in the two words "competence" and "compete." Rather than thinking about competing against someone else, focus on competing with yourself. Each practice session is an opportunity to compete against the standard that was set at the prior practice session. When you *deliberately* practice, every moment is an opportunity to reach just beyond where you were before.[15] Deliberate practice is different from casual practice and playing or singing something over and over without intention or mindfulness. To practice deliberately, push yourself beyond your comfort zone and become comfortable with taking risks. If you are not stretching yourself or reaching higher, you are not growing and improving. The clearer your mental representation is, the more ready you are to identify mistakes and diagnose a problem.[16] If you miss your target, evaluate, try again, or change your strategy. Look for solutions, such as slowing down the tempo, changing up the rhythm, or isolating variables to simplify the phrase. Focus on fundamentals and scaffold your practice session so that the final product is built one level at a time.

The more you consistently practice a skill, the more you wire and program your brain to be able to achieve that skill with ease. When you first practice something new, you begin to carve a neural pathway in your brain, increasing the myelination of those neurons and the speed that information travels. Then the more you practice, the more defined the pathway becomes.[17] Naturally, ensemble rehearsals led by the teacher are opportunities to direct group structured practice as well. We should model through our rehearsal strategies both how to practice individually and how to rehearse as a section. When my students ask why we keep repeating something, I respond, "We are myelinating our brain!" This is how we grow our skills and level of competence.

Practicing is often a solitary task that we do on our own, but practicing together is a great way for student leaders to support and model for the students that they get to collaborate with. Practicing in pairs is a lot of fun, and students can alternate giving feedback to each other. Sectional rehearsals led by students can include moments for group practice and shared feedback. Because of the importance of hearing or seeing the goal that students are aiming for, the student leader needs to be able to provide a model for the other students to imitate as well as provide constructive, helpful comments. Brendon Burchard writes, "The fastest way to get better at something is to have a coach tell you where you can improve. A third party watching you is important to skill development because you can't improve what you can't see—when you're in the picture, you can't see the frame."[18]

Student leaders can also raise the bar for everyone in the group through teaching their peers and giving constructive feedback and feedforward. Feedback focuses on what was just demonstrated and points out what went well and what needs to be improved. Feedforward focuses on solutions and moving towards a goal rather than focusing on what is wrong.[19] Both feedback and feedforward are important skills for teaching and leading. In all interactions, it is important that the student leaders teach and communicate in a respectful and supportive manner. I recommend hosting mock teaching and feedback sessions so that students can practice with your guidance prior to leading independently. In the next section, let's look at some strategies for peer teaching, feedback, and feedforward.

Peer Teaching Strategies

1. The upbeat to teaching is the preparation and mindset of the teacher. Be sure to plan and envision what and how you want to teach and what the outcome will be for those that you teach.

2. Demonstrate the entire skill or musical phrase.

3. Break the task down into smaller steps, chunks, or skills.

4. Do the skill with your peer.

5. Give specific, constructive feedback and feedforward.

6. Repeat or move on to the next step.

7. Show appreciation and give praise.

Additionally, to check for understanding and to empower the learners, ask them to demonstrate and become the teacher. Essentially, switch roles.

Peer Feedback and Feedforward Strategies

1. The upbeat to giving feedback and feedforward is to listen and watch carefully so that you notice what went well and what can be improved. Aim to formulate comments that are the most helpful, constructive, and likely to create forward momentum.

2. Be respectful and encouraging.

3. Be specific. Rather than only saying "good job," share details about what went well. Likewise, specifically diagnose what needs to change or be improved and how to make that happen.

4. Focus on providing solutions rather than only identifying problems. Of course, students still need to know what went wrong in order to understand what to change or modify.

5. Ask for input, feedback, and feedforward from those you are teaching and leading. The student leader should check in with those they are teaching to discover whether their

methods of teaching are helpful or should be adjusted. Ask questions to ensure everyone is understanding what you are communicating.

Vignette

Tyler Ehrlich
Decatur High School Band Director
Emory University Wind Ensemble Conductor, Decatur, Georgia

"Do we teach music, or do we teach students?"

After completing my undergraduate and graduate degrees, I began the exciting adventure of full-time student teaching. I was only a few days into it before I realized some of these students do not care about becoming better musicians. To me, this was a huge revelation. While I'd had great musical training, I did not have a single tool in my toolbox to teach students *why* they should care about making great music. While struggling with the disconnect between my students and me, I also spent time considering the age-old question, "Do we teach music, or do we teach students?" A shift in mindset answered this question and solved the apparent artistic apathy.

"We teach students the art of music." Students come before music.

The only way to prioritize competence is to first build connections with our students. The veteran teacher knows this, but the student-teacher (me!) certainly did not. I invested a lot of time to create opportunities to build these essential relationships. Through a leadership camping retreat, eating meals with kids, and planning other casual opportunities (e.g., a band pool party, movie, or arcade visit) I found more opportunities to form strong ties with my students. We cannot expect students to prioritize their own artistic competence if there is no relationship with the adult standing in front of them. Once that bond is forged, students respect and witness the passion with which we teach. And from there, they are primed to care about making great music and are motivated to develop their competence as young musicians.

What about our competence as teachers? This is where our own education is key, through graduate school, summer symposiums, music education conferences, conducting workshops, and other opportunities. I remember attending multiple sessions that Dr. Arau taught at the Conn-Selmer Institute in 2019. Many of his concepts, exercises, and recommendations I've taken to heart, and I have seen a dramatic impact in how my students develop their own competence both as instrumentalists and as peer leaders.

Perhaps the most significant thing I've changed is holding leadership training year-round, and most importantly, as a component of our band camp. We discuss our three band goals: (1) love like family, (2) lead with positivity, and (3) strive for mastery. Students learn that everyone's best is different, and while there can only be one first chair player, we can all strive to be our own true best. We acknowledge that the most important leadership positions are the students on our logistics crew. While we can rehearse without a section leader, a drum major, or perhaps even the band director, we cannot rehearse without water coolers, speakers, or yard line markers. We talk about how to develop our competence as performers and learn the elements of deliberate practice.

While I know that it would take more time than I will be on this earth to be the world's most competent educator, I try to remember (and remind my students of) what James Clear, author of *Atomic Habits*, calls "the power of tiny gains." If we can develop our competence by 1 percent per day, we will improve by 37 percent over the course of the year. That spark pushes me to continually grow and, as such, be a better educator for my students.

Application

1. Choose an area where you would personally like to grow your competence. It could be related to music education— such as score study, conducting, ear training, playing an instrument better—or it could be something outside the field of music education such as knitting, water skiing, or golf. Intentionally apply deliberate practice strategies so that you can treat your own growth and learning as a lab that can positively impact how you teach your students to grow their own competence.

2. Encourage your students to grow their competence in the areas they will need to model as leaders. This can include music performance skills, marching skills, and/or communication skills. Teach students to break down the larger skill into smaller stepping stones so they can master the skill one step at a time.

3. Be mindful of your self-talk and mindset when deciding to develop competence in a particular area. Catch yourself using negative and downgrading language, and revise your thoughts to be encouraging and supportive. Practice reframing self-talk with your students.

4. Teach your students the science of myelin wrapping to understand how skills are acquired. Diminish the importance of talent and emphasize the development of skills so that students learn they have unlimited potential.

Journal Questions

1. In what ways would you like to grow your competence in teaching and leading? What steps will you take to improve in these areas? What resources do you need to gather the knowledge or coaching that will help you achieve at the next level?

2. Reflect on a student who surprised you by surpassing your expectations and achieving a much higher level of competence as a musician and/or leader. How does this make you feel?

3. Reflect on how the mindset and confidence level of students affects their motivation and drive to grow in their own competence.

Quotes

Motivation is what gets you started. Habit is what keeps you going.

> — Jim Ryun
> as quoted in Hoda Kotb's *This Just Speaks to Me*, p. 9

The only thing more important than the will to win is the will to prepare to win.

> — Vince Lombardi
> as quoted in T. W. Lewis's *Solid Ground*, Chapter 7

Success is the sum of small efforts, repeated day in and day out.

> — Robert J. Collier
> as quoted in Don Soderquist's *The Wal-Mart Way*, p. 162

Success is giving 100 percent of your effort, body, mind, and soul to the struggle.

> — John Wooden
> as quoted in Brendon Burchard's *High Performance Habits*, p. 267

You should never view your challenges as a disadvantage. Instead, it's important for you to understand that your experience facing and overcoming adversity is actually one of your biggest advantages.

— Michelle Obama

as quoted in Brendon Burchard's *High Performance Habits*, p. 271

ENDNOTES

1. Brendon Burchard, *The Charge: Activating the 10 Human Drives that Make You Feel Alive* (New York: Free Press, 2012), 59.
2. Daniel Coyle, *The Talent Code: Greatness Isn't Born. It's Grown. Here's How* (New York: Bantam Dell, 2009), 40.
3. Anders Ericsson and Robert Pool, *Peak: Secrets from the New Science of Expertise* (Boston: Houghton Mifflin Harcourt, 2016), 168.
4. T. Harv Eker, *Secrets of the Millionaire Mind: Mastering the Inner Game of Wealth* (New York: HarperCollins, 2005), 182.
5. Kate Whiting, "Here are 10 of Nelson Mandela's Most Inspirational Quotes," World Economic Forum, July 18, 2019, https://www.weforum.org/agenda/2019/07/nelson-mandela-south-africa-quotes-madiba-inspiration/.
6. Brendon Burchard, *The Charge: Activating the 10 Human Drives That Make You Feel Alive* (New York: Free Press, 2012), 63.
7. Daniel Coyle, *The Talent Code: Greatness Isn't Born. It's Grown. Here's How.* (New York: Bantam Dell, 2009), 175–176.
8. James Clear, *Atomic Habits: An Easy & Proven Way to Build Good Habits & Break Bad Ones* (New York: Avery, 2018), 17.
9. Ibid., 20
10. Scott Shickler and Jeff Waller, *The 7 Mindsets To Live Your Ultimate Life* (Hartford, CT: Publish Your Purpose Press, 2011/2019), 27.
11. Brendon Burchard, *The Charge: Activating the 10 Human Drives That Make You Feel Alive* (New York: Free Press, 2012), 73.
12. Carol S. Dweck and Ellen. L. Leggett, "A Social-Cognitive Approach to Motivation and Personality," *Psychological Review* 95, no. 2, 256–273.

13. Jon Gordon, *The Power of a Positive Team: Proven Principles and Practices that Make Great Teams Great* (Hoboken, NJ: John Wiley & Sons, 2018), 31.
14. Anders Ericsson and Robert Pool, *Peak: Secrets from the New Science of Expertise* (Boston: Houghton Mifflin Harcourt, 2016), 80.
15. Ibid., 97–100.
16. Ibid., 75.
17. Daniel Coyle, *The Talent Code: Greatness Isn't Born. It's Grown. Here's How.* (New York: Bantam Dell, 2009), 40.
18. Brendon Burchard, *The Charge: Activating the 10 Human Drives That Make You Feel Alive* (New York: Free Press, 2012), 72.
19. Marshall Goldsmith, "Try Feedforward Instead of Feedback," October 29, 2015, https://www.marshallgoldsmith.com/articles/try-feedforward-instead-feedback/.

Chapter 11

THE 4 C'S OF UPBEAT LEADERSHIP: CONNECTION

You can have all the knowledge and skill and credibility
in the world but if you cannot connect with others, build
a relationship with others, and impart that knowledge to
others, it has little value.

— John C. Maxwell

Madison had made up her mind. She was going to drop out of band. During a break on the third day of band camp, she walked down the music hallway on her way to tell the news to her high school band director in his office. She was sad because she had always loved being in band. At her middle school before her family moved into the new district, band was her home away from home, but now in a new place, Madison felt like she didn't know anyone, and no one seemed to even notice her. The first few days of band camp were reserved for the freshmen and the older student leaders, and much of the time was spent with the students in her section—the tuba players—all of whom, other than her, happened to be boys. It hurt Madison to be ignored, and she almost felt invisible, as if she could disappear and no one would care.

This is how Madison was feeling when, just thirty feet away from the band director's office, she saw a friendly student named Sean walking towards her. Sean changed the course of Madison's life by doing one simple thing. He said, "Hi."

"Hi."

That's all.

Then Madison said, "Hi." The conversation continued naturally. Sean said, "Hey, I'm Sean. What's your name?"

Madison replied, "I'm Madison. I'm a freshman and I play the tuba."

Sean said, "Oh, that is so cool! I play the trumpet and I'm one of the drum majors. What do you like to do when you're not in band?"

And because of something that started off with just a simple "hi," Madison changed her mind. She never made it to the band director's office to drop out of band. That one connection with Sean led to more and more connections with other students, to the director, to the music, to performing, and to what Madison would eventually refer to as "her band family." Two years later, Madison auditioned and made the all-state band on tuba, and then in her senior year she became the tuba marching band section leader. That is when I met her.

Madison shared this story with me a few years ago while I was a guest student leadership teacher at her high school band camp. It was the first day of band camp with just the section leaders and first-year marchers. That morning, before the younger students arrived, as Madison told me and the other student leaders this story from her past, all the original emotions that she felt—the pain, loneliness, sadness, disconnection—made her tear up. Another section leader gave her a hug to comfort and encourage her to make it through telling the entire story. Later that afternoon, Madison came inside for a student leadership session after leading her tuba section members through a playing and marching sectional, and she was surprised by what had happened. She told us, "None of the freshmen tubas will talk to me."

In my conversation with the student leaders, we discussed how being real, authentic, and vulnerable with section members can open a pathway to build trust and connection. Seeing this situation as an opportunity to build connections, I asked Madison if she would be willing to share her story with all the freshmen marchers the next day at camp. She said she would, and then to show their support, all the student leaders decided that they would also share their own stories from their first year in marching band—their struggles, the fun times, the hard times, the joy, the pay-off from working hard, and the friendships they had made. That evening, the student leaders planned out what they would each say. Although they were nervous to speak so openly about their experiences, some expressed that they were excited to remove any barriers to connection or communication that being older and having a leadership title can create.

We kicked off the following morning with a meeting in the band room with the freshmen and student leaders. One by one, student leaders courageously stood up and shared their own stories. You could feel the energy in the room shift as a sense of relief and ease came over the freshmen who realized they were not alone in feeling anxious or nervous. They learned that others before them had gone through the same process with similar feelings and that sticking with band was rewarding and worthwhile. Madison bravely spoke from her heart, and I could see in the eyes and body language of the freshmen tuba players that they were taking in every word. The students cheered for Madison afterwards, emboldened and inspired by her courage and vulnerability.

After this meeting, all the students went outside to practice marching fundamentals. Later during the lunch break, I asked Madison how it was going with her tuba section. Madison grinned and laughingly said, "Well, Dr. Arau, now the tubas won't stop talking to me!"

• • •

Isn't that a great story?! Thank goodness Madison happened to bump into a student who knew the importance of connection at just the right time! Teaching and learning music are about so much more than just the music. Our students crave to be a part of something bigger than themselves and they desperately want to be noticed and valued. As music educators, we model the importance of connection by how we reach out, listen to, and honor each student's individual voice. Our students, in turn, strengthen the web of connections in the ensemble by how they interact with each other. If Madison had not run into Sean at that crucial moment, the story might be quite different. Sean exemplifies how a student leader, or any engaged student for that matter, can proactively extend a hand and ensure that another student feels welcomed and that they belong.

I love writing about the third C of Upbeat Leadership—*connection*—because it is essential to every aspect of our lives. Humans thrive on connection for survival. From the moment we are born, when we need to be held and cared for, the desire and need for connection never goes away. Many students join music ensembles because of connections they have made either with their music teacher or with friends who are also joining. Indeed, many students continue to stay involved in music because of the many layers of connections that are formed over time. **Music classrooms and ensembles that make connection central to learning, culture, and leadership are contexts for communities where students and teachers thrive.**

We began exploring the 4 C's of Upbeat Leadership with a deep dive into the first C: *character*. Character encompasses *who* we are. Our character is our essence and the foundation that the other C's are built upon. The second C, *competence*, allows us to earn trust from those we are leading based on our skills and ability to demonstrate and role-model. Competence is the *how*. However, in order to be able to motivate, inspire, persuade, and influence others, we must be able to connect. That is why the third C is *connection*. We are drawn to the members of the ensemble, the director, the music, performing, and the feeling that comes from being part of excellence. Take a moment to reflect on your own "why" for choosing to become a music educator and a musician. You likely became a music teacher because of a combination of all or some of the connections you felt to music, your instrument, your music teachers, your friends in the ensemble, or the magic you felt in performances. This connection energized you, and you wanted more of it. **Connection is a powerful feeling and gives meaning to what we do in life; therefore, connection is the "why" of the 4 C's of Upbeat Leadership.** As Brené Brown writes, "We are psychologically, emotionally, cognitively, and spiritually hardwired for connection, love, and belonging. Connection, along with love and belonging (two expressions of connection), is why we are here, and it is what gives purpose and meaning to our lives."[1]

The connections made through music matter so much. Even though social media digitally connects us to people around the world, people feel lonelier and more disconnected than ever before due to a lack of "meaningful human connectedness."[2] Because of technology, so much of how we communicate today is device to device rather than heart to heart, eye to eye. Thankfully, we have music to bring us together spiritually and physically so that we can still get the reward of connection and belonging we long for.

As music educators, we get to experience one of the most incredible forms of connection through the art of conducting music. Conducting an ensemble is an opportunity to conduct energy. We can equate what we do as music conductors to how electricity is conducted. To conduct is to lead. When we conduct ourselves, we are taking responsibility for our actions. We choose how to conduct ourselves. The conductor of a train makes sure everyone is on board by announcing, "All aboard!" The conductor drives the engine of the train and makes sure all the passengers are accounted for. When electricity is conducted, it passes from one point to the next, just as a train passes from one station to the next. As conductors, we also lead and move the ensemble from one musical location to the next, and as we do that, we infuse the players with our energy. When the energy channels are open, the players send their energy towards the conductor, creating an energy loop that energizes the performers, the conductor, the music, and the audience. This is why live performances can feel so electric. The audience becomes part of the energy exchange—feeling the energy from the performance while also sending their personal energy to the performers. This sensation connects everyone in a kinetic, shared experience. In those moments, everyone in the room feels the physical and emotional connection.

The connection we feel when making, rehearsing, conducting, and creating music is a model for how we can create connections beyond music. It is vital that leaders make connection a priority. **If leaders can't connect, communicate well, and relate with others, they will find when they look around that they are merely taking a walk by themselves rather than leading.** Like character and competence, the capacity to connect with others can be grown, practiced, and developed. No matter where our connection skills are today, they can be continually improved, and our music program is an ideal place for building these connections. Within each music class, ensemble, and/or program, there is truly a web of connections to be woven.

The Web of Connections

Let's look at just some of the connections that arise when we place a student leader at the center. Although you may need to point them out at first, your students can then clearly see how the interconnectedness is integral to the success of everyone in the web of connections. **For this section I will write as if I am addressing a student in your music class.**

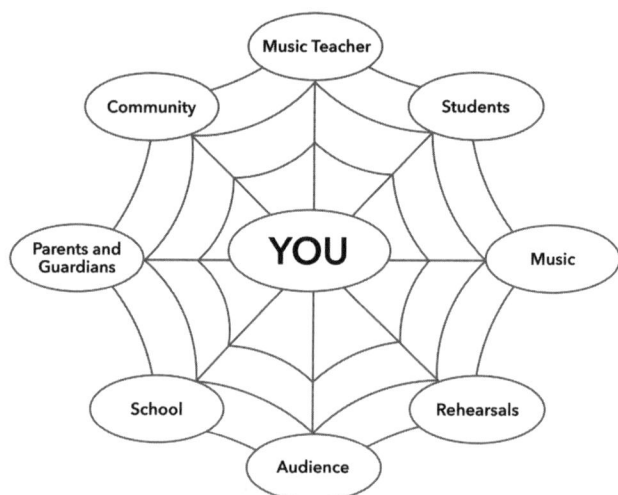

Web of Connections

Connection to You

I know it may seem unusual to include the connection to ourselves when talking about the role that connections play in leadership and in music, but it is actually the most important and fundamental connection. Becoming more conscious and aware of how our thoughts, attitudes, and feelings influence how we communicate and interact with others is a major key to successful leadership. The more we understand ourselves, show compassion for ourselves, and honor our own unique voice, the more we will have to give and contribute to others. It has been said that we cannot give what we do not have, and I believe this to be true. How we treat others is often a reflection of how we treat ourselves, and we ought to treat ourselves as well as we treat others. **Treat yourself with the same kindness and compassion that you aspire to give and show others.**

Another way to think of this is that how we lead others reflects how we lead ourselves. Leadership comes from within, yet our focus is usually on how we lead others and what actions we are taking as a leader. However, *who* we are—our thoughts, attitudes, character, integrity, and values—inform, influence, and impact our leadership decisions. You may find that taking a moment to mindfully breathe a few slow, deep breaths in and out of your nose, and allowing your thoughts to come and go and accepting your thoughts non-judgmentally, helps you to ground and center yourself. Or you may prefer to play or sing a piece of music that opens up a connection to your heart. Writing your thoughts down in a journal or mindfully walking in nature may also expand your sense of connection to yourself. Think about what brings purpose and meaning to your life. How do you want to show up in the world? As a leader, how would you like to be a positive influence and make a difference?

Connection to the Music Teacher

Connecting to your music teacher can be a lot of fun! Connect as much as you can in class and in rehearsals by being fully present, engaged, and enthusiastic. Come to class as prepared as you can so that you can connect more with your teacher through eye contact and conversation while making music. You can learn a lot about music and leadership from your teacher, so go out of your way to ask questions and discuss topics that you are interested in learning more about, and feel free to share what you know with your teacher! The great thing about being a teacher is that every day we have an opportunity to learn from our students. I would encourage you to ask your teacher how you can be of service and help, because there is always something that needs to be done. It is often during the times that we are involved in doing odd jobs, such as organizing music and cleaning up the music room, when the greatest conversations and connections naturally occur. Some music classes and ensembles have more than one director and additional staff. Be friendly, welcoming, and supportive of all the music educators. They are there to help every student be successful.

Connection to Students

Reach out and intentionally connect with the members of your section, group, and ensemble. If you have tended to wait for others to seek you out, as a leader it is important to courageously take the first step to connect. Sometimes the first step is as easy as raising your hand, waving, smiling, and saying "hi" to someone you have not met before. Every student wants to feel that they belong, that they are part of a group that values and cares about them. Don't wait for others to extend their hands to you; be the initiator and extend your hand first. Leaders take the first step to connect. Sharing stories of past musical or marching struggles that you have faced can help level the playing field and ease the anxiety of younger or less experienced members. We all connect and relate to stories, so sharing about a particular experience with feeling can build a connection and bridge. Rather than viewing yourself as a "leader," think of yourself as a "mentor" to assist and help other students. **Instead of leaders and followers, focus on the spirit of togetherness that happens when everyone is a "collaborator" working towards the common goal of musical excellence.**

Connection to Music

What a joy it is to make music! Think back to those pieces you have listened to, played, or created that have stuck with you, where you can imagine the performance as if it is happening now—the sound, the feeling, the spark. The connections that are possible through the performance of music are almost inexpressible. Remarkably, so many connections are made before we even begin playing a piece of music. With musical compositions, composers begin with a connection or an inspiration. They may connect to a folk song they want to arrange, a painting, a moment in history, a particular message, lyrics, or an emotion they wish to express. This initial connection becomes embedded in their composition, which makes its way to your music stand so that you get to make the notes on the page come to life. Notice how the music makes you feel and then wholeheartedly lean in and express your feelings through your singing and playing. The deeper the connection you can make to the music, the more fulfilling the experience. Openly broadcast your feelings and connections with music to inspire and encourage the other students in your ensemble to also get excited about the opportunity to make music. Music brings us together. Music tells stories that remind us of our common humanity. Music unites us. Music reflects who we are and paints an image of who we can become. **Music expresses, reveals our true nature, speaks from the heart, and lets us know that we are not alone.**

Connection to Rehearsals

The connection in performance begins well before the concert. Heart-to-heart, human-to-human connections begin in the classroom with the interactions and exchanges between the teacher and the students and amongst the students themselves. Every day is an opportunity to create a shared experience. The process of growth, learning, connections, and preparation in rehearsals is the upbeat to the concert that makes for a memorable experience. From the moment the ensemble sight-reads a piece in rehearsal, open your heart channel so that emotional expression is part of the journey beginning on day one and not something that is added the week before the concert when all the details on the page are buttoned up and taken care of. The energy that touches your soul should be embraced as an essential element that you strive to express at a higher level in each subsequent rehearsal. Even when a deep connection is only made for a few fleeting seconds in rehearsal, we all will have tasted it. That feeling of energy is the ember that motivates us to stoke the timber, creating more sparks and fanning the flames for more.

Connection to the Audience

Connecting with the audience in a performance can be electric, magical, and extremely rewarding. The pay-off in performance makes all the hard work, attention to detail, and extra effort worthwhile. In rehearsals, we experience many connections with the conductor, the music, the other musicians, our own emotional and mental connection to the music, and the acoustics of the space where we rehearse. When we perform in front of an audience, our level of commitment, passion, and connection is often heightened. The audience members, who are typically hearing the performance of a piece for the first time, get to listen, feel, see, and experience the music from a fresh perspective. Their emotional response and energy can be felt by the performers on the stage, elevating the rush of pride and satisfaction that we love to feel in live concerts. Smile at the audience, acknowledge them, and thank them afterwards for supporting you and your ensemble.

Connection to School

The music program is a source of pride for your school. The band, choir, and orchestra are some of the most visible organizations representing the school to the community. As a member of the music program, you not only represent music, but you also represent the excellence of your school. Share with the other students the importance of showing your pride for your ensemble by putting forth your best self at school and in the community. Make doing well in all your classes a goal and consider setting up a tutoring system for students to help each other out in their non-music classes as well as in music classes. The other teachers in the school will come to view the music students as role models, which in turn increases the respect and support for what you get to do in music.

Connection to Parents and Guardians

Successful music programs rely on the support of parents and guardians, whose support for their children is sustained in many ways—through lessons, instruments, encouragement, attending concerts, building props, fundraising, feeding the ensemble at events, transportation. This list could go on and on. Always go the extra mile to express appreciation by actually saying thank you, and don't take what they do for granted. Be a role model for the other students and create a culture of gratitude by leading by example.

Connection to the Community

In addition to connecting with the community at concerts, shows, halftime performances, pep bands, and/or parades, collaborate with your teacher to find additional ways to serve and give back to the community. Consider forming chamber ensembles that can volunteer to perform at senior centers, the mall, or the grocery store. Promote and broadcast all the positive ways that your band, choir, or orchestra contribute to the greater good of the community and ask news reporters to report on how your musical group contributes to and benefits your community. Show appreciation and gratitude to community members for their support at performances and during fundraising events. **Instead of asking the community how they can serve your group, ask community members how your ensemble can serve them.** This will strengthen ties and connections to the community and ultimately reap rewards for everyone.

Teamwork
(back to addressing the teacher)

We reach out to connect with others because we cannot do everything alone. Great success is never achieved in solitude. We do our best when we work together as a team. I have found that the following ideas and principles have had a positive impact on the feeling of connection and the strengthening of teamwork in ensembles. Naturally, other than performing a solo, all the work we do in music is done in a group or a team, so the tenets of teamwork readily apply. Legendary former UCLA basketball coach John Wooden used to share with his players that the success of the team takes "10 hands" to score a basket.[3] I love this philosophy. Passing the ball amongst all five players on the path to scoring has more meaning than when one person, acting as the hero, does it alone. How does this apply to music and leadership? The student leader should focus more on collaboration and cooperation than on doing everything by themselves. Furthermore, their aim should be to create a culture in which competition amongst the musicians is minimized and celebration is emphasized. Celebrate the growth and achievement of each other without feeling that someone else's success diminishes your own.

Empathy and respect for diversity, essential qualities of an Upbeat Leader, can be practiced and developed through listening deeply and truly seeking to understand. Brené Brown defines empathy as "connecting with the emotion that someone is experiencing, not the event or the circumstance."[4] Effective leaders try to feel how others feel and find a common ground in order to build connection and a healthy community. Honor each other's cultures, backgrounds, religions, colors, and genders. Connect before you lead and care before you critique. The importance of connecting and showing interest in others is highlighted by this well-known saying, often credited to President Theodore Roosevelt: "Nobody cares how much you know until they know how much you care." Choose to be curious, interested, and fascinated by the members of the group. You can find what you are looking for, especially if you look for positives in others.

Differences of opinion amongst individual members of the team should be encouraged, because a more creative solution or strategy oftentimes arises from the mixture of thoughts and ideas. Always be respectful of other opinions and try to learn from others. Take time to listen first and try to understand where your team members are coming from before asking them to see the world your way. Be respectful and open-minded. Leonardo da Vinci once said, "I do not care that I am right; what I care about is getting the right answer."[5] We can learn from our team members and even make a better decision when we do.

Student leaders should also model a caring disposition, showing compassion and respect so that the other members of the group will mirror the same behavior and treat each other well. Members of the group will respond better to the leader when the leader comes from a caring, supportive, and encouraging place. Strive to create a sense of belonging for every member of the group by welcoming them wholeheartedly and encouraging them to be themselves. Team members will rise to the level of expectations and the level of commitment, dedication, and skill of the leader, and they will respond better to the leader when the leader is supportive and authentic.

When possible, lead, support, guide, and empower members by delegating responsibilities to give others an opportunity to shine. The leader should take responsibility when the team does not achieve its goals and give the credit to the group when it does. Recognize the importance of every member of the group and remember the words of Helen Keller, "Alone we can do so little; together we can do so much."[6]

Communication Circles

Breaking the ice and getting to know each other is crucial for the success of any group. Here is a fun activity that is particularly effective at the beginning of the year or for an event in the summer prior to the school year starting. I learned this highly engaging activity from Tim Lautzenheiser, and I have used it with every grade level and adults successfully.[7] Here are the basics for kicking it off.

1. Ask students to number off as ones and twos.

2. Stand in the center and ask the ones to make a circle around you. Once the circle is established and evenly spread out, ask the ones to face away from the center.

3. Ask the twos to find a one to be their first partner. If there is an uneven number, two students can pair up as one. The twos form the outer circle and the ones form the inner circle.

4. The teacher or student leader standing in the center shares the topic of discussion or question. Everyone is silent while awaiting the conversation piece.

5. The ones respond first.

6. After about twenty to thirty seconds, the teacher claps once and loudly says "switch!" Then the ones stop talking and the twos respond to the topic or question.

7. After about twenty to thirty seconds, the teacher claps three times and calls out, "change!"

8. All the students stop talking and the ones take one step to their left (counterclockwise) so that they are facing a new partner. The twos stay where they are.

9. Steps 4–8 are repeated multiple times until the teacher feels that there has been enough time for students to have a lot of fun and to get to know each other better.

Here are some sample questions for the beginning of the school year. For the sake of simplicity, I will use the noun "band." Use the name of whatever group is appropriate: band, choir, orchestra, jazz band, jazz choir, music, school, fine arts, sport, etc.

1. What are you looking forward to this year in band?
2. Share something fun that you got to do this summer.
3. What is one of your funniest memories from being in band?
4. Share what it felt like when you chose your instrument for the first time.
5. What are challenges that you foresee this year in band, and what are some solutions and ways to handle them?
6. What are opportunities that you foresee this year in band, and what can you do to make the most of them?
7. Share a struggle that you have had in band but that you worked through and overcame.
8. What do you love the most about being in band?
9. What can you do to help make everyone feel welcome in the band?
10. What are your personal goals for this year in band?
11. What goals do you have for your section?
12. What goals do you have for the entire band?
13. Share something positive about the person in front of you. (I recommend using this same directive three or four times in a row).
14. *Without talking*, share something positive about the person in front of you. (You will want to repeat this many times, as it always brings much joy and creativity. For questions 13 and 14, I recommend picking up the pace to about ten seconds per student response).

Effective Communication

How we communicate influences how we connect with others. We communicate with our words, our body language, our tone of voice, our actions, our behavior, our music, and our art. We communicate messages by how we show up, the attitude we bring, and what we broadcast through the energy that we share with others. We communicate on social media, in texts, messages, emails, and videos. Whatever the form of communication we use, we are communicating a message. An Upbeat Leader understands that communicating well is key to building strong connections.

Here are some communication tips to share with your students.

- When communicating face to face, your attitude, words, tone of voice, posture, facial expressions, eye contact, and smile impact how others will respond to you.
- Our words matter because language affects us at a cellular level. The things we say, read, and hear can literally change our physiology.[8] Choose your words carefully, as it is difficult to take back something after it has been said. This is equally important with written text. Use motivating language as much as possible to emphasize that we are in this together. Words such as "we," "let's," "us," "together," and "join us" inspire connection and break down any barriers or separation that can happen between a leader and member. Focus on what "we get to do" and use the word "yet" when the group is making progress but has not yet attained the goal, as in, "We are not there *yet*." Avoid using

language that emphasizes hierarchy and separation, such as, "I want you to do . . ." or "Do this for me."

- Communicate clearly with a friendly and encouraging tone of voice. If you communicate with a harsh, irritable, or condescending tone of voice, your message will be received defensively and with irritation. **Just like the tone of an instrument affects the sound of the ensemble, your tone of voice when communicating affects the connection and "sound" of the conversation.**

- Communicate with a confident and open posture. If possible, have your heart face the person you are speaking to, because where your heart goes, energy flows.

- Use your facial expressions, eye contact, and smile to give emphasis, meaning, and sincerity to what you are communicating. Consider practicing communicating in the mirror so you become more aware of how your facial expressions may be perceived.

- Listening well is equally important to how well you communicate your message. Listen to fully understand, not to respond. Instead of formulating a response while the other person is talking, try to see what they are sharing from their point of view.

- Maintain eye contact and an open posture while listening. Avoid crossing your arms as this sends a stand-offish message.

- While the other person is speaking, nod to show you are listening and integrate elements of what they communicated in your response.

- Listen more than you speak, and remember the wisdom of Greek stoic philosopher Epictetus: "We have two ears and one mouth so that we can listen twice as much as we speak."

How We Throw the Ball Affects How the Ball Is Received

Here is a fun game that teaches an important principle about communication. This works great with groups ranging from five to over a hundred people.

1. Ask the students if they agree that as musicians and leaders, we tend to be creative. Ask the students if we tend to focus on what we want to create rather than what we don't want. Generally, the responses are a hearty "Yes!" Then say, "However this begins is not how it needs to end."

2. Tell the students that you need to go get your "prop," and then walk to retrieve your "prop" from behind something that is out of the view of the students. Your "prop" is an imaginary basketball that you can start dribbling as if you were bouncing a real basketball. Then toss or throw the "basketball" to a student. Hopefully they catch it, and then they will either throw it back to you or to another student.

3. In the beginning, most students pass around the imaginary basketball, but after a while, a student usually changes the prop to something else—a baseball, football, soccer ball, beach ball, frisbee, volleyball—and this change makes the game more fun. If the ball gets passed back to you, you can turn it into a footlong sub sandwich and take a bite out of

it before passing the sandwich to a student. The possibilities are truly endless. Some have turned the prop into a kitten, a cup of water, or even a saxophone, for example.

4. Once enough students have had a chance to interact with the "ball" or it is thrown "out of bounds," you can bring the game to a close and share the important leadership and communication message that the game teaches.

5. The message is, "How we throw the ball affects how the ball is received." If I throw the ball to you with great speed, you have to catch it quickly with snap reflexes. If I gently lob a ball to you, you can catch it gently, which in contrast may feel like slow motion. **Just as changing how we throw a ball affects how the receiver catches the ball, how and what we communicate affects how others will catch or receive our message.** How and what we say affects how others listen to us. How we welcome others will impact whether they feel that they belong or not. How we lead affects how others follow. Just as we can choose our upbeat, we also choose how we throw the ball.

Connect through Vulnerability

This chapter's opening story about Madison illustrates the role that vulnerability plays in opening up channels of communication and building trust. When Madison told a story of how she felt when she was a freshman in the marching band, the other students found her more relatable and approachable. Leaders should find ways to normalize struggles, challenges, and even common feelings and emotions that members of the group may be experiencing. As Madison discovered, telling stories of our personal struggles is not necessarily easy. It may, in fact, feel scary, risky, or like a show of weakness, but the display of appropriate vulnerability comes across to others as courage. When we put ourselves out there through sharing a personal story or reaching out, we risk being rejected or hurt. Without a doubt, it does take courage to connect, and it is rewarding and central to being an effective Upbeat Leader.

According to Brené Brown, "Vulnerability is the core of all emotions and feelings. To feel is to be vulnerable. To believe vulnerability is weakness is to believe that feeling is weakness."[9] She continues, "Vulnerability is the birthplace of love, belonging, joy, courage, empathy, and creativity. It is the source of hope, empathy, accountability, and authenticity."[10] When Madison opened up to the younger students in the room about her own emotional path in band, the other students felt something in common with Madison, which built a bridge of trust between them. It is helpful for the leaders to let the new students know that they are not alone in their feelings of insecurity, self-doubt, or loneliness. By sharing their own stories of struggle and how they grew from the experience, the student leaders give courage to the members of the group. Usually when one student bravely shares a challenge they have faced, others will feel more comfortable and emboldened to talk about their own personal challenges, strengthening connections amongst all the students.

The Principle of Value

Like Madison, all of us want to feel that we matter and that our presence in the world has meaning and makes a difference. We want to feel connected to others, to a group, or to a cause that is greater than ourselves. In fact, when we don't feel connection, we feel disconnection and loneliness, and those feelings hurt. In musical ensembles, if students do not feel connected, they will often withdraw and eventually drop out of the group, reflecting Brené Brown's assertion that "connection is why we're here. We are hardwired to connect with others, it's what gives purpose and meaning to our lives, and without it there is suffering."[11] A goal for student leaders is to take the initiative to reach out and make sure that every member of the group feels valued. This begins with looking for something nice or positive to say to a student, even something as simple or superficial as "I like the color of your shirt."

Being noticed makes us feel special. It feels good to share something positive with someone else in the same way that it feels good to receive a positive comment or feedback. I call this exchange the *principle of value*. When you share with someone that you value them, they feel better about themselves *and* their value of you is elevated. In this positive state, the value of both individuals rises in an upward spiral, eventually leading to both becoming the best version of themselves. The initiator does not need to expect a positive comment in return about themselves, but when it does happen, it raises the good feelings and value of both people to an even higher degree.

The *principle of value* gives validation to others; it reinforces that they matter, that they are valued, and that they belong. When we celebrate and accept others for being who they *are* instead of insisting that they change to fit in, we create a welcoming space where everyone can thrive. Student leaders should encourage their team members by letting them know they believe in them and that they are grateful to be in the group with them. Proactively starting off an interaction with a positive comment is an example of what it means to lead with positivity.

Positive Bumper Cars

Rather than simply encouraging students to be positive, I love creating situations for the students to experience what it feels like to embody the *principle of value* when they are leading with positivity. I call this game *positive bumper cars*. Here are the instructions and guidelines. Feel free to make adjustments to suit your situation and space.

1. You will need an open space without any obstructions like chairs or stands. The students should stand (if they are able) and spread out so they are all separated by at least a few feet.

2. Ask the students if they have ever been on a bumper car ride at a theme park, fair, or carnival.

3. Explain that they are going to play a game similar to bumper cars but that this is called "positive bumper cars." Have fun with this. I like to pretend that everyone is a transformer and that they become their own car. I simply ask the students to raise their elbow out to the side so that they can lightly tap each other's elbows as they mill about and connect with as many students as possible.

4. At this point, it is helpful to model what an exchange could look like. As the teacher, you should walk over to a student and, with permission, lightly tap elbows and share the first positive thing about the student that pops into your mind.

It might be "Nice glasses," "I like your shoes," or "Thank you for your smile." Generally that student will then share a positive thought about you, but if not, encourage them to at least say something nice back to you. Let the students know that after an exchange where one student points out a positive and then the other student says something nice in return, they both should move on to connect with others. Encourage them to get out of their comfort zone to connect with people they don't know as well.

5. I have found that the most challenging aspect about running this game is bringing it to an end because the students end up having such a great time and there is a lot of laughter, making it difficult for the students to even hear the teacher. I recommend practicing the ending ahead of time. I ask the students if they are familiar with Transformers, and generally they are. I point out that at the end I will be calling out "Positive bumper cars is coming to a close. Please shut down." When they hear me say "Please shut down," they should stop talking and collapse their positive bumper car down as if they were a Transformer and await further instructions.

6. After simulating the ending, you are almost ready for the game to start. First give the students a goal to make at least five connections during the next two minutes. Then: "Positive bumper cars now begins!"

7. During those two minutes, you can participate or monitor the activity.

8. When it is time to end the game, move to the center of the group and announce, "Positive bumper cars is coming to a close. Please shut down." Once the students have quieted

down, you can engage them in a spontaneous conversation about how they feel. They will feel fantastic! For two minutes the students have been focused on noticing the positives in others and receiving positive comments from their peers. This experience has stimulated their prefrontal cortex, flooding them with the feel-good brain chemicals: dopamine, oxytocin, endorphins, and serotonin. As you explain that this is what it feels like to *lead with positivity*, ask them if they would like to feel and live this way all the time—noticing what is good in others and looking for the positives. Let them know that they *can* when they choose what to focus on, and, together, they can intentionally choose to create a culture that uplifts, encourages, and celebrates every member of the group.

Vignette

Kelley Burroughs
Band Director
Ocoee Middle School, Cleveland, Tennessee

As a middle school band director, I get the privilege of starting many students on their band journey. One of the first communications I send home is a letter that is mailed to the student at the end of fifth grade telling them what instrument they will be playing and welcoming them to the band family. Once school begins, my amazing co-teacher, Spencer Hughes, and I encourage our students to connect with one another as well as to our school community.

One of the most meaningful ways we do this is through a mentorship program with our special education class. The students work together to teach a student to play a band instrument. These students are included in the winter and spring concerts. As they get to know each other through sharing music, it's amazing to see how the friendships form. They high five each other in the hallway. They eat together in the cafeteria. The mentors send Valentine's and birthday gifts to their new friends. Friday Funday is probably the best day of the week, filled with Boomwhacker play-alongs and dance parties.

I will never forget when one student decided she wanted to play the trombone. Her mentors patiently tried to get her to make a sound from August to October. Nothing was working. She was unable to buzz her lips. Still her mentors persisted. Then one day the student made the tiniest little sound. The entire room stopped. Everyone looked at the group and the girl's face said it all. "I did it!" I had tears in my eyes as the whole room erupted in celebration for her accomplishment.

We never charge admission to our concerts, but at each winter concert we take up donations for The Caring Place, which coordinates charitable giving for the greater community. This simple act reminds students that we are part of a bigger community and that we are responsible for each other. Our students are also encouraged to donate to other band programs when they experience a natural disaster or loss.

Because middle school kids need lots of structure, our students always have a starter on the board when they enter class. On Fridays we always ask, "What did you learn this week in band?" This gives students an opportunity to reflect on their hard work and find something they accomplished. We also ask, "What are you looking forward to in band class?" This helps us gauge how connected they are to the program. If a student is looking forward to playing a pep band song, we try to teach a pep band song that is accessible to their grade level. The third question we always ask is some kind of get-to-know-you question. Have you ever asked a middle school student what their third favorite dinosaur is? You should.

Our students also connect through different themes that arise in our classes. Last year we spent a great deal of time debating possums and their value to the universe. This year we gave our students the "pig personality test." Spencer, my co-director, unintentionally drew the funniest pig you have ever seen. This has become a "thing" in our classroom this year. The students submitted over 180 names for the pig and then voted to call it "Snoop Hog." One student came in with stickers that his dad made of the pig and we also had keychains made. They really enjoy having things that are unique to band, our own private jokes. It makes the sense of family much stronger.

I was lucky enough to teach my own three children in band, and they called me mom in class. Other students began calling me mom too. This makes me extremely happy. Because you know mom has high expectations of you. Mom expects you to behave. Mom will set you straight. And mom loves you. When you become a part of the Ocoee band, you become part of a family. We stand up for each other. We support each other. We laugh together, and best of all, we make music together. How lucky we are to be able to share this with our incredible students!

Application

1. Highlight the various connections that occur in a daily rehearsal or music classroom. Invite your students to share the connections they feel to the music, the composer, the lyrics, or the emotions that are expressed.

2. Take time to share gratitude for your students so that they feel valued and that they matter.

3. Encourage your students to notice the good in others and to lead with positivity. Play the positive bumper car game and/ or communication circles so that the students experience the *principle of value* firsthand.

4. Take the lead with building trust by sharing a vulnerable story of overcoming a challenge to invite more authentic and open communication.

5. Play the *throw the imaginary ball game* to illustrate that how we throw the ball affects how the ball is received and that how we communicate, connect, and lead affects how others will respond to us.

6. Select music that you and your students will connect to emotionally so that you can discuss the power of connection through music.

Journal Questions

1. In what ways do you feel connected to your students, and how do you feel you could take that connection to a deeper level?
2. How do you let your students know that you care about them, value them, and honor them? What role does gratitude play in your music room?
3. What can you do to increase your passion and connection to the music and to your students?
4. How can you create an atmosphere that makes connection central to the culture of your classroom and ensemble?

Quotes

It is one thing to communicate to people because you believe you have something of value to say. It's another to communicate with people because you believe they have value. People's opinion of us has less to do with what they see in us than it does with what we can help them see in themselves.

— John C. Maxwell
The 21 Irrefutable Laws of Leadership, pp. 118–119

People don't care about how much you know until they know how much you care.

> — Theodore Roosevelt
> as quoted in John C. Maxwell's
> *The 21 Indispensable Qualities
> of a Leader*, p. 103

A crucial measure of our success in life is the way we treat one another every day of our lives.

> — P. M. Forni
> *Choosing Civility*, p. 4

We are psychologically, emotionally, cognitively, and spiritually hardwired for connection, love, and belonging. Connection, along with love and belonging (two expressions of connection), is why we are here, and it is what gives purpose and meaning to our lives.

> — Brené Brown
> *Daring Greatly*, p. 68

The meeting of two personalities is like the contact of two chemical substances: if there is any reaction, both are transformed.

> — Carl Jung
> *Modern Man in Search of a Soul*, p. 49

ENDNOTES

1. Brené Brown, *Daring Greatly: How the Courage to Be Vulnerable Transforms the Way We Live, Love, Parent, and Lead* (New York: Gotham Books, 2012), 68.
2. Frank John Ninivaggi, "Loneliness: A New Epidemic in the USA," Psychology Today, February 12, 2019, https://www.psychologytoday.com/us/blog/envy/201902/loneliness-new-epidemic-in-the-usa.
3. John Wooden and Steve Jamison, *Wooden on Leadership* (New York: McGraw-Hill, 2005), 123–124.
4. Brené Brown, *Daring Greatly: How the Courage to Be Vulnerable Transforms the Way We Live, Love, Parent, and Lead* (New York: Gotham Books, 2012), 81.
5. Scott Shickler and Jeff Waller, *The 7 Mindsets to Live Your Ultimate Life* (Hartford, CT: Publish Your Passion Press, 2011/2019), 67.
6. Ibid., 70.
7. Tim Lautzenheiser, *Classic Leadership: A Curriculum for the Development of Student Leaders* (Chicago: GIA Publications, 2014), 42.
8. Judith E. Glaser, *Conversational Intelligence: How Great Leaders Build Trust and Get Extraordinary Results* (Brookline, MA: Bibliomotion, Inc., 2014), 83.
9. Brené Brown, *Daring Greatly: How the Courage to Be Vulnerable Transforms the Way We Live, Love, Parent, and Lead* (New York: Gotham Books, 2012), 33.
10. Ibid., 34.
11. Ibid., 8.

Chapter 12

THE 4 C'S OF UPBEAT LEADERSHIP: CLARITY

Music is powered by ideas. If you don't have clarity of ideas,
you're just communicating sheer sound.[1]
— Yo-Yo Ma

During my senior year in high school, I started to notice that my vision was changing. The first sign was when I wrote down the wrong homework problems while reading the whiteboard in my physics class. What a disappointment the next day to discover that I had done the wrong homework! After I made a similar mistake in calculus, I decided to sit closer to the front of the room, hoping it was just a fluke.

Summer passed and then I was off to college. I knew my vision was declining even more when I embarrassed myself walking across the university campus. "Hi, Scott!" I said happily to the student coming towards me. He looked away uneasily, and as I got closer, I realized he was very much *not* Scott. Social mishaps like this happened quite a few more times before I was willing to admit that

I needed glasses. I waited until my holiday break at home for an eye doctor appointment and then selected my first pair of glasses. I remember the magical moment when I put on the glasses and drove back to my parents' house, marveling at the clarity of the street signs. Even the speed limit signs sparkled with the clear definition of the numbers. I could distinguish the outlines, the variations of green, and the texture of the leaves on trees, and every color I saw was radiant. The contrast from blurry vision to absolute clarity was stunning, and while I had tried putting off the inevitable, I was truly grateful to be able to see clearly again.

• • •

Just as having clear vision helps when navigating social cues and context, having a clear vision helps navigate life. It helps us to see the road, the signs, and the other drivers. Most importantly, clear vision allows us to see where we are going and where we are headed. **Clear vision is more than the ability to read directions and see the way forward; clear vision is about having direction and *believing* that you will arrive at your destination.**

Leaders need a clear vision—they need to see the future with clarity. Imagine looking through a window that is covered with dirt. Until the window is cleaned and the dirt washed away, we can't clearly see what is on the other side. This is why the fourth C of Upbeat Leadership is *clarity*. A person can have a stalwart character, a high level of competence, and a propensity to connect and communicate, but without clarity, they will not be able to lead the group forward. If the leader is uncertain about where they are headed or why it matters, they will not be very successful in getting there. **A leader with clarity**

communicates the vision, leads the way, and inspires the team to go in the same direction.

Clarity brings the first three C's of Upbeat Leadership together. Our *character* determines our values, our *competence* determines what we can do, and our *connection* creates belonging. Clarity clearly defines the character, the skills, and the community that are essential to where the group is going. Clarity comes from awareness of our values, dreams, and what brings meaning. Clarity of purpose clearly communicated leads to clarity of action. Much like character, competence, and connection, clarity can be developed. Encourage your students to develop their own clarity of values, vision, and goals so they can more effectively lead themselves and others.

A Vision Is Future-Oriented

When we hear of people having a vision, they usually describe something that has not yet come to be. A vision is future-oriented and can be seen in the mind's eye prior to its realization. Great leaders have vision. Martin Luther King Jr., Steve Jobs, and Nelson Mandela had dreams and visions that they clearly communicated, igniting a massive following.

A vision can be small and safe or enormous and audacious, and the leader is the carrier of the message. Founded in a belief that it will be accomplished, the vision represents forward motion. By focusing on what you want to create rather than what you don't want, you paint a picture of what the group can grow into, what it can aspire to be. It takes courage to envision a brighter future. Avoid the temptation to just accept the status quo. Dream of more for yourself and the group.

While vision may be future-oriented, it still impacts us today. **An inspired vision ignites a spark in us to think and act the way we would if the vision were already a reality.** Ask yourself, "If I had already achieved my vision, how would I think and act today?" The answer to that question is your guide for how to act in the present moment. How do you want to *feel* in the future when you reach your destination? Let the anticipation of that feeling motivate you to move forward. What are your current strengths and weaknesses? And in what ways will you and your group need to grow, learn, and develop to make the vision a reality? **Don't see a vision as an impossible dream. See it as an inevitable destination, a natural result of the habits of thought, behavior, and actions lived every day moving forward.**

Former NFL coach of the Tampa Bay Buccaneers and the Indianapolis Colts, Tony Dungy, writes in *The Mentor Leader*, "Vision paints the picture of where we want to be, what we want to look like, what we hope things will be like in the future."[2]

Creating a Vision

Years ago, when I first had the opportunity to teach leadership to the Westwood High School marching band in Austin, Texas, the directors and I decided that by the end of our leadership camp we wanted to create a vision for the band. We divided the student leadership team into five groups and each group reflected on the values that were important to them and the band. Initially, the vision statements were multiple sentences, but after a few rounds of sharing and revision, the student leaders and teachers chose just three words to inspire them. "Pride. Passion. Family." Those three words defined what was already important to them and inspired them to do and be more in those three areas. Once the vision was created, the students latched onto its significance and meaning so that those three words could focus their goals and motivate their thoughts and behavior.

Creating a vision for your music program is like planning a family vacation. The purpose for a family vacation may be to add some fun to life, to take a break from the daily routines, or to explore the countryside and sights along the way. But a deeper purpose may be to create an opportunity to unite and strengthen the family. Think about the steps in the process. You begin by thinking about and dreaming of all the places you would like to go. You may even surf the Internet looking for desirable, beautiful, and adventurous destinations. You talk with your family members about where they would like to go and why. Once you all decide *where* you want to go, you start dreaming of all the possibilities to make this vacation special. Your vision is the destination. Your mission is to unite the family. The preparation for the trip, the route you plan, and the stops along the way are metaphors for the goals that you set to make your vision and mission become a reality.

Let's say you decide you want to travel from your hometown of Sacramento to Los Angeles. I grew up in Sacramento and actually remember a family trip much like the one described here! Your route may include visits to San Francisco and Monterey on the coast to enjoy the beaches, parks, piers, shopping, and the views. Then you may decide to continue back inland to Yosemite so you can spend a couple days hiking and absorbing the natural beauty of the rivers, waterfalls, wildlife, flowers, and rock formations. For the next phase of your trip, you drive to your ultimate destination: Los Angeles. Your vision began with seeing you and your family in Los Angeles and then you planned the journey, the process, to get to your destination. Dreaming of a vision opened so many exciting possibilities because you took the time to reflect, imagine, and create.

Our music programs and ensembles can feel like a family. It's no wonder that students and directors refer to their groups as their band family, orchestra family, or choir family. When planning a family vacation, just like creating a vision and mission for your music ensembles, you will get more buy-in when you ask your family members to share their ideas for destinations. Involve everyone in the discussion and work towards creating a vacation experience that all will be excited about and can get behind.

The vision should reflect what is important to the teacher *and* the students and clearly communicate where the group is headed. While the teacher or conductor can create a vision and share it with all the students, I find that collaboratively creating a vision leads to a higher level of buy-in, motivation, and enthusiasm from everyone. As discussed in Chapter 7, Creating an Upbeat Culture, empowering students to be part of the imagining and creation of the vision, mission, and values of the group is a win-win. The process of creating a vision can be blended with the mission (purpose) and values (what matters) of the organization as well. The final product should inspire, motivate, and demonstrate pride in the organization. A vision for the future is exciting and motivating when you have a burning desire to achieve it. Motivation and desire stem from a sense of purpose. What is that purpose that moves you and can rally and unite your students?

Believe It to See It

The process of creating a vision generates many ideas that represent how the students feel and what they believe is important. Encourage your students to dream big and think beyond what they have always done. The past need not limit the present. Even though many of the suggestions won't make it into the final vision statement, those contributions can become part of the goals that will be written to help make the vision a reality.

It is important that you and the students actually believe in the vision, so stay in the dream mode for a while and keep the conversation positive. What holds many back from achieving big goals is that they have been taught they need to see it to believe it. However, **great leaders believe it before they see it.** In the early 1960s, President John F. Kennedy proclaimed that by the end of the decade the United States would put a man on the Moon. Of course, this had never been done before. No one had ever seen it, and the technology and understanding had just begun to be developed in 1958. JFK shared his message and vision, harnessed to a belief that was so strong and a vision so clear that it motivated an entire country to make this dream a reality.

A leader with clarity sees the vision become a reality in their mind and believes it will happen. Military strategist and philosopher Sun Tzu (544–496 BCE) wrote over 2,500 years ago in *The Art of War*, "Victorious warriors win first in their minds and then go to war. Defeated warriors go to war first and then seek to win."[3] Sun Tzu was describing the importance of our upbeat, mindset, and clarity of vision for our success as leaders. **Not only do leaders believe in themselves but they also believe in those they are leading.** Their faith in and high expectations for their team are essential to making steady progress. Team members can sense when their leader doubts their ability to achieve a goal, which is why leaders need to be confident that their teams have what it takes to move forward. It takes courage to believe in a vision yet to be manifested, and it takes confidence to communicate the vision. In order to inspire others, although it is challenging, we must have an unwavering clarity of vision to lead the way. As Jon Gordon writes in *The Power of a Positive Team*, "For the vision and purpose to come alive, it must have meaning for each team member."[4] Student leaders need to be able to clearly communicate the vision to their group so that everyone understands the direction and purpose to then support the vision with enthusiasm. **The vision gives direction to the goals and action steps that follow.**

Music Program Vision and Mission Statements

In my collaborations with music programs, I have found that creating a vision-mission statement should come before deciding on goals. What is the big picture, direction, and purpose that supports and inspires all the actions and decisions that follow?

If you would like to create three separate statements, this is how to differentiate them.

Vision focuses on *where* we are going.
Mission focuses on *why* we do what we do.
Values focus on *what* is important to us.

Many groups have found that combining elements of the vision, mission, and values into one inspirational statement works great as well. If the process and the outcome motivate and lead to greater clarity and purposeful action, your group will find success.

Here is a general strategy that has worked successfully in the past to help groups create their vision-mission statements.

1. Start off in a large group. I have facilitated the creation of vision-mission statements with an entire ensemble or program and also with just the student leadership team and directors. Both approaches work well, but if you have the opportunity, work with the group as a whole first, and then work with the smaller teams.

2. Engage the students in a conversation about where the program *is* and where they would like to see it *go*. Talk about the strengths of the program and areas that need some attention for improvement. Encourage the students to dream big.

3. Try to find similarities and points of agreement with the students. This is a perfect opportunity for the director or directors and staff to talk about the values, dreams, and visions they have for the program. Work to find similarities and points of agreement with the students.

4. Share some examples of vision-mission statements from other music organizations (see below) or professional companies or athletic organizations to provide a model for what students will be developing. Here are two examples. Feel free to add more that resonate with you.
   • Southwest Airlines: "To become the world's most loved, most flown, and most profitable airline."[5]
   • Starbucks: "To inspire and nurture the human spirit— one person, one cup, and one neighborhood at a time."[6]

5. Divide the students into groups. I have found that five to eight students per group works well. Give the groups some time to brainstorm ideas for the creation of a vision-mission statement. I recommend writing on poster board or butcher paper with markers so they can easily present the visual of their first draft to the full group.

6. Each group presents their first draft. The other students should be encouraged to take notes on what each group presents and keep an open mind so they can learn from each other.

7. After sharing, the groups begin anew, experimenting with the ideas from their notes on the other groups. They may even decide to continue to use some of their original ideas.

8. When the second drafts are ready to be presented, the students and teacher(s) may be gravitating towards a particular statement. If it feels like the groups would benefit from a third return to the drawing board, you can opt for that. Otherwise, engage the entire group in a discussion to work towards creating a vision-mission statement that resonates with everyone and gets you and your students excited for the future.

9. After the vision-mission is finalized, the students can begin the process of making individual, section, and full ensemble goals to make the vision and mission a reality. The process of student goal setting is described later in this chapter.

10. Begin taking action to accomplish these goals.

Example Vision and Mission Statements

Friendship, positivity, passion, perseverance, excellence, and inspiration are important values to the Jeffersonville High School Band in Jeffersonville, Indiana. Following the collaborative process of vision-mission creation, the students and directors Adam Miller and Miko Martinez came up with a statement that provides a clear direction and purpose for everyone in the program.

Jeffersonville High School Band Vision-Mission Statement

Through our **Friendship**, we create **Positivity**.
Through our **Passion**, we will **Persevere**.
Through our **Excellence**, we **Inspire** the world around us.

The Jeffersonville Band integrates this statement into their daily rehearsals with cheers led by a student leader who calls out "Through our" and the band cheers, "Friendship." The student leader continues to call out what is not in bold, and the other students respond with the words in bold. The students also set goals and action steps connected to this set of meaningful statements, which gives clarity to the student leadership team and guides their thoughts, decisions, behavior, and leadership. It was important to the students and directors that their vision-mission statement apply to life within band and life outside of band; hence, the final clause, "we inspire the world around us."

Jay Gephart, director of bands at Purdue University, asked me to help guide the student leadership team of the Purdue "All-American" Marching Band in the creation of a new vision-mission statement. After training on the 4 C's of Upbeat Leadership, we began the process of innovating a new vision-mission. It was important to the students to include the values that distinguish Purdue's traditions, their focus on academics, and their desire to entertain the audience. Here is what they created.

Purdue University "All-American" Marching Band
WE:
Uphold a Tradition of Excellence
Develop Scholars and Leaders
Entertain, Connect, and Inspire

Following a leadership session with me, Director of Bands Peter Lillpopp and his Fort Hays State University marching band student leadership team in Hays, Kansas, created the following statements to guide their goals and the culture they strive to create.

Fort Hays State University Marching Band

Vision Statement: A thriving and developed marching band whose primary goal is to entertain Tiger fans and represent the university on gameday.

Mission Statement: To provide performance opportunities that serve the Tiger community while inspiring confidence in the band's leadership, critical thinking, problem-solving, collaboration, communication, marching, and musical skills.

Value Statement: The Fort Hays State Tiger Marching Band is driven by its members' commitment, adaptability, and overall experience. The band values diversity and a family atmosphere. As a result, the marching band has developed a collaborative and vibrant environment among music majors and non-music majors. Responsibility, respect, accountability, honesty, positivity, technological innovation, creativity, and hard work are valued characteristics that marching band members share. Our members lift one another to achieve individual and band goals.

Challenges and Solutions

Many teachers have been part of an organization or staff development collaborative session to create a vision or mission statement. The process can be a positive step toward deciding on mutually agreed upon values and what the group stands for. The problem is that days or weeks later most members of the group simply won't recall what the statement was. Unless the vision is integrated, becomes part of daily decisions, and is kept at the forefront of everyone's minds, it will be forgotten.

The vision needs to be followed by action and purposeful intent. A vision has meaning if you *make* it meaningful. **Your program's vision can either be a collection of words strung together, or it can become the fabric upon which your music program is sewn.**

So, what are the challenges to anticipate and their potential solutions?

1. **Challenge:** People are often resistant to change and tend to fall back into their comfort zone and what has been done before. It is difficult to motivate change if it feels like it goes against the tradition or culture of the program.

    Solution: Buy-in from the student leaders is integral to motivating the entire group to move in the direction of the vision. Honor students' thoughts and opinions by giving them a voice and empowering them to play an integral role in shaping the future of the ensemble.

2. **Challenge:** People will give lip service to a vision without willingness to put in the individual effort toward achieving the vision.

    Solution: Enthusiasm for the vision is contagious. Paint a vivid picture so students can see and feel the reward and energy that will come from reaching for the vision and mission. Celebrate the daily achievements along the way.

3. **Challenge:** Unclear goals and/or unclear action steps.

    Solution: The stepping stones of daily actions need to be clear. Without clear goals and concrete, sequential action steps for students, the vision will not be achieved. Invite students to create their own goals so they feel empowered and are given a voice in the process.

Student Leadership Vision and Goals

In addition to creating a vision and mission for the music ensemble or music program, students should be encouraged to set personal goals that align with the group's vision and goals. Student leaders need to have a vision for their own growth and improvement. Who do they want to become? How will their actions today be part of their ideal future self? **Leading is not just about helping those that we lead get to a destination; Upbeat Leadership is simultaneously about the growth and development of the leader.** Achievement happens when the entire team learns and grows together.

Goals should inspire you and motivate action. Just as your upbeat—your attitude—precedes your actions, thinking of goals that will take you to the next level requires reflection and an unwavering belief that you will do whatever is necessary to achieve your goal. Goals can include improving or mastering a particular skill, such as improving range on an instrument, and personal growth, such as being kinder to yourself and others.

Begin by answering these questions.

- Where are you now? What is your level of competence, attitude, mindset, connections, etc.?
- Where would you like to go? What would you like to achieve, create, develop, master, etc.?

Next, create **UPBEAT** goals. Remember that an Unwavering Positive Belief Energizes Actionable Thoughts.

- U = **Unwavering:** Your clarity and unbreakable commitment, determination, and perseverance will keep you on course to stick with your action plan and achieve your goals even if you encounter challenges or failure. Because you are unwavering, you get to see struggle as an opportunity to improve rather than as a sign to give up.

- **P = Positive:** Approach your goals with an "I can" attitude. Positive goals move you and your group forward, make a difference in your life and the lives of others, and open up possibilities to create further solutions.

- **B = Belief:** Your belief in yourself and belief in the importance of your goal will power you through challenges and obstacles that may get in the way. Your belief will allow you to create a mental representation, an image in your mind of reaching your goal, allowing you to visualize a clear path to accomplishment. Your belief gives purpose, meaning, and significance to your goal, which will motivate you to act confidently with intention. Your belief and upbeat mindset inspire passion and fuel the fire to reach for your goal.

- **E = Energizes:** Energy is required to convert your goals and dreams into action steps that will propel you forward. Your unwavering positive belief excites, inspires, motivates, and directs your next step.

- **A = Actionable:** Action is required to achieve goals. Goals that are actionable require a commitment to doing the work that is necessary, being consistent, and following through. Sticking with an action plan requires resilience, grit, and persistence. Reaffirm your intention every day to take one more step on the path towards achieving your goal.

- **T = Thoughts:** Creating goals, designing actions, and choosing your attitude happens in your mind. Focus on the positive impact that achieving your goal will have on you and others.

*U*nwavering
*P*ositive
*b*elief
*e*nergizes
*A*ctionable
*T*houghts
Upbeat®**Goals**

Student leaders should break their goals down into smaller tasks and objectives that can be achieved in a reasonable timeframe. Encourage them to create a clear plan by writing down goals and action steps and consistently referring to them, noting their progress along the way. Keep sight of the big picture while going after the daily goals. Let students know that it is okay to fall, and when they stumble, they can get back up, shake it out, learn from it, and keep on going.

In addition to creating a personal vision and goals, student leaders should collaborate with their section or team members to devise group goals. **Goals should ignite their inner flame and inspire them to aim for the stars.** Communicate the goals, purpose, and vision clearly so that everyone remembers where they are headed and why they are putting in the effort. According to motivational author Jon Gordon, "The research shows that when people know how they are contributing to a shared vision and a bigger purpose, engagement and passion soars."[7] Being upbeat about UPBEAT goals motivates everyone to put their best foot forward every day towards making progress and climbing to the next highest peak.

Five Steps to Reach the Summit

Clearly defining your vision, mission, values, and goals is essential to leading successfully. However, a clear vision must be accompanied by mindsets, behaviors, and action steps that will help you achieve your goals. Revisit your vision and goals daily when you set your intention in the morning and again throughout the day.

Ask yourself, "What is my mountain?"

Your mountain is a challenge, goal, or destination you would like to reach. This could be your personal or group goal. Once you have clarity about what you would like to accomplish, follow these five steps to reach the summit. Draw on all 4 C's of Upbeat Leadership—character, competence, connection, and clarity—to guide your thoughts and actions. Together, teachers and their students will find that although there will be obstacles along the way, continuing the climb and the view from the top will make the effort rewarding and worthwhile.

Step 1: Preparation

Luck is what happens when preparation meets opportunity.[8]
— Ancient Roman philosopher Lucius Annaeus Seneca

- Set your intention and choose your upbeat.
- Have a clear picture of the map where you are headed.
- In your mind, anticipate obstacles and plan ahead for them so you are not surprised and are able to devise solutions.
- See yourself taking initiative, being proactive, and responsive rather than reactive along the way.
- Decide what you will need to bring with you on this climb. It may be your music and instrument, or it may be courage and a positive mindset. Perhaps all four?

Step 2: Teamwork

- For a group vision or goal, work together as a team. For an individual vision or goal, enlist others to support you and help you be accountable for staying on course.
- Notice the positive attributes in your climbing partners and instill a sense of pride in those you lead.
- Ask for help and support each other. Be thoughtful and encouraging of each other, even when the climbing gets tough.
- While remaining focused on the goal, honor different viewpoints and care for the well-being of every member of the team.
- Express gratitude to your teammates and remember that *together* we can be so much more.

Step 3: Enjoy the Journey

- Find joy in the pursuit of your goal.
- Treasure the journey and the process—even the hard times—and realize that the climb is part of a bigger purpose.
- Approach every step forward with enthusiasm.
- Appreciate and recognize the little things along the way, including the progress and improvement, no matter how small.
- If you fall, get back up and ask yourself what you learned from the stumble.

Step 4: Sense of Purpose

When you know your why and you know the way,
you won't let obstacles get in the way.[9]
— Jon Gordon

- Imagine how you will feel when you accomplish your goal and allow that feeling of anticipation to inspire and motivate you and your team.
- Stay upbeat and positive by focusing on your vision.
- When the trail gets steep and challenging, and it will, get back in touch with your sense of purpose and "why" for taking the journey.
- If others on the journey with you want to give up or turn back, remind them of why continuing on the pathway matters.
- Although there may be those who tell you that you can't do it or you should be doing it another way, believe and trust in yourself and don't let them get you down.

Step 5: Celebrate Success

- Celebrate the stepping stones of success, not just the arrival at the summit, to motivate and inspire your team.
- When you reach the summit, show gratitude to the team rather than taking credit yourself.
- Take time to enjoy the summit and take in the view and feeling of accomplishment.
- Soak in the feeling of accomplishment, reflect on the hard work, and draw on this success to inspire you to seek new heights.

What mountain will you climb next?

Vignette

Brittany Dacy
Associate Director of Bands
Westwood High School, Austin, Texas

The Westwood Band has always been a welcoming place for all students to come together and share their love for music. We have worked to create the open and inclusive environment but never really had a clear mission statement or uniting idea to explain this magic. Even as a student some years ago, I knew it was home but wouldn't have been able to tell you why.

My second year on staff we brought Dr. Arau to leadership camp, hoping to get the clarity of purpose we knew our band family needed. Through Dr. Arau's student-based leadership, students created the goals and overall theme for the program that year, giving them ownership, increasing buy-in, and providing them the opportunity to be proud of their hard work the upcoming year. Before nailing down any concrete goals, we were looking for a mission statement or slogan to guide our ideas. As the students worked on the values of the Westwood Band, things like *pride in performance, passion for music* while supporting others, and most importantly, our *band family* kept coming up. However, the students were struggling with how to get all these concepts into one concise and clear sentence.

Finally, one of our drum majors, James, said, "What if we only use the three words: pride, passion, family?" There was a spark in the room—something changed immediately. Dr. Arau's jaw dropped, all the students got quiet, the staff became excited. We were finally ready to define the identity of the band program that was already there. All the hyper-focus on wording left and the students instead started talking about all the different ways to interpret these values. They realized how the three words applied so well in any number of situations. We talked more about the order, and it became clear that family had to be last because it was the thing that you remembered most about band and was the most important. Our band is, was, and always will be a family. That day at our student leadership camp in the middle of July, the Westwood culture was defined and embraced. We finally had the clarity we needed to deepen and strengthen our band culture.

Our students, staff, and community have fully embraced this vision. "Pride, Passion, Family" is now on our band logo, staff email signatures, and on the trailer we take to marching band shows and contests. First-year students know they're walking into a welcoming environment where they can feel safe and will be instantly embraced as part of the family. We have leaned on these words in times of struggle and success. In the pandemic, we used these words to align our curriculum so our students could still have what they value most. We are using these words to come back from the pandemic and serve our students and each other with care and compassion. We have an alumni band that adds the word "legacy" to our slogan as well. "Pride, Passion, Family" unites us and it helps our students feel safe and successful. Our band director emeritus, Jack Green, tells our alumni "Welcome home" when they come back to visit, and they sure come back in droves! "Pride, Passion, Family" is home.

Application

1. Meet with your student leaders or your entire ensemble and create a vision-mission statement using the steps shared in this chapter. Be clear on what is important to you and the direction that you would like to see the group head.
2. If your group already has a vision-mission statement, spend time reconnecting to its meaning and significance with your students so that it fuels and motivates the action necessary to fulfill its promise.
3. In addition to having your students make goals connected to the vision-mission statement, set your own intentions and goals to make the dream a reality.
4. Promote the vision-mission by making posters to place in the music room, write it on T-shirts, include it on all emails, and plaster it on your music program's website and social media. Say, chant, sing, or cheer the vision daily with your students so that it becomes woven into the fabric of the group's identity.

Journal Questions

1. The fourth C of Upbeat Leadership is *clarity*. How clear is your vision for yourself as a music educator? Are you clear on who you are and who you would like to aspire to become? Take a moment for yourself to reflect on how you would like to grow and develop as a music educator.

2. What are your hopes and dreams for your music program? How can you more clearly communicate your vision for the music program to your students, their parents, and your administration in order to enlist their support?

3. What is your mountain? What challenge would you like to confront, climb, and summit? Make a plan using a combination of UPBEAT goals and the Five Steps to Reach the Summit.

Quotes

Be more intentional about who you want to become. Have vision beyond your current circumstances. Imagine your best future self and start acting like that person today.

— Brendon Burchard
High Performance Habits, p. 65

Dream lofty dreams and, as you dream, so you shall become. Your vision is the promise of what you shall one day be; your ideal is the prophecy of what you shall at last unveil.

— James Allen
The Complete Collection, p. 107

Having a clear plan is as important as motivation and willpower.

— Brendon Burchard
High Performance Habits, p. 60

The greatest danger for most of us lies not in setting our aim too high and falling short, but in setting our aim too low and achieving our mark.

— Michelangelo
as quoted in Scott Shickler and Jeff
Waller's *The 7 Mindsets to Live Your
Ultimate Life*, p. 41

In the long run, men hit only what they aim at.

— Henry David Thoreau
as quoted in Tony Dungy's
The Mentor Leader, p. 53

Endnotes

1. CelloBello, "Yo-Yo Ma interview: On Practicing," YouTube Video, 5:45, October 23, 2017, https://www.youtube.com/watch?v=qsnrWNYMFvI.
2. Tony Dungy with Nathan Whitaker, *The Mentor Leader: Secrets to Building People and Teams That Win Consistently* (Carol Stream, IL: Tyndale Momentum, 2010), 32–33.
3. Mark Divine, *The Way of the SEAL: Think Like an Elite Warrior to Lead and Succeed* (White Plains, NY: Reader's Digest Adult Trade Publishing, 2013/2018), 57.
4. Jon Gordon, *The Power of a Positive Team* (Hoboken, NJ: John Wiley & Sons, 2018), 37.
5. "Purpose, Vision, and The Southwest Way," Southwest Airlines website, accessed September 3, 2021, http://investors.southwest.com/our-company/purpose-vision-and-the-southwest-way.
6. "Our Company," Starbucks website, accessed September 3, 2021, https://www.starbucks.com/about-us/.
7. Jon Gordon, *The Power of a Positive Team* (Hoboken, NJ: John Wiley & Sons, 2018), 38.
8. Scott Shickler and Jeff Waller, *The 7 Mindsets to Live Your Ultimate Life: An Unexpected Blueprint for an Extraordinary Life* (Hartford, CT: Publish Your Purpose Press, 2019), 75.
9. Jon Gordon, *The Power of a Positive Team* (Hoboken, NJ: John Wiley & Sons, 2018), 25.

CODA

Now this is not the end. It is not even the beginning of the end. But it is, perhaps, the end of the beginning.[1]

— Winston Churchill

Thank you for being on this upbeat journey with me. I hope that you have found some fresh ideas and strategies in these twelve chapters to ignite your passion, to inspire new approaches for amplifying student engagement and enthusiasm, and to lead you toward a blueprint to build, sustain, and reach higher through student leadership. Personal growth is never-ending. We never reach a point where we say to ourselves, "I made it. I am as good as I will ever be." This is unlike reaching our maximum physical height when we can eventually say, "This is it." Then as we get older and start to get shorter, we can look back at that high point! Personal growth, as opposed to physical growth, keeps going as long as we are open to learning and excited about reaching higher and higher. I used to think we were born with a certain level of potential that we would spend our lives striving to attain. I now know that when we get to a higher level of growth, there are always more summits to climb.

One of the challenges with reading personal growth books is that we may get inspired in the moment, but unless we integrate the messages and actions into our daily thinking and behavior, we end up making next to no lasting changes. We will fall back to our old programming, habits, and comfort zone. And yet every day is a new opportunity to choose our upbeat. Reading a book will not necessarily lead to a lasting change but making a daily decision to reclaim our upbeat will. We often unintentionally give away our personal power, choices, and control. However, we can reclaim these things by exercising our ability and freedom to choose our upbeat, our thoughts, and our attitude. Living an upbeat life does not make our problems and challenges go away. Nor does it mean that we won't have downbeat moments or days. What it does mean, however, is that when we are intentional about choosing our upbeat from the moment we wake up and throughout the course of our day, we will be able to discover solutions, respond from a calm center, and shine a light on the goodness of others.

The suggested small shifts in **Part 1: IGNITE!** can make a tremendous difference for us personally. We began our journey together focusing on a pathway to reframe how we view our own lives. We talked about the impact of our upbeat, the Power of G.E.T., supercharging our morning, and sustaining our upbeat all day. We discussed strategies to reframe how we approach the little things and the big things in our lives, refilling our cup so that we can pour into others from a place of vitality and strength. We gave ourselves permission to take care of ourselves through self-care strategies such as mindful breathing, mindful walking, and mindful eating, and we recognized how being fully present and appreciative in the moment rekindles our passion. Without taking time to pause, reflect, and connect to our inner selves, our thoughts, and our heart, we might just become someone who goes through the motions without being centered and feeling fully alive.

Part 2: INSPIRE! broadened our focus so that we can more fully inspire our students. We began with discussing how our mindset affects every aspect of our teaching, including why, how, and what we teach. Our mindset is contagious and affects how our own students feel about their own abilities to learn, grow, and take on challenges as well as how they respond to struggle and failure. An upbeat mindset classroom is one where every moment provides an opportunity for our students to take a step forward, and if they stumble, they have the courage to get back up, learn from it, and keep going. We then explored how key mindfulness practices work to create classrooms where our students are present, aware, and focused on what they are learning while simultaneously nurturing a space where self-compassion and compassion for others is central to the learning environment. Next, we discussed how to create an upbeat culture that honors and respects all students while propelling the group to the next level of connection, care, and excellence.

In **Part 3: LEAD!** we took a close look at a blueprint for developing a successful student leadership program. Creating a Leadership Symposium empowers students and gives them ownership and intrinsic motivation to continue the progress and growth of the music program. By teaching and reinforcing the 4 C's of Upbeat Leadership—character, competence, connection, and clarity—students are given the knowledge, mindset, and skills to be successful as leaders in and outside of the music room.

We did not choose to teach because it is easy. We chose to teach because students need us and because nothing tends more to the human heart than listening, performing, studying, and creating music together. Yet that special power within is often clouded by doubt, stress, insecurity, and a dependence on what other people think of us. I hope that in this moment you can suspend worry and thoughts that you are not good enough (you ARE!), or that you have no control over your own life (you DO!). Look within at who you are. Who are you at your core? Not how others define or categorize you but who you truly are. And while you look within, tap into your desires, your drives, and who you want to become. What brings you joy? What excites you about life? What are your hopes and dreams? These may be deep secret dreams that you have suppressed and never shared before. I want you to acknowledge who you are meant to be—who you are meant to become. You will feel a resonance, a vibration in your energy in the same way that you feel a sensation of wonder when a chord is played perfectly in tune, and the harmonic series comes alive over the primary notes of the chord, ringing in the hall well after the release. You will know you have found your life's path when you notice that you lose a sense of time and enter that state of flow.

We choose our thoughts. We choose our attitude. We choose our upbeat. Instead of focusing on what you don't want, focus on what you want to create. What we focus on expands. What we focus on grows. See possibilities and recognize that we are all in this together. We are a community with a common cause to support, serve, lead, and teach our students through the greatest gift, the gift of music. Music brings people together. Music reflects and creates community. Music expresses what words cannot. **Yes, we have to count when playing music, but we can always count *on* music to be there for us when we need it.**

First Lady Abigail Adams wrote in a letter to Thomas Jefferson, "Great necessities call forth great leaders."[2] I say, "Great necessities call forth great teachers." We need you now more than ever. If there was ever a time that we needed great music teachers, it is now. James Sherman wrote, "You can't go back and make a new start, but you can start right now and make a brand new ending."[3] We can all start and begin anew right now. No matter what has happened in the past, we can create and direct a new future. It begins with choosing our upbeat. Let's dream together of the difference we will make sharing the beauty of music while helping our students discover what already lies within.

Endnotes

1. Winston Churchill, "The End of the Beginning," speech made at the Lord Mayor's Luncheon, Mansion House, The Churchill Society London, November 10, 1942, http://churchill-society-london.org.uk/EndoBegn.html.
2. Abigail Adams's letters to Thomas Jefferson, as quoted in John W. Gardner, *On Leadership* (New York: Free Press, 1990), 39.
3. James R. Sherman, *Rejection* (Golden Valley, MN: Pathway Books, 1982), 45.

JOIN THE UPBEAT COMMUNITY

I hope that you will keep this book nearby as a source of inspiration, ideas, strategies, and personal reflection. If you have found the content to be of value, please join me in sharing it with others. Let's get connected and build the Upbeat Community so that together we can inspire positivity through leadership and music around the world.

Join the mailing list for upcoming events and get access to more resources and materials on leadership, mindset, mindfulness, culture, conducting, rehearsing, and more at **www.upbeatglobal.com**.

Contact Matthew Arau for guest speaking, teaching, coaching, and conducting: matthew@upbeatglobal.com

Facebook:
- Upbeat Global: https://www.facebook.com/pages/category/Motivational-Speaker/Upbeat-Global-110885907220776/
- Matthew Arau: https://www.facebook.com/matthew.arau

- Upbeat Leaders: https://www.facebook.com/groups/238379780620680
- Mindfulness for the Music Educator: https://www.facebook.com/groups/621448305418621

Instagram:
- Upbeat Global (@upbeat.global)
- Matthew Arau (@matthew_arau)

LinkedIn:
- https://www.linkedin.com/in/matthew-arau-92801346/

Twitter:
- @MatthewArau
- @Upbeat_Global

YouTube:
- Upbeat Global

GRATITUDE

I have saved writing my thank you's until the very end. Although I begin and end every day with a focus on gratitude, my desire to fully share my appreciation in print has made this more difficult than I had imagined. The ideas and content of this book have been influenced by so many people in my life, and I know I could never do them all justice in a few pages of acknowledgments. I would like to begin by sharing my heartfelt gratitude for Merilee, my family, and every teacher, student, mentor, friend, and colleague that I have ever had. You helped shape my thoughts and who I have become.

I am not exaggerating when I say this book would not have been possible without the support, encouragement, love, and brilliance of Merilee. Even the word to describe my philosophies on leadership, mindset, and culture, *upbeat*, was originally her idea. Her positive attitude, humor, and love of life have lifted me up during the year-long process of completing this manuscript and her influence and suggestions are embedded throughout. Merilee is my upbeat, the source, the light, and my muse. Thank you, Merilee. I love you forever.

I am grateful to my parents, José and Suzanne, for your love and support throughout my entire life and for always encouraging me and believing in me. Thank you to my siblings, María, José, and Javier, for inspiring me by how you make a positive difference every day. Thank you to Uncle George for stretching my mind and encouraging my interest in mindfulness and leadership. Thank you to Judy for being such a supportive and loving mother-in-law.

Thank you to Tim Lautzenheiser for your gracious foreword and continuous support and encouragement. It is because of your role modeling, servant leadership, and inspiration over many decades that I recognized the importance of fostering a student leadership program. Getting the opportunity to speak and teach alongside you has been an honor.

I would like to give a hearty thanks to all the amazing music educators who graciously contributed vignettes to broaden the personal touch of *Upbeat!* In the order of the chapters that they are in: Mark Stice, Alley Lacasse, Elizabeth Weismehl, Lesley Moffat, Jayson Gerth, Adam Miller, Jared Cassedy, Nate Sletten, Cameron Jenkins, Tyler Ehrlich, Kelley Burroughs, and Brittany Dacy.

Thank you to everyone who read through parts of the manuscript and gave your feedback, including Dan Miles, Alley Lacasse, Cameron Jenkins, Elizabeth Weismehl, and Mark Stice.

Thank you to Jayson Gerth, with an eagle-eye for detail, who offered valuable edits and suggestions throughout this entire process. So grateful to you for your visit from Iowa to our home in Wisconsin to talk about the book in person.

My sister María is a master of writing and language. She elevated the level of clear communication in my writing and spent hundreds of hours poring through the book before the final editing process, fine-tuning my grammar, finding citations, and stretching me to dig deeper. Thanks to WhatsApp and Google Docs, we have been able to connect daily on the book from Portugal to Wisconsin.

Thank you to every teacher and administrator who has invited me to work with your students or educators. I have learned so much from you and each one of those opportunities.

Thank you to the Upbeat Team. I couldn't have done this alone, and it has been so much fun and an honor to collaborate with you. A shout-out goes to Tyler Jaques for his special contributions to the Five Steps to Reach the Summit.

Thank you to Scott Rush who has believed in the importance of this project from the moment he read the first draft of the opening chapters and felt compelled to share my early work with Alec Harris at GIA Publications. Scott, you encouraged me to stay true to my voice, and I am very appreciative of you.

Thank you, Alec Harris, for your enthusiasm for the message of *Upbeat!* and for taking a chance on me as a first-time book author. It has been a dream of mine to write for you and GIA.

Massive gratitude is extended to my editor at GIA, Bryan Gibson, for always being positive, patient, and supportive even when I was behind on meeting deadlines. With a smile on your face, you never doubted that I would finish the book on time.

Thank you to Jeremy Fermin and Tenacity Digital for your creative graphics and to Martha Chlipala at GIA Publications for your exceptional work on the cover, layout, and design of the book.

Thank you to Scott Edgar, who encouraged me to write this book and for believing in the importance of weaving mindfulness together with social and emotional learning in music education.

Thank you to Scott Sheehan and Keith Hodgson for being such supporters and promoters of the *Upbeat!* message.

Thank you to the teachers who have been part of my online VanderCook College of Music course, Mindfulness for the Music Educator, from whom I learned so much and for cheering me on when I shared that I wanted to write a book on the topic of mindfulness and music education.

I would like to thank my past music teachers, including Wayne Reimers, Mark Tulga, Craig Faniani, Steve Jordheim, Ken Schaphorst, Bob Levy, Nick Keelan, Mike Ross, Allan McMurray, and Don McKinney. To Steve Jordheim, thank you for your enthusiasm when you heard about the Loveland High School Leadership Symposium. Who knew that a breakfast in Denver, Colorado, would lead to a career teaching leadership around the world?!

Thank you to Max McKee, Scott McKee, and all the faculty and staff at the American Band College and the Western International Band Clinic. Max, you represent to me what it looks like to have a dream and follow through to make it a reality. Thank you to all my incredible mentors, including Cecil Gutierrez, Sherree McLaughlin, Larry Wallace, Paula Crider, Anthony Maiello, Jay Gephart, Colonel Mike Bankhead, J. Steven Moore, Dick Mayne, Ray Cramer, Larry Livingston, Mark Fonder, Andy Mast, Dixie Detgen, Joe Brice, Tom Leslie, Bruce Dinkins, W. Dale Warren, W L Whaley, and Ralph Hultgren.

A special thank you to Colonel Lowell Graham. I wanted to let you know that "Yes, I remember!"

Thank you to Brian and Leila Pertl for your dear friendship, inspiration, and support.

Thank you to Mary Shada, Danielle Youngblood, Rick Frei, and Lucille Steiner for your incredible support and friendship that began years ago when I was a high school band director and has continued to this day.

Thank you to the folks at Conn-Selmer for giving me the opportunity to serve our profession on a broader level—Tim Lautzenheiser, Mike Kamphuis, Erin Cole Steele, Frank Troyka, Elisa Janson Jones, William Earvin, and Steve Zapf.

To John Stoner, thank you for seeing something within me before I saw it in myself. Your belief in me has meant the world.

Thank you to our loving and affectionate Dachshund-Chihuahua, Olive, who rested on my lap during much of the writing process. Olive has truly been a writing partner!

And finally, thank you to you, the reader, for traveling this journey with me. Although we may not have met *yet*, I look forward to the day when our paths do cross and we *get* to say hello. Wishing you peace, happiness, fulfillment, and joy.

With gratitude,
Matthew

BIBLIOGRAPHY AND
INSPIRATIONAL READING LIST

Abel, Ernest L., and Michael L. Kruger. "Smile Intensity in Photographs Predicts Longevity." *Psychological Science* 21, no. 4 (2010): 542–544.

Achor, Shawn. *Big Potential: How Transforming the Pursuit of Success Raises Our Achievement, Happiness, and Well-Being.* New York: Currency, 2018.

———. *The Happiness Advantage: The Seven Principles of Positive Psychology That Fuel Success and Performance at Work.* New York: Crown Business, 2010.

———. "The Happy Secret to Better Work." TED Talk, May 2011. https://www.ted.com/talks/shawn_achor_the_happy_secret_to_better_work.

Adams, Chris. "Can People Really Multitask?" ThoughtCo., February 17, 2019. https://www.thoughtco.com/can-people-really-multitask-1206398.

Alda, Alan. *If I Understood You, Would I Have This Look on My Face?: My Adventures in the Art and Science of Relating and Communicating.* New York: Random House Trade Paperback Edition, 2018.

Allen, James. *The Complete Collection*. Create Space Independent Publishing Platform, 2018.

Allman, Peter. *Shrink-Proof Your Life: Top Ten Ways to Stay Off the Therapist's Couch*. Self-published, 2016.

Antanaityte, Neringa. "How to Effortlessly Have More Positive Thoughts." TLEX Institute. Accessed September 28, 2021. https://tlexinstitute.com/how-to-effortlessly-have-more-positive-thoughts/.

Arau, Matthew. "Developing the Right Mindset." *The Instrumentalist* 72, no. 10 (May 2018): 18–23.

———. "Mindset Reset: Mindfulness and Positive Thinking Strategies for the Music Educator." *Nebraska Music Educator* 79, no. 1 (July 2020): 37–42.

———. "Reflect, Restore, Recharge." *The RIMER Rhode Island Music Educators' Review* 63, no. 2 (Spring 2021): 27–31.

———. "Reflect, Restore, Recharge, Create." *Teaching Music* 29, no. 2 (October 2021): 42–48.

Arau Ribeiro, María del Carmen, André Nusselder, Nataša Brouwer, Natália Gomes, and Noel Lopes. "An International Student Workshop on Design Thinking in Time of Corona: Redesigning an International Event as an Online Interactive Learning Experience." In *Innovative Teaching Methods: Practical Teaching in Higher Education*, edited by Lidia Pokrzycka. Lublin: Maria Curie-Sklodowska University Press, 2020.

Arnall, Judy. *Discipline Without Distress*. Calgary, Alberta, Canada: Professional Parenting Canada, 2008.

Atchley, Paul. "You Can't Multitask, So Stop Trying." Harvard Business Review, December 21, 2010, https://hbr.org/2010/12/you-cant-multi-task-so-stop-tr.

Bajaj, G. J. *Love Begets Wealth*. Self-published. 2008.

Barenboim, Daniel. *Music Quickens Time*. London: Verso, 2008.

Brackett, Marc. *Permission to Feel: Unlocking the Power of Emotions to Help Our Kids, Ourselves, and Our Society Thrive*. New York: Celadon Books, 2019.

"Breathing Life Into 'Inspire.'" Merriam-Webster. Accessed September 5, 2021. https://www.merriam-webster.com/words-at-play/the-origins-of-inspire.

Breathnach, Sarah Ban. *Simple Abundance: A Daybook of Comfort and Joy*. New York: Warner Books, 1995.

Brown, Brené. *Dare to Lead: Brave Work. Tough Conversations. Whole Hearts*. New York: Random House, 2018.

———. *Daring Greatly: How the Courage to Be Vulnerable Transforms the Way We Live, Love, Parent, and Lead*. New York: Gotham Books, 2012.

———. *The Gifts of Imperfection: Let Go of Who You Think You're Supposed to Be and Embrace Who You Are*. Center City, MN: Hazelden, 2010.

Brown, Les. *The Courage to Live Your Dreams*. Gildan Media, 2021.

Brown, Peter C., Henry L. Roediger III, and Mark A. McDaniel. *Make It Stick: The Science of Successful Learning*. Cambridge, MA: The Belknap Press, 2014.

Bunting, Michael. *The Mindful Leader: 7 Practices for Transforming Your Leadership, Your Organisation and Your Life*. Milton, Queensland, Australia: John Wiley & Sons, 2016.

Burchard, Brendon. *High Performance Habits: How Extraordinary People Become that Way*. Carlsbad, CA: Hay House, 2017.

———. *The Charge: Activating the 10 Human Drives that Make You Feel Alive.* New York: Free Press, 2012.

———. *The Student Leadership Guide, 4th edition.* Garden City, NY: Experts Academy Press, 2009.

Cain, Susan. *Quiet: The Power of Introverts in a World that Can't Stop Talking.* New York: Broadway Books, 2013.

CelloBello. "Yo-Yo Ma interview: On Practicing." YouTube Video, 5:45, October 23, 2017. https://www.youtube.com/watch?v=qsnrWNYMFvI.

Chang, Larry. *Wisdom for the Soul: Five Millennia of Prescriptions for Spiritual Healing.* Washington: Gnosophia, 2006.

Chödrön, Pema. *Start Where You Are: A Guide to Compassionate Living.* Boulder, CO: Shambhala, 2018.

———. *When Things Fall Apart: Heart Advice for Difficult Times.* Boulder, CO: Shambhala, 2016.

Churchill, Winston. "The End of the Beginning." Speech made at the Lord Mayor's Luncheon, Mansion House, The Churchill Society London, November 10, 1942. http://churchill-society-london.org.uk/EndoBegn.html.

Cirino, Erica. "What Are the Benefits of Hugging?" Healthline, April 11, 2018. https://www.healthline.com/health/hugging-benefits.

Clear, James. *Atomic Habits: An Easy & Proven Way to Build Good Habits & Break Bad Ones.* New York: Avery, 2018.

Colvin, Geoff. *Talent is Overrated.* New York: Penguin, 2010.

Cornett, Vanessa. *The Mindful Musician: Mental Skills for Peak Performance.* New York: Oxford University Press, 2019.

Covey, Stephen M. R., with Rebecca Merrill. *The Speed of Trust: The One Thing that Changes Everything*. New York: Free Press, 2006.

Covey, Stephen R. *The 7 Habits of Highly Effective People: Restoring the Character Ethic*. New York: Fireside, 1990.

Coyle, Daniel. *The Culture Code: The Secrets of Highly Successful Groups*. New York: Bantam Books, 2018.

———. *The Talent Code: Greatness Isn't Born. It's Grown. Here's How*. New York: Bantam Dell, 2009.

Croce, Pat. *Lead or Get Off the Pot! The Seven Secrets of a Self-Made Leader*. New York: Fireside, 2004.

Csikszentmihalyi, Mihaly. *Flow: The Psychology of Optimal Experience*. New York: Harper Perennial Modern Classics, 1990/2008.

Dalai Lama and Desmond Tutu with Douglas Abrams. *The Book of Joy: Lasting Happiness in a Changing World*. New York: Avery, 2016.

Dalai Lama and Howard C. Cutler. *The Art of Happiness: A Handbook for Living*. New York: Riverhead Books, 2009.

Daskall, Lolly. *The Leadership Gap: What Gets Between You and Your Greatness*. New York: Portfolio/Penguin, 2017.

Demos, John N. *Getting Started with Neurofeedback*. Norton Professional Books, 2005.

Dethmer, Jim, Diana Chapman, and Kaley Warner Klemp. *The 15 Commitments of Conscious Leadership: A New Paradigm for Sustainable Success*. Chicago: Conscious Leadership Group, 2014.

Divine, Mark. *The Way of the SEAL: Think Like an Elite Warrior to Lead and Succeed*. White Plains, NY: Reader's Digest Adult Trade Publishing, 2013/2018.

————. *Unbeatable Mind: Forge Resiliency and Mental Toughness to Succeed at an Elite Level.* Self-published, 2015.

Duckworth, Angela. *Grit: The Power of Passion and Perseverance.* New York: Scribner, 2016.

Duhigg, Charles. *The Power of Habit: Why We Do What We Do in Life and Business.* New York: Random House, 2014.

Dungy, Tony, with Nathan Whitaker. *The Mentor Leader: Secrets to Building People and Teams That Win Consistently.* Carol Stream, IL: Tyndale Momentum, 2010.

Dweck, Carol S. *Mindset: Changing the Way You Think to Fulfil Your Potential.* London: Robinson, 2012/2017.

————. *Mindset: The New Psychology of Success.* New York: Ballantine Books Trade Paperback Edition, 2008.

————. "The Perils and Promises of Praise," *Educational Leadership* 65, no. 2 (October 2007): 34–39.

————. "The Power of Believing that You Can Improve." TEDx, November 2014 https://www.ted.com/talks/carol_dweck_the_power_of_believing_that_you_can_improve.

Dweck, Carol S., and Ellen L Leggett. "A Social-Cognitive Approach to Motivation and Personality." *Psychological Review* 95, no. 2: 256–273.

Dyer, Wayne W. *Change Your Thoughts—Change Your Life: Living the Wisdom of the Tao.* Carlsbad, CA: Hay House, 2007.

————. *The Power of Intention: Learning to Co-create Your World Your Way.* Carlsbad, CA: Hay House, 2004.

Edgar, Scott N. *Music Education and Social Emotional Learning: The Heart of Teaching Music.* Chicago: GIA Publications, 2017.

Eker, T. Harv. *Secrets of the Millionaire Mind: Mastering the Inner Game of Wealth*. New York: HarperCollins, 2005.

Elliot, Elisabeth. *Through Gates of Splendor*. Carol Stream, IL: Tyndale Momentum, 1981.

Elrod, Hal. *The Miracle Morning: The 6 Habits That Will Transform Your Life Before 8 a.m.* London: John Murray Learning, 2016/2017.

Emmons, Robert A., and Michael E. McCollough. "Counting Blessings Versus Burdens: Experimental Studies of Gratitude and Subjective Well-Being in Daily Life." *Journal of Personality and Social Psychology* 84, no. 2 (February 2003): 377–389.

Ericsson, Anders, and Robert Pool. *Peak: Secrets from the New Science of Expertise*. Boston: Houghton Mifflin Harcourt, 2016.

Forni, P. M. *Choosing Civility*. New York: St. Martin's Griffin, 2010.

Frankl, Viktor E. *Man's Search for Meaning*. Boston: Beacon Press, 1959/2006.

Fredrickson, Barbara L. *Positivity: Top-Notch Research Reveals the Upward Spiral That Will Change Your Life*. New York: Three Rivers Press, 2009.

Gallwey, W. Timothy. *The Inner Game of Tennis: The Classic Guide to the Mental Side of Peak Performance*. New York: Random House Trade Paperback Edition, 1974/2008.

Gardner, John W. *On Leadership*. New York: Free Press, 1990.

Gielan, Michelle. *Broadcasting Happiness: The Science of Igniting and Sustaining Positive Change*. Dallas, TX: BenBella Books, 2015.

Glaser, Judith E. *Conversational Intelligence: How Great Leaders Build Trust and Get Extraordinary Results*. Brookline, MA: Bibliomotion, Inc., 2014.

Goldsmith, Marshall. "Try Feedforward Instead of Feedback." October 29, 2015. https://www.marshallgoldsmith.com/articles/try-feedforward-instead-feedback/.

Goleman, Daniel. *Emotional Intelligence: Why It Can Matter More than IQ.* New York: Bantam Books, 1995.

Gordon, Jon. *The Energy Bus: 10 Rules to Fuel Your Life, Work, and Team with Positive Energy.* Hoboken, NJ: John Wiley & Sons, 2007.

———. *The Power of Positive Leadership: How and Why Positive Leaders Transform Teams and Organizations and Change the World.* Hoboken, NJ: John Wiley & Sons, 2017.

———. *The Power of a Positive Team: Proven Principles and Practices that Make Great Teams Great.* Hoboken, NJ: John Wiley & Sons, 2018.

———. *You Win in the Locker Room First: The 7 C's to Build a Winning Team in Business, Sports, and Life.* Hoboken, NJ: John Wiley & Sons, 2015.

Goyder, Caroline. *Find Your Voice: The Secret to Talking with Confidence in Any Situation.* London: Vermillion, 2020.

Green, Barry, and W. Timothy Gallwey. *The Inner Game of Music.* New York: Doubleday, 1986.

Gutman, Ron. "The Hidden Power of Smiling." TED Video, filmed March 2011. https://www.ted.com/talks/ron_gutman_the_hidden_power_of_smiling.

Hanh, Thich Nhat. *Peace Is Every Step: The Path of Mindfulness in Everyday Life.* New York: Bantam Books, 1991.

Hanson, Rick. *Just One Thing: Developing a Buddha Brain One Simple Practice at a Time.* Oakland, CA: New Harbinger Publications, 2011.

Hardy, Benjamin. *Personality Isn't Permanent: Break Free from Self-limiting Beliefs and Rewrite Your Story*. New York: Portfolio/Penguin, 2020.

Harvey, Steve, with Jeffrey Johnson. *Act Like a Success, Think Like a Success: Discovering Your Gift and the Way to Life's Riches*. New York: HarperCollins, 2014.

Hawn, Goldie, with Wendy Holden. *10 Mindful Minutes: Giving Our Children – and Ourselves – the Social and Emotional Skills to Reduce Stress and Anxiety for Healthier, Happier Lives*. New York: Perigee Trade Paperback Edition, 2012.

Helmstetter, Shad. *What to Say When You Talk to Your Self: Powerful New Techniques to Program Your Potential for Success*. New York: Gallery Books, 1986/2017.

Hendricks, Karin S. *Compassionate Music Teaching: A Framework for Motivation and Engagement in the 21st Century*. Lanham, MD: Rowman & Littlefield, 2018.

Hicks, Ester, and Jerry Hicks. *Ask and It Is Given: Learning to Manifest Your Desires*. Carlsbad, CA: Hay House, 2004.

Hill, Napoleon. *Think and Grow Rich*. New York: Jeremy P. Tarcher/Penguin, 1937/2005.

Hinshaw, Robert E. *Living With Nature's Extremes: The Life of Gilbert Fowler White*. Boulder, CO: Johnson Books, 2006.

Hoerr, Thomas R. *The Formative Five: Fostering Grit, Empathy, and Other Success Skills Every Student Needs*. Alexandria, VA: ASCD, 2016.

Hof, Wim. *The Wim Hof Method: Activate Your Full Human Potential*. Boulder, CO: Sounds True, 2020.

Holiday, Ryan. *Stillness Is the Key*. New York: Portfolio/Penguin, 2019.

Kotb, Hoda. *This Just Speaks to Me*. New York: G. P. Putnam's Sons, 2020.

Jennings, Patricia. *Mindfulness for Teachers: Simple Skills for Peace and Productivity in the Classroom*. New York: W. W. Norton & Company, 2015.

Jordan, James. *The Musician's Soul: A Journey Examining Spirituality for Performers, Teachers, Composers, Conductors, and Music Educators*. Chicago: GIA Publications, 1999.

Jordan, James, Mark Moliterno, and Nova Thomas. *The Musician's Breath: The Role of Breathing in Human Expression*. Chicago: GIA Publications, 2011.

Jung, Carl. *Modern Man in Search of a Soul*. London: Routledge, 2001.

Kabat-Zinn, Jon. *Mindfulness for Beginners: Reclaiming the Present Moment – and Your Life*. Boulder, CO: Sounds True. 2016.

———. *Wherever You Go, There You Are: Mindfulness Meditation in Everyday Life*. New York: Hachette Books, 1994/2005.

Kahneman, Daniel. *Thinking, Fast and Slow*. New York: Farrar, Straus and Giroux, 2011.

Katie, Byron, and Stephen Mitchell. *Loving What Is: How Four Questions Can Change Your Life*. New York: Random House, 2008.

Kerpen, David. *The Art of People: 11 Simple People Skills That Will Get You Everything You Want*. New York: Crown Business, 2016.

Kraft, Houston. *Deep Kindness: A Revolutionary Guide for the Way We Think, Talk, and Act in Kindness*. New York: Tiller Press, 2020.

Lagos, Leah. *Heart, Breath, Mind: Train Your Heart to Conquer Stress and Achieve Success*. Boston: Houghton Mifflin Harcourt, 2020.

Lautzenheiser, Tim. *Classic Leadership: A Curriculum for the Development of Student Leaders.* Chicago: GIA Publications, 2014.

———. *Everyday Wisdom for Inspired Teaching.* Chicago: GIA Publications, 2005.

———. *Music Advocacy and Student Leadership: Key Components of Every Successful Music Program.* Chicago: GIA Publications, 2005.

———. *The Art of Successful Teaching: A Blend of Content & Context.* Chicago: GIA Publications, 1992.

Lautzenheiser, Tim, Patrick Sheridan, Scott Lang, and Jon Gomez. *Leadership Success.* Chicago: GIA Publications, 2004. DVD.

Leahy, Robert L. *The Worry Cure: Seven Steps to Stop Worry from Stopping You.* New York: Three Rivers Press, 2006.

Lemov, Doug, Erica Woolway, and Katie Yezzi. *Practice Perfect: 42 Rules for Getting Better at Getting Better.* San Francisco: Jossey-Bass, 2012.

Lewis, T. W. *Solid Ground: A Foundation for Winning in Work and Life.* Scottsdale AZ: T. W. Lewis Company, 2020.

Lyubomirsky, Sonja, Kennon M. Sheldon, and David Schkade, "Pursuing Happiness: The Architecture of Sustainable Change." *Review of General Psychology* 9, no. 2 (n.d.): 116.

Maxwell, John C. *Everyone Communicates, Few Connect: What the Most Effective People Do Differently.* Nashville: Thomas Nelson, 2010.

———. *Failing Forward: Turning Mistakes into Stepping Stones for Success.* Nashville, TN: Thomas Nelson, 2000.

———. *Intentional Living: Choosing a Life That Matters.* New York: Center Street, 2015.

———. *The 21 Indispensable Qualities of a Leader.* Nashville: Thomas Nelson, 1999.

———. *The 21 Irrefutable Laws of Leadership: Follow Them and People Will Follow You.* Nashville: Thomas Nelson, 1998/2007.

McGonigal, Kelly. *The Upside of Stress: Why Stress is Good for You and How to Get Good at It.* New York: Avery, 2015.

———. *The Willpower Instinct: How Self-Control Works, Why It Matters, and What You Can Do to Get More of It.* New York: Avery, 2012.

Mehrabian, Albert. *Nonverbal Communication.* Piscataway, NJ: Aldine Transaction, 1972.

Mehrabian, Albert, and Susan R. Ferris. "Inference of attitudes from nonverbal communication in two channels." *Journal of Consulting Psychology* 31, no. 3 (1967): 248–252. https://doi.org/10.1037/h0024648.

Miller, Kori D. "14 Health Benefits of Practicing Gratitude According to Science." Positive Psychology, February 27, 2021. https://positivepsychology.com/benefits-of-gratitude/.

Mollick, Lynn. "Robert Leahy Speaks on Cognitive Therapy for Worry and Rumination." NJ-ACT. Accessed September 28, 2021. https://www.nj-act.org/workshops/past-workshops/12714-robert-leahy-ph-d/.

Nestor, James. *Breath: The New Science of a Lost Art.* New York: Riverhead Books, 2020.

Nevarez, S. Michele. *Emotionally Intelligent Habits.* Hoboken, NJ: Wiley, 2021.

Ninivaggi, Frank John. "Loneliness: A New Epidemic in the USA." Psychology Today, February 12, 2019. https://www.psychologytoday.com/us/blog/envy/201902/loneliness-new-epidemic-in-the-usa.

Normandie, Jaclyn M. *The Mindful Musician: Finding a Healthy Balance.* Middletown, DE: Normandie Publishing, 2021.

"One Smile Can Make You Feel a Million Dollars." Scotsman, March 4, 2005. https://www.scotsman.com/health/one-smile-can-make-you-feel-million-dollars-2469850.

Palmer, Parker J. *Let Your Life Speak: Listening for the Voice of Vocation.* Hoboken, NJ, John Wiley & Sons, 1999.

———. *The Courage to Teach: Exploring the Inner Landscape of a Teacher's Life.* San Francisco: Jossey-Bass, 2007.

Pascual-Leone, A., D. Nguyet, L. G. Cohen, J. P. Brasil-Neto, A. Cammarota, and M. Hallett, "Modulation of Muscle Responses Evoked by Transcranial Magnetic Stimulation During the Acquisition of New Fine Motor Skills." *Journal of Neurophysiology* (September 1, 1995). https://journals.physiology.org/doi/pdf/10.1152/jn.1995.74.3.1037.

Peale, Norman Vincent. *The Power of Positive Thinking.* New York: Fireside, 1952/2003.

Pink, Daniel. *Drive: The Surprising Truth About What Motivates Us.* New York: Riverhead Books, 2009.

Porath, Christine. *Mastering Civility: A Manifesto for the Workplace.* New York: Grand Central Publishing, 2016.

Proctor, Bob. *The ABCs of Success: The Essential Principles from America's Greatest Prosperity Teacher.* New York: Jeremy P. Tarcher, 2015.

Purushothaman, Dr. *Character Quotes.* Kollam, Kerala, India: Centre for Human Perfection, 2015.

Rath, Tom, and Donald O. Clifton. *How Full Is Your Bucket: Positive Strategies for Work and Life.* New York: Gallup Press, 2004.

Ray, Darby Kathleen. *Theology that Matters: Ecology, Economy, and God.* Minneapolis: Fortress Press, 2006.

Ricci, Mary Cay. *Mindsets in the Classroom: Building a Culture of Success and Student Achievement in Schools.* Waco, TX: Prufrock Press, 2013.

Robbins, Mel. *Stop Saying You're Fine: The No-BS Guide to Getting What You Want.* New York: Three Rivers Press, 2011.

Robbins, Tony. *Awaken the Giant Within: How to Take Immediate Control of Your Mental, Emotional, Physical & Financial Destiny!* New York: Simon & Schuster Paperbacks, 1991/2013.

———. "The Midnight Workout." Medium, February 15, 2017. https://medium.com/thrive-global/the-midnight-workout-d870c24305b0#:~:text=The%20great%20John%20Wooden%20once%20said%3A%20"Be%20more,what%20he%20does%20when%20no%20one%20is%20watching.

Robinson, Lawrence, Melinda Smith, and Jeanne Segal. "Laughter is the Best Medicine." Help Guide, July 2021. https://www.helpguide.org/articles/mental-health/laughter-is-the-best-medicine.htm?pdf=13511.

Safwan, Ahmed. "How the First 20 Minutes of Your Day Can Set You Up for Success." Entrepreneur, July 13, 2017. Accessed September 16, 2021. https://www.entrepreneur.com/article/291907.

Seligman, Martin E. P. *Authentic Happiness: Using the New Positive Psychology to Realize Your Potential for Lasting Fulfillment.* New York: Free Press, 2002.

———. *Flourish: A Visionary New Understanding of Happiness and Well-being.* New York: Atria Paperback, 2013.

———. *Learned Optimism: How to Change Your Mind and Your Life.* New York: First Vintage Books, 1990/2006.

Shenk, David. *The Genius in All of Us: New Insights into Genetics, Talent, and IQ*. New York: Anchor Books, 2010.

Sheridan, Patrick, and Sam Pilafian. *Guide to the Breathing Gym*. Mesa, AZ: Focus on Music, 2021.

Sherman, James R. *Rejection*. Golden Valley, MN: Pathway Books, 1982.

Shickler, Scott, and Jeff Waller. *The 7 Mindsets to Live Your Ultimate Life: An Unexpected Blueprint for an Extraordinary Life*. Hartford, CT: Publish Your Purpose Press, 2019.

Sinek, Simon. *Leaders Eat Last: Why Some Teams Pull Together and Others Don't*. New York: Portfolio/Penguin, 2017.

——. *Start with Why: How Great Leaders Inspire Everyone to Take Action*. New York: Portfolio/Penguin, 2009.

Smith, Emily Esfahani. *The Power of Meaning: Finding Fulfillment in a World Obsessed with Happiness*. New York: Broadway Books, 2017.

Soderquist, Don. *The Wal-Mart Way*. Nashville: Thomas Nelson, 2005.

Stone, Douglas, and Sheila Heen. *Thanks for the Feedback: The Science and Art of Receiving Feedback Well*. New York: Viking Penguin, 2014.

Syed, Matthew. *Bounce: Mozart, Federer, Picasso, Beckham, and the Science of Success*. New York: Harper Perennial, 2010.

Thoreau, Henry David. *Walden*. Princeton, NJ: Princeton University Press, 1989.

Tough, Paul. *How Children Succeed: Grit, Curiosity, and the Hidden Power of Character*. Boston: Mariner Books, 2012.

Tracy, Brian. *Change Your Thinking, Change Your Life: How to Unlock Your Full Potential for Success and Achievement*. Hoboken, NJ: John Wiley & Sons, 2003.

Wakin, Daniel J. "The Maestro's Mojo. *The New York Times*, April 6, 2012. https://www.nytimes.com/2012/04/08/arts/music/breaking-conductors-down-by-gesture-and-body-part.html.

Washington, Booker T. *The Story of the Negro: The Rise of the Race from Slavery, Vol. 1.* New York: Doubleday, Page and Company, 1909.

Washington, Booker T. *Up from Slavery.* Dover Publications, 1901/1995.

Weil, Andrew. *Spontaneous Happiness: A New Path to Emotional Well-Being.* New York: Little, Brown and Company, 2011.

Whiting, Kate. "Here are 10 of Nelson Mandela's Most Inspirational Quotes." World Economic Forum, July 18, 2019. https://www.weforum.org/agenda/2019/07/nelson-mandela-south-africa-quotes-madiba-inspiration/.

Wiltermuth, Scott S., and Chip Heath. "Synchrony and Cooperation." *Psychological Science* 20, no. 1 (January 2009): 1–5.

Wooden, John, and Steve Jamison. *Wooden on Leadership.* New York: McGraw-Hill, 2005.

Zander, Rosamund Stone, and Benjamin Zander. *The Art of Possibility: Transforming Professional and Personal Life.* New York: Penguin Group, 2000.

Ziglar, Tom. *Choose to Win: Transform Your Life One Simple Choice at a Time.* Nashville, TN: Nelson Books, 2019.

Ziglar, Zig. "Change What Goes Into Your Mind." Ziglar. Accessed September 5, 2021. https://www.ziglar.com/quotes/you-are-what-you-are-and-where-you-are/.

———. *Goals.* New York: Simon & Schuster Audio, 1995.

————. *See You at the Top—25th Anniversary Edition*. Niles, IL: Simon & Schuster Audio, 1989. Compact disc.

Zimmermann, Manfred. "Neurophysiology of Sensory Systems." In *Fundamentals of Sensory Physiology*, edited by R. F. Schmidt, 68–116. Berlin: Springer Berlin Heidelberg, 1986.

Index

ABOUT THE AUTHOR

(Photo by Ken Cobb)

Dr. Matthew Arau, founder of Upbeat Global and Upbeat! Leadership Workshops, Coaching, and Keynotes, is an Associate Professor of Music and the Chair of the Music Education Department and the Symphonic Band conductor at the Lawrence University Conservatory of Music in Appleton, Wisconsin. In addition, Dr. Arau is on the graduate conducting faculty of the American Band College of Central Washington University and on the graduate mindfulness faculty at VanderCook College of Music. He also serves as a Conn-Selmer Education Clinician, an Education Consultant for Connect through Music, and as Member-at-Large on the NAfME Council for Band Education.

Dr. Arau has guest conducted and presented on student leadership, mindfulness, growth mindset, rehearsal techniques, and creating positive cultures in person in over twenty-five states and four continents in person. He has presented at the International Midwest Band and Orchestra Clinic, the Western International Band Clinic, the NAfME National Conference, numerous state and regional music education association conferences, and the Conn-Selmer Institute. He has conducted honor bands in Australia, Greece, Cyprus, and Malaysia, and all-state honor bands across the United States.

Dr. Arau draws on a deep reservoir of fifteen years of experience as a successful middle school and high school band director in Loveland, Colorado, where he led his bands at Walt Clark Middle School and Loveland High School to numerous championships and honor performances and pioneered the Leadership Symposium.

Dr. Arau earned his D.M.A. in wind conducting and literature from the University of Colorado Boulder, his M.S. in music education from the American Band College at Southern Oregon University, and a B.M. in music performance (jazz studies), music performance (classical), and music education and a B.A. in government from Lawrence University. Discover more about Dr. Matthew Arau at www.upbeatglobal.com.